Englishness

Englishness

Twentieth-Century Popular Culture and
the Forming of English Identity

Simon Featherstone

Edinburgh University Press

© Simon Featherstone, 2009

Edinburgh University Press Ltd
22 George Square, Edinburgh

Typeset in Sabon and Futura
by Servis Filmsetting Ltd, Stockport, Cheshire, and
printed and bound in Great Britain by
the MPG Books Group

A CIP record for this book is available from the British Library

ISBN 978 0 7486 2365 5 (hardback)

The right of Simon Featherstone
to be identified as author of this work
has been asserted in accordance with
the Copyright, Designs and Patents Act 1988.

Contents

Acknowledgements   vi

Introduction: Being English   1
1   Thinking about England   9
2   Reviving England   28
3   Festivals   47
4   Journeys   66
5   The North   84
6   Race   103
7   Sport   121
8   Voices   140
9   Romance   159
Conclusion   178

Bibliography   183
Index   197

Acknowledgements

I would like to thank the following people who have helped me in various ways with the writing of the book: David Bownes, Tess Buckland, Will Burdett, Lawrence and Catherine Dixon, Ann Featherstone, C. P. Lee, John Moffatt, Malcolm Taylor, Eva Salgado Sánchez, Max Tyler, Andrew Tolson, Debbie Walker and the staff at the Rochdale Museum Service, and Ruth Willats. Jackie Jones has provided me with consistent support and wise advice. Tracy Cruickshank gave up a hard-earned holiday to read a draft and, as ever, to put me back on the right track.

The book is dedicated to my mother and to my father.

Introduction: Being English

In the weeks before 23 April it is now possible to buy a range of gifts – cards, mugs, sweatbands – displaying the red cross of St George. This commercial celebration of the English national saint is a relatively recent phenomenon, traceable to the resurgence of the George Flag as a sporting emblem during the 1996 European Football Championships, but also indicative of a new popular performance of nationhood. The nature of this discourse can be judged by the verse of one of the cards available in 2007:

> On St George's Day
> Petal by petal
> A bud becomes a rose
> Year by year
> England's greatness grows.

The sentiment is simultaneously affirmative and cautious. England is imagined not as a blooming rose but as an opening bud, the sign of a young nation, therefore. For a country that has tended to see itself as ancient this seems strange, but perhaps acknowledging the consequences of United Kingdom devolution over the last ten years, the card industry poet registers a need for a new England to emerge and to celebrate itself through the post. Quite what an appropriate St George's Day greeting might be is unclear and staff of my local card shop were unable to describe a typical purchaser, but the fact of its commercial existence marks a development in the expression of English identity.

The St George's Day card recalls another ambivalent English popular text of the early twenty-first century, overheard at the Trent Bridge Test Match against Australia in August 2005. The England cricket team was in the unusual position of being able to win an Ashes game and a section of the crowd (young, male and drunk) was in celebratory mood. The men sang the following chorus, borrowed from the grim repertoire of England football fans:

With St George in my heart keep me English,
With St George in my heart I pray,
With St George in my heart keep me English,
Keep me English till my dying day.

Even delivered with slurred relish on a warm afternoon, the song, like the verse in the card, spoke more in hope than in the bold national assertion that the moment seemed to demand. At the centre of the lyric lies worry, not confidence. Its prayer – for the lyric retains the hymnal mode of its source – is that the English national saint might forestall any alarming change of nationality during a lifetime. The singer, it implies, might one day wake up as someone else – not English, without nationhood or, most worryingly of all perhaps, of another nation. Hoping to be 'kept' English is hardly a trenchant assertion of the integrity of national identity, just as the bud not yet blooming only promises an English rose.

These are trivial items with which to begin a discussion of a century of national cultural representation, but triviality forms part of the problem of Englishness that will be discussed here. The routine expressions of the national question – the political meanings of the St George flags, the difficulties with national anthems, the discriminations between being English and being British – are predictable, easily packaged and wearisome. What does it really matter if Englishness is found, lost, never existed or is roughly the same as Britishness, whatever in turn that may be? In an era of an intensification of the politics and rhetoric of globalism, internationalism and devolution it might seem rather late to examine the absence of national identity in a country that historically dominated so many others. And yet the English are persistently, if incoherently, interested in 'who they are'. A genre of publishing has grown up around the fascination. Over the last four years alone there have appeared Kate Fox's *Watching the English: The Hidden Rules of English Behaviour* (2004), A. A. Gill's *The Angry Island: Hunting the English* (2005), Christopher Winn's *I Never Knew That About England* (2005), Colin Irwin's *In Search of Albion* (2005), Peter Ashley's *Unmitigated England: A Country Lost and Found* (2006), Sue Clifford's *England in Particular* (2006) and Billy Bragg's *The Progressive Patriot: A Search for Belonging* (2006). As their titles suggest, the England of these books is variously unknown, lost or sought after. For the English who read about being English also like to be told how hard it is to say who they are.

These popular expressions of nationhood, whether in books, cards or songs, suggest the continued relevance of an English national identity to the English and the difficulty of its definition and expression. Tom Nairn, perhaps the most acute and certainly the most exasperated political commentator on the case of England over the last twenty-five years, has also put the argument for the necessity of a new English national settlement. Whilst nationalism remains the most significant cultural expression of social identity, a fact made clear by the proliferation of new European nations over the last twenty years, England's uncertainty about itself remains an anomaly. As the same process develops within the United Kingdom, Nairn argues, the problem of England is 'now bearing down rapidly upon its inhabitants and knocking upon its own historical door' (Nairn 2002: 102). Any answer to that summons must go beyond a simplistic fascination with the quirks of Englishness and engage fully with difficult histories of governance, class, imperialism and gender.

England's evasion of popular nationalism, as Nairn and other historians have suggested, is partly explained by a historical willingness to subordinate national expression to broader domestic and global structures of colonial and imperial power. Such a process has also led to the absence of the cultural imperatives that shaped the intellectual foundations of other national revivals in the United Kingdom. England has no threatened indigenous language such as Welsh or Gaelic; it has no urgent need to record and preserve residual social formations or traditional cultures that might encode national identity; and it acknowledges no tradition of resistance to an outside cultural hegemony that is represented in the United Kingdom by England itself. Nationalist intellectual endeavour is normally directed towards the questioning of dominant ideologies and discourses, and tends by its nature to oppose rather than to study history's victors. The popular and academic cultural impetus that shaped the School of Scottish Studies at the University of Edinburgh in the 1950s, for example, did not exist in England. A School of English Studies on the Scottish model still sounds scarcely credible. What would its curriculum be? Who would study it? Who would teach there? Where would it be based? English Studies, in an academic context, still signifies English literary studies, a limitation of national focus that, as Perry Anderson, Francis Mulhern and Brian Doyle have variously suggested, represents precisely the avoidance of broader political and cultural questions that has been so characteristic of English intellectual history (Anderson 1968; Mulhern 1979; Doyle 1989).

Academic approaches to questions of Englishness have been notably cagey, reflecting both the potential embarrassments and anachronisms of the subject and the right-wing politics that had become so forcefully associated with the flag of St George. Robert Colls and Philip Dodd's innovative study of the making of modern English cultural identity, *Englishness: Politics and Culture 1880–1920* (1986), significantly did not lead to any proliferation of Englishness studies and no book on the subject with a comparable range has been published since. However, in retrospect it was the beginning of a more sustained if diffuse scholarship of English culture. Until quite recently, literary studies continued to be the most important conduit for the discussion of English identity as Alison Light's *Forever England* (1991) and Anthony Easthope's *Englishness and National Culture* (1999) demonstrated. By the turn of the twentieth century, though, other disciplines had also begun to approach the English question. Linda Colley's *Britons: Forging the Nation* (1992) initiated a 'national turn' in British historiography, and two later studies, Robert Colls' *Identity of England* (2002) and Krishan Kumar's *The Making of English National Identity* (2003), were specifically concerned with the historical construction of Englishness.

The importance of national representation was also emphasised in academic disciplines that developed in the 1980s and 1990s. Andrew Higson's *Waving the Flag* (1995) argued for the importance of cinema in shaping English/British identity, for example, and Christine Gledhill and Gillian Swanson's *Nationalising Femininity* (1996) emphasised the feminising of English identity in its study of film during the Second World War. Tony Mason's *Sport in Britain* (1989) and Richard Holt's *Sport and the British* (1989) explored the relationship between sport and national identity, a field of enquiry that expanded notably during the 1990s. Emergent academic interests in English regional identities, particularly northern identities, also encouraged considerations of their role within broader national formations as in Patrick Joyce's *Visions of the People* (1991), Robert Colls and Bill Lancaster's *Geordies* (1992) and Dave Russell's *Looking North* (2004).

Whilst Englishness Studies remains a fantasy, the various academic perspectives upon England, along with the popular discussions of English identity and a range of political interventions, combine to form a refreshingly unenclosed and informal cultural project. The angry nationalist revivalism of Simon Heffer and Roger Scruton, the patriotic revisionism of Billy Bragg, the ironic journalism of Jeremy Paxman and Gill, the popular anthropology of Fox, the idiosyncratic Marxism of Nairn and the reflections on nationhood and race by Stuart Hall and Paul Gilroy, make Englishness a diverse and surprisingly heterogeneous field for study and argument, and one that has not yet sealed its roads or hedged its borders. This book is intended to contribute to these popular and academic debates. It reviews the resources for studying Englishness and makes its own survey of the way English national identity has been defined and expressed in popular cultural performances of the twentieth century. The films, songs, variety shows, strikes, dances, football and cricket matches, political speeches, riots, novels and festivals that figure here are necessarily eclectic, but they also serve to show the main preoccupations of the stories that England has been telling itself about itself, to adapt Clifford Geertz's phrase. Those stories, as the initial examples suggest, are rarely coherent narratives, though they sometimes try to be. More often they represent moments of struggle in an English experience of modernity and tradition that remain unresolved into coherent national form and expression.

The focus of the nine chapters is upon performances of national identity. Performance is a term that acknowledges the acts of invention and construction that have been implicit in the very notion of national identity since the classic work of Eric Hobsbawm and Benedict Anderson on the subject (Hobsbawm and Ranger 1983; Anderson 1983). But performance here is also meant literally, with many of the case studies dealing with real performances on stages, sports fields and political platforms. They range across a century of English modernity, from the mass culture of the music halls in the 1890s to that definitive state expression of the problem of national identity, the Millennium Dome. The coverage of the period between is neither chronological nor entirely even in its distribution, the chapters sometimes emphasising continuities in English identity across decades and at other times focusing upon a significant period of cultural development. The aim is to establish the range and congruence of the resources of English self-representation.

Place is also important. One of the themes of the book is the suppressed significance of regional identity in both the establishment and the problematising of Englishness. The examples, therefore, reflect the cultural diversity of 'provincial England' as well as describing the formation of dominant national discourses in the metropolitan centre of London and the 'deep English' landscapes of the southern counties. Performances in Wigan, Blackpool, Trowell, Dunston and Leamington Spa and journeys along old and new English roads combine to make a more complex map of national culture. Also present are the foreign places that have often caused the English to worry about themselves – the Empire and Commonwealth, Europe in its various guises and the United States, a constant reference point of desire and threat for English popular culture since the 1920s.

The book begins by defining theories of Englishness, though the coherence implied by the term is frequently absent from the discussions of an identity more often rendered by appeals to instinct and tradition than by definition and analysis. The five theories considered here suggest the range of political and cultural discourses that contest English identity. The fringe of Anglo-Saxon revivalists, the Far Right traditions represented by the British National Party and the conservatism of Heffer and Scruton form one edge of the attempts at post-devolutionary English revivalism. These are offset by the persistent influence of George Orwell's anti-theories of Englishness and the Marxist analysis of England's absent national centre by Anderson and Nairn. A contrasting critique of England's elusive identity is provided by the developing tradition of postcolonial studies, beginning with C. L. R. James in the 1930s and developing in the sociology of Stuart Hall and Paul Gilroy in the post-*Windrush* era of emigration from the Caribbean and the Indian subcontinent. The gender politics of Englishness has also been an ambivalent feature of its evasions of nationalist definition. The classic abrogation of English patriarchy, Virginia Woolf's *Three Guineas* (1938), is considered against the radical conservative philosophy of the Women's Institutes and the dissenting women's voices of post-Second World War cultural studies which traced a feminised tradition of national representation in the writing, cinema and biographies of English modernity. The conflicts and meeting points of these arguments about Englishness are represented in the eight chapters that follow.

Chapter 2 considers three private initiatives of national recovery in the main period of English revivalism, the first decade of the twentieth century. Robert Baden-Powell's Boy Scouts and the English folk-dance movements founded by Cecil Sharp and Mary Neal drew upon both traditional and modern resources for such revivals. They also suggest the disruptive influence of conflicts about class, gender and race in their development of a new vision of Englishness. Chapter 3 studies two later state-sponsored interventions in national identity. The Festival of Britain and the Millennium Experience, though notionally British, were firmly metropolitan English in their conception and siting, a formative tension in their projection of national cohesion. Fifty years apart, they illustrate the difficulties of managing a public repertoire of English/British representations, the first in a context of postwar reconstruction and imperial decline, the second in one of cultural globalisation and British devolution. The third case study, the Miners' Strike of 1984–5, offers a contrasting model of national representation. The last great British industrial conflict of the twentieth century defined opposing versions of national identity and history that were played out in English (and British) regions normally ignored in discussions of nationhood. Its alternative topography of modernity and its re-affirmation of older traditions and performances of local identity and struggle provide a counter-discourse to the public statements of national coherence implied by the two official national festivals.

The next two chapters examine representations of English place as sites for the performance and the iteration of national identity. A study of the genre of the literary topographical journey suggests the selective ways in which Englishness was defined in the first half of the century. Travelling to 'discover England' established an ideology of ruralism and historical continuity underpinned by an unacknowledged and exclusive modernity of vision and communication. These discursive acts of travel also highlighted contradictions and evasions in English self-representation, problems of national definition that are central to the national journeys of Edward Thomas, H. J. Massingham and C. E. Montague, and to Michael Powell and Emeric Pressburger's cinematic adaptation of the genre, *A Canterbury Tale* (1944). Chapter 5 argues the importance of English regionalism in the construction of national identity. Concentrating on the North West, a region frequently omitted from the maps of the English journeys discussed in Chapter 4, it considers the role of the North in George Orwell's and Mass-Observation's social anthropology projects of the 1930s. It also examines the challenge to such representations shaped by contemporary Northern popular performers. The work of the comedians Gracie Fields and Frank Randle affirmed a distinctive northern modernity that emphasised economically and culturally distinct regional identities whilst, in the former's case, articulating a distinct national alternative to dominant transatlantic forms of song and film.

The following two chapters consider questions of Englishness and otherness, Chapter 6 focusing on questions of race and Chapter 7 on international sport. The development of a postcolonial Englishness is traced through the histories of the Caribbean political activists and theorists Marcus Garvey and C. L. R. James, an emigrant history that is offset by a study of the black English boxer Randolph Turpin, whose troubled relationship with provincial England and ambivalent encounters with African-America in the 1950s counterpoint the main trajectory of postwar studies of emigration. The chapter also examines the construction of a newly racialised Englishness in the postwar period, a development embedded in legislation, in the populist regional politics and oratory of Enoch Powell and in the civil disturbances in West London in the summer of 1958. Chapter 7 focuses on international football and cricket and their limited but eloquent performances of English nationhood in direct competition with the sporting styles of other cultures. It examines the cultural meanings of three famous moments – the Adelaide Test Match against Australia during the 1932–3 'bodyline' series, the English football team's defeats by Hungary in 1953 and 1954, and Paul Gascoigne's tears in the semi-final of the 1990 World Cup. The questions of style, modernity and masculinity that emerge from these contests also incorporate broader cultural conflicts concerning colonial politics, postwar European nationalisms and English self-perceptions in domestic games structured through social and economic difference.

The final two chapters consider English voices and English sexuality. Beginning with the role of elocution in English education and broadcasting, Chapter 8 traces the role of speech, accent and dialect in formations of national identity and the importance of strategies of mimicry. These cultural contests of voice are compared with the history of the English singing voice in the second half of the chapter. Cecil Sharp's work on folk-song and the career of the music-hall songwriter Edgar Bateman suggest competing versions of national song in the first quarter of the century. This contest between an imagined traditional purity and a realised mass cultural voice was supplanted by American popular song styles which, from the 1920s onwards, forced new accommodations of style and national self-presentation.

The complex interaction of Englishness, popular culture and tradition also shapes the last chapter. This considers the relationship between English identity and sexuality by a study of three classic representations of modern romance. D. H. Lawrence's *Lady Chatterley's Lover* (1929), David Lean's film *Brief Encounter* (1945) and the media-defined romance narratives of Lady Diana Spencer in the 1980s and 1990s suggest ways in which heterosexual English bodies articulated themes of national identity in periods of cultural crisis and change. Lawrence's narrative of a cross-class relationship is developed in the context of the aftermath of the First World War and within the territory of the East Midlands coalfields. Lean's film of provincial desire also engaged with issues of wartime social change and, like Lawrence's novel, had a subsequent role as the centre for popular and academic debates about Englishness and sexuality. Lady Diana Spencer's narratives of romance, awkwardly poised between biographical reality and national melodrama, encoded a fin-de-siècle reappraisal of monarchy through discourses of gender and sexuality. Her sudden death also provoked conflicting representations of English tradition and modernity, an instability reinforced by the rapidity of the forgetting of that moment and its meanings in the years that followed.

Chapter 1

Thinking about England

'There is no available formula for a post-British England', writes Tom Nairn, looking ahead to the day when the English, shorn of the high political disguises of Great Britain and the United Kingdom, will have to deal with themselves as a nation rather than as an undeclared senior partner in a quasi-feudal multinational arrangement (Nairn 2000: 28). However, one of the enduring strengths of the English state has always been its avoidance of classic modes of nationalist description, representation and symbolism. Its resistance to definition and particularly its willingness to subsume national identity within the geopolitical organisations that it silently dominated – Great Britain, the Empire, the United Kingdom – produced a resilient, contradictory anti-nationhood, the very denial of nationalism allowing strategic assertions of national power. But whilst the English, in popular political terms, remain a nation that has not spoken yet there has always been a lot of talk about that not speaking. As Nairn suggests, England lacks a popular nationalist politics, but that lack has itself generated distinctive formulas of national representation and debate. This chapter examines five ways of thinking about England involving elegy, empiricism, anti-intellectualism, gender and race that have influenced the representation of nationhood in the twentieth century. They continue to shape contemporary debates, popular and academic, about what it is to be English.

Declining England

English nationalism, pure English nationalism, is difficult to find, such has been the encroachment of Britain upon the politics of England. Even the two political parties most virulent in their nationalist agendas, the British National Party and the UK Independence Party, adopt the disguises of Britain and the United Kingdom in their titles despite being active only in England. For a really English approach to nationhood it is necessary to turn to groups like Ða Engliscan Gesiðas and Steadfast, two organisations that vividly demonstrate just how difficult it is to be English. Founded in 1966, Ða Engliscan Gesiðas aims to restore 'the just spiritual foundation that England lost in 1066' when it was 'tainted with the curse of the Norman Bastard, William, born of the Harlot' (Phillips 2000: 47, 39). The effects of this Norman curse were such that they led one of the group's activists, the Church of England clergyman John Lovejoy, to compare the endangered lot of the English to that of the Aboriginal peoples of North-West Australia. It was a condition that he attempted to offset by making long-distance runs through the North of England 'in hope of meeting people and awakening an interest in the Old English basis of our identity' (Lovejoy 2000: 89). Steadfast, less committed to Anglo-Saxon history, is nevertheless concerned to challenge 'prejudice against the English; to expose misrepresentation of the English [and] to fight injustice and discrimination that disadvantages the English' (Linsell 2001: 427). *An English Nationalism* (2001), the theoretical tract written by its ideologue Tony Linsell, develops theories of the biological basis for English identity and analyses the threats that it continues to encounter, including the 'crippling burden of guilt and shame that has been unfairly heaped on [it] during the past forty years'. 'Always the English are retreating', he laments, 'handicapped by an ever-declining population' (Linsell 2001: 13, 401).

The two organisations' emphases on the details of Norman heresy and on English fertility problems no doubt hinder their passage into mainstream political debate. But such eccentricities disguise the ways in which their ideas form part of a broader and more influential English nationalist discourse that shares their fears and resentments, if not their more arcane commitments to celebrating the 'Anglo-Saxon diaspora' and reviving the Anglo-Saxon language through audio tapes (Linsell 2001: 13). *This England*, a magazine launched in 1968 and still publishing forty years later with the same editor, Roy Faiers, suggests how the preoccupations of Steadfast and Ða Engliscan Gesiðas can be moulded into a more readily marketable form. It described itself in its first issue as 'a wholesome, straightforward and gentle magazine that loves its own dear land and the people who have sprung from its soil'. 'Instead of politics', the first editorial promised, 'we shall bring you the poetry of the English countryside' (*This England*, 1.1, 1968: 3). 'England's loveliest magazine' went on to pursue an unchanging policy of high production values, rural photographs, patriotic poetry and a celebration of timeless English values and craftsmanship delivered to a readership claimed on the magazine's front covers in 1998 to be 'two million patriots all over the World'. Yet the politics that were disavowed in the first issue gradually surfaced over the years and in a form that would characterise an influential strand of popular English nationalism in the late twentieth century.

By the 1980s Faiers had developed the magazine's always energetic royalism to embrace openly neo-conservative social and economic policies in his editorials, even as the shire horses walked the fields in the photographs and timeless parish rituals were celebrated in the features. In Winter 1981, for example, when 'economists [were] predicting national ruin [and] the trade unions [were] threatening all sorts of disruption', the magazine opened up its Cheltenham properties to offset 'the appalling effects of Britain's heart-rending Abortion Act', sheltering mothers 'safe from scornful tongues and the pressures of the lucrative abortion industry' (14.4, 1981: np). In 1997, anticipating Prime Minister John Major's imminent loss of power, Faiers intervened in an editorial that lamented the lack of 'a Briton of compelling stature able to grab the reins of power, unite the country, and steer this scepter'd isle back to its rightful place on the world scene'. Evoking a nation 'hamstrung by ditherers and deceivers', he ended with the plea '*Will ye no come back again . . . Maggie?*' (30.1, 1997: np). By 2006 *This England* was also establishing explicitly anti-European positions ('Don't Let Europe Rule Britannia: A Non-Political Campaign Sponsored by *This England*') and making comparable non-political contributions to questions of ethnicity. 'My pals were mainly called Harry, Les, Fred, Bill and Johnny', recalled Faiers in 2006, 'but the most commonly listed non-Christian name for baby boys on the nation-wide Register of Births in modern Britain is now Mohammed! Make of that what you will . . .' (39.1, 2006: 22).

The organisation that made the most of Faiers' long career of presenting non-political Englishness was the British National Party. Attempting to consolidate a patchy electoral presence in the decaying urban fastnesses of Burnley, the Isle of Dogs and Barking, the BNP sought to re-brand itself in the1990s as a traditional English party. The German National Socialist reference points of its precursor organisation the National Front disappeared, as did party newspapers with names like *Bulldog* and *Spearhead*. In October 2001 they were replaced by the glossy magazine *Identity* which aspired to the production values and replicated a good deal of the content of *This England*. Nick Griffin, the BNP leader, also adopted the embattled tone of Faiers and Linsell, representing his party as one committed to 'human rights, working for the democratic enfranchisement of the dispossessed British majority' (Griffin 2002: 7). To pursue this end Griffin encouraged members to develop a political ideology drawn from 'home-gown [*sic*] thinkers like G. K. Chesterton and Hilaire Belloc' (two writers well represented in *This England*) as it sought to revive 'the most spied-upon, browbeaten, cowed people in the world' (Griffin 2002b: 7; Griffin 2002a: 5). The party also began to organise 'family weekends' in the English country-side and to encourage the revival of English folklore, 'celebrating Mayday with Jack in the Green and other archetypal creatures from our ethno-cultural subconscious', as Griffin puts it (Griffin 2007: 7).

The 'traditional turn' of the BNP was a rejection of one set of polit-ical contradictions in favour of another. Nazi reference points had always been incongruous in a national identity that, as Paul Gilroy noted, has increasingly located itself in the historical imaginary of English resilience and solidarity during the Second World War (Gilroy 2004: 97). At the same time, though, for an English neo-fascism with electoral bases in Barking and Burnley to refashion itself by reference to Mayday traditions and the eccentric Catholic conservatism of Chesterton and Belloc suggests the remarkable paucity of English nationalism's ideological and discursive resources as it retreated from the modern environments of its core support to seek visions of revival. It is a limitation of representation shared by England's nationalist intellectuals and populists alike, as the work of Simon Heffer and Roger Scruton suggests.

Heffer, once columnist for the *Daily Mail* (circulation 2,353,000) and latterly for the *Daily Telegraph* (circulation 882,400), provides a populist version of the nationalism of *This England* and Steadfast. His polemical purpose is to rouse 'a rigour-free appeasement addicted English', as he puts it in *Nor Shall My Sword: The Reinvention of England* (1999), an 'English' contribution to the devolution debates of the late 1990s (Heffer 1999: 32). Like Ða Engliscan Gesiðas and the BNP, he offers an analysis of a weak England, undermined by its own cultural generosity and lack of guile. 'The English (unlike their Scottish cousins) are a simple and politically unsophisticated people', he claims. They have 'tended more than is good for them to think of themselves as British' (11, 13). The various Scottish, Welsh and Northern Irish devolutions, Heffer argues, offer England the chance to re-imagine itself by reference to living traditions of English culture and values too long subsumed within an over-indulged Britishness. Shakespeare, Milton, Elgar, Constable, Montgomery and Churchill are summoned alongside Geoffrey Chaucer, Thomas Tallis, Henry Yevele and Inigo Jones as inspirations for a twenty-first-century English Renaissance (though the identity of Henry Yevele might pose a problem for some of his readers) (48, 127).

The philosopher Roger Scruton, former editor of the *Salisbury Review*, a journal that represented the only sustained attempt at an intellectual grounding of late twentieth-century English nationalism, also called upon premodern, ruralist resources to define that national vision. First published in 1982, the *Review*'s project 'to conserve the image of authority in an age of licence' entailed the aggressive reversal of a perceived dominance of leftist philosophical discourse, the recovery of 'lost' conservative voices, the re-establishment of the Anglican faith as central to nationhood and an intellectual assault upon 'enemies within' – state secondary education, legacies of postwar socialism and the Welfare State (*Salisbury Review*, 10.1, 1991: 2). Despite the sophistication of its philosophical engagement with European Marxism, the *Review* always appealed to belief and conviction when it came to defining the Englishness that it intended to revive. In a 1993 editorial, for example, it is the sacredness of English institutions – the monarchy, the Church of England, Common Law – that is at issue and that is inevitably threatened. 'The idea of England is a religious idea', Scruton asserts, and one imperilled by the secularist supra-nationalisms of Europe. 'There was no process of "nation building" in the United Kingdom', he writes proudly in his 'memorial address' *England: An Elegy* (2000). Identity was instead 'founded on a loyalty to England: not a nation or a doctrine or a state, but a *country*, the place where we belong' (Scruton 2000: 5).

If, in Benedict Anderson's influential assertion, all nations are 'imagined communities', the Englands of Scruton, Heffer, the BNP and Ða Engliscan Gesiðas are more imaginary than most. Their projection of a persisting, though constantly endangered, premodern rural England involves an act of impersonation and denial that has been an integral part of the theorising of England over the last century. Scruton, like his political elder Enoch Powell the product of a provincial grammar school, projects himself into an alternative feudal nation – 'the rural society that still provides the core experience of England', as he puts it (*Salisbury Review*, 10.4, 1992: 41). That 'core experience', though, can be established only by acts of mimicry and masquerade that aim to insert patriots within an essential English tradition that lies beyond their origins and which is always almost lost to contemporary England. Heffer's account of a young Powell's journey, dressed in hunting pink, to the Old Berkeley East meet via the Metropolitan Line and suburban trains is a startling representation of this determined manufacture of English tradition (Heffer 1998: 109).

The confusions and contradictions of an English nationalism defined by intangible spiritual inheritance, ruralist fantasy and political contradiction have not affected its general influence, even if they have thwarted its explicitly political goals. The 3.5 million members of the National Trust and the enduring support for an unreformed monarchy indicate a generalised but powerfully ingrained national attraction to something resembling the pastoral and feudal identity that Scruton articulates. Nevertheless, the limitations of this range of representation are plain. Martin J. Wiener, in his influential polemic *English Culture and the Decline of the Industrial Spirit 1850–1980* (1981), argued that such imagined traditions were the late nineteenth-century product of an alliance between emergent capitalism and residual aristocratic territorial interests. It was a compact, Wiener suggests in language sympathetic to the neo-liberal discourses of the time, that stalled the development of the modernising entrepreneurial energies that had been so notable a factor in mid-nineteenth-century England. The English, he argues, persuaded themselves that their character and culture 'was not naturally progressive, but conservative; its greatest task . . . lay in taming and "civilizing" the dangerous engines of progress it had unwittingly unleashed' (Wiener 1981: 6). Yet the popular conservative Englishness expressed by Heffer, Faiers, Scruton and now the BNP remains trapped in the contradictory model of neo-liberal economics and a rhetoric of 'traditional' conservative values rooted in the southern shires. Celebrating 'folkways' is about as practical as learning to speak Anglo-Saxon for redefining contemporary English nationhood. It is this impracticality of conservative ruralist strategies of nationhood that goes some way to explaining the continuing importance of George Orwell to debates about English identity.

Ordinary England

George Orwell is probably the most influential twentieth-century theorist of Englishness. This is an Orwellian sentence: assertive, slightly qualified and unsupported by any evidence. And, as with many of Orwell's sentences, it contains both a truth and a deception. Nearly sixty years after his death in 1950, theorists of Englishness (and Britishness – Orwell never made much of a distinction), including Prime Ministers of the Right and the Left (John Major most famously, Gordon Brown most recently), have continued to use his essays as points of reference and authority. This is because Orwell offers a definition of England that mixes populism, patriotism and radicalism in a convincing voice and a supple syntax. His is an Englishness in discursive political motion, providing perspectives that can be applied equally to common-sense Labourism, nostalgic Conservatism, cautious Liberalism, anti-Americanism and Euro-scepticism. His work remains an improbably useful resource for a nation that still finds it hard to say exactly what it is.

'The English are not intellectual', Orwell claimed in his essay 'The Lion and the Unicorn' (1941), 'they have a horror of abstract thought, they feel no need for any philosophy or systematic "world-view"' (Orwell 1970a: 77). It is a national trait that he did his best to embody in wartime essays that developed a theory of Englishness through a denial of the possibility of any such theory. 'The Lion and the Unicorn', 'The Art of Donald McGill' (1941) and 'The English People' (published in 1947, but written in 1944) are celebrations of an Englishness defined by common sense, idiosyncrasy, anti-authoritarian commonality, instinctive fairness and inarticulate patriotism. His own writing seems 'English' in just these ways, trusting to feelings and an inherent reasonableness. 'When you come back to England from any foreign country', he writes in 'The Lion and the Unicorn', 'you have immediately the sensation of breathing a different air' (75). It is a national sensation developed through the celebrated series of evocations that follow: 'solid breakfasts and gloomy Sundays, smoky towns and winding roads, green fields and red pillar-boxes' and, in a detail dubiously deployed by Prime Minister Major in 1993, 'the old maids biking to Holy Communion through the mists of the autumn morning' (Orwell 1970a: 76, 75; Seldon 1997: 370). Such imagist poetry replaces any clear statement of social and political meaning. Yet the rhythms and the details of the landscape that he evokes are careful and strategic, assimilating traces of conflicting traditions of radicalism, conservatism, modernity and tradition, and admitting the nation's limitations whilst celebrating its cultural securities in a time of extreme crisis. He evokes 'green fields' but only in conjunction with 'smoky towns' which are in their way picturesque rather than grimly industrial. The red pillar-boxes and the bicycle become emblems of a nineteenth-century modernity now comfortably settled within a traditional English frame. It is a statement in miniature of the ambivalent national politics that Orwell came to represent.

As Raymond Williams has argued, the Orwell of these essays is a complex and careful rhetorician who constructs his own English persona within the national identity that he evokes (Williams 1971: 16–28). His style – lucid, winning, funny – embodies and disguises the deceptions of Eric Blair, the 'real' George Orwell. Combining Etonian assertiveness with a 'popular' simplicity of syntax and vocabulary and an apparent absence of intellectual method, he seems to bridge the great economic and political divides that were his concern. But the careful selection of memorable details and of national characteristics was

calculated to maintain a contradictory politics that could simultaneously acknowledge social and imperial injustices and recast the nation
as a 'family with the wrong members in control' (Orwell 1970a: 88).
This rendering of social and economic disparity and exploitation into an
accommodating metaphor of a family argument is entirely in keeping
with Orwell's earlier celebration of the 'privateness of English life' and
his wartime commitment to distancing his politics from the Right-Left
polarities of the 1930s (77). The Englishness essays explore the means
of recasting 'ordinary' English experience beyond such politics and
within a new sense of nationhood of 'emotional unity' even as he defines
England in the same paragraph as 'the most class-ridden country under
the sun' (87). Orwell's rhetorical skills shaped an unlikely conduit that
connected popular radicalism – his sense of a quiet English social revolution being accelerated by the war – to the conservative attachment to
Scruton's '*country*, the place where we belong'.

'Patriotism and intelligence will have to come together again', Orwell
writes in 'The Lion and the Unicorn', and part of his contribution to this
meeting is his distinction between that patriotism and nationalism (96).
Nationalism, he argues in an essay of 1945, depends upon a hierarchical classification of identities and a competitive discrimination of values
between nations. It consequently makes wars. Patriotism, on the other
hand, is a 'devotion to a particular place and a particular way of life,
which one believes to be the best in the world but has no wish to force
upon other people' (Orwell 1970b: 411). It is this anti-theory of a
benign, instinctive commonality that transcends class, region and ideology that is the aspect of Orwell's work that has proved most attractive
to British politicians and to some cultural historians. John Major turned
to 'The Lion and the Unicorn' whilst attempting to distance himself
from the divisive national politics of his predecessor, Margaret Thatcher.
Gordon Brown did the same when he sought to articulate 'the future of
Britishness' through national 'core values' – 'liberty, responsibility and
fairness' – in order to offset nationalist successes, particularly in
Scotland (Brown 2006: 5). Orwell it is who stands at the bar in the first
sentence of Robert Colls' *Identity of England*, and as recently as 2006
Billy Bragg is to be found praising 'The Lion and the Unicorn' as 'the
greatest book on Englishness ever written' (Bragg 2006: 196).

The very qualities that make Orwell attractive across political
divides, however, have also made him a controversial figure in post-
Second World War cultural studies and particularly for the English Left.
Raymond Williams, under interrogation by *New Left Review* in the
1970s, identified 'the dreadful stuff from the beginning of the war' as
amongst the most damaging legacy of Orwell's protean performances

and a betrayal of the more radical positions that he had established in the 1930s (Williams 1979: 391). Twenty years on Christopher Hitchens was engaged in rescuing Orwell from such accusations of betrayal, emphasising the particular historical contexts of that 'stuff' and asserting the continuing relevance of his internationalist radical commitments (Hitchens 2002). Orwell should not really be as useful or as controversial nearly sixty years after his death – no other national theorist of his generation has remotely the influence that he continues to exert. That he does so suggests the skill of his management of his contradictory positions, the persistence of those contradictions in early twenty-first-century England and the absence of a theory of national identity that can challenge his rhetorical appeal.

Absent England

It was all that Orwell represented – or appeared to represent – for the Left that provoked a third significant discourse of Englishness. In the 1960s and 1970s, Perry Anderson and Tom Nairn, political theorists associated with *New Left Review*, developed a complementary questioning of British national culture in a series of essays published in that journal. Like Orwell's essays on England, they emerged from periods of crisis. Anderson's 'Components of the National Culture' was published in the summer of 1968 in the wake of the May uprisings in Paris and other European capitals, Enoch Powell's so-called 'rivers of blood' speech on immigration in April (which isn't referred to) and the student 'revolt' at the University of Essex (which is). The essay is both a polemical piece that affirms solidarity with the domestic revolutionary student movement and a survey of the modern failures of English radicalism that preceded it. The lack of any revolutionary traditions in England, Anderson suggests, is bound up with a broader intellectual incapacity to countenance such change. Britain, unlike the rest of Western Europe, lacked an indigenous sociology and Marxism, he argues. This 'absent centre' in the intellectual and political life of the nation that gives the essay its title initiated a reactionary vicious circle of inertia. The historical and cultural conditions that constrained working-class radicalism also rendered a revolutionary intelligentsia impossible and doomed England to a stunted modernity, isolated from the European developments which were shaping the insurrections on the streets of Paris and Berlin. England, Anderson laments, lacks the intellectual tools to understand and so to change itself because the energies that might have led to a genuinely radical national culture were diverted into parochial obsessions with literary criticism and linguistic philosophy. Instead of Walter Benjamin there was George Orwell; instead of Antonio Gramsci there was A. J. Ayer. The 'twentieth century itself becomes the impossible object', he concludes. 'The era of revolutions is, necessarily, unthinkable' (Anderson 1968: 56).

Anderson's lament for the lack of modernity in English thought and politics, its essential un-Europeanness, foreshadowed the structuralist and deconstructive turn in British intellectual life a decade or so later. It also exacerbated a schism within British Marxism, leading the historian E. P. Thompson to defend the 'peculiarities of the English', those 'certain strengths and humane traditions in British life which Other Countries . . . whose Marxism is mature and whose salesmanship is high-powered, do not always display' (Thompson 1978: 56). Anderson's co-editor at *New Left Review*, Tom Nairn, also took the 'peculiarities of the English' seriously whilst sharing his colleague's frustrated sense of an Englishness limited by restrictive intellectual and political resources and ambitions. Nairn, unlike the resolutely internationalist Anderson, argued that England did indeed need a nationalism. However, it was to be one informed by European models and by the emergent nationalist traditions of the British Isles rather than by the quasi-feudal visions propounded by Enoch Powell or the equivocal populism of George Orwell. *The Break-Up of Britain* (1977; revised edn. 1981), written in the context of abortive Scottish and Welsh devolution legislation and the deepening crisis in Northern Ireland, includes chapters on Powell and on the 'English Enigma'. Like Anderson's 'absent centre', Nairn's 'enigma' registers England's idiosyncratic national identity and its lack of a cultural narrative through which radical change could be articulated. 'There is no coherent, sufficiently democratic myth of Englishness', he writes, 'no sufficiently accessible and popular myth-identity where mass discontents can find a vehicle' (Nairn 1981: 294).

Nairn was also the first intellectual of the Left to insist upon the importance of 'Britain' and the 'United Kingdom' as powerful invented identities committed to preserving what he called the 'permanent immaturity' of political experience in England (Nairn 1988: 137). 'British', a term used interchangeably with English as much by Anderson as by Orwell, is for Nairn a sign of the complex, distorting history of Englishness and its colonialism rather than a trivial imprecision of usage. ' "England" and "Britain" may seem much the same thing to the English and to distant observers', he notes tartly in *After Britain* (2000). 'They never do, to immigrants or other archipelago dwellers' (Nairn 2000: 39–40). 'Britain', for Nairn, is a uniquely constructed nation, one 'forged', in Linda Colley's suggestively ambiguous term, through acts of

English incorporation that took place before and beyond the main phase of European nation-building in the nineteenth century. 'There never have been "Britons" . . . any more than there were "Austro-Hungarians" before 1917', he argues, for Britain was defined by 'state-way[s] rather than folk-way[s]' (Nairn 1981: 369; Nairn 2000: 177). However, unlike Austro-Hungarianness, Britishness did not collapse with the end of the empire that it had been invented to accommodate and extend. The success of Britain as a popular 'state-way', Nairn argues, became England's problem.

Through age, use, relative social stability and (unexpectedly, perhaps) immigration, Britain nearly became a viable national identity having been 'worn long enough to feel almost like the "nature" evoked by nationalists' (Nairn 1997: 110). England, at a state level at least, invested so much in the forging of Britishness, an identity that few beyond England acknowledged anyway, that the possibility of its own emergence as an operable nation remained in doubt – hence the bizarre historicism of Ða Engliscan Gesiðas and the strenuous rural fantasies of *This England*. Hence also some other strange consequences. In 1924 the Conservative Party Leader Stanley Baldwin began a speech to the Annual Dinner of The Royal Society of St George by expressing 'a feeling of satisfaction and profound thankfulness that [he could] use the word "England" without some fellow at the back of the room shouting out "Britain" ' (Baldwin 1926: 1). Englishness, for Baldwin, had become an identity that could not speak its name except in the privacy of a private club devoted to that purpose. But through the improvised polit-ical history that Nairn descibes, British identity came to have uses that Baldwin could not have anticipated. The sociologists Les Back, Tim Crabbe and John Solomos recorded a black Londoner's response to the black footballer Ian Wright donning a St George's flag during the England-Argentina game in the 1998 World Cup: 'I thought "What the fuck is he doing – has he lost his mind completely!" I mean the St George Cross! That's the worst thing for a black person because accord-ing to them people you can't be black and English. Maybe Britishness would be something else because you can be "black British" but English? Never!' (Back, Crabbe and Solomos 2001: 255).

Postcolonial England

Lez Henry's interpretation of Wright's performance gives popular expression to one of the most significant theoretical approaches to Englishness in recent times. The development of postcolonial studies in the last twenty-five years has provided new perspectives upon what Stuart Hall has called 'that great unspoken British value – "whiteness" ' (Hall 1999–2000: 7). Issues of race, imperialism and postcolonialism are crucial but frequently unarticulated elements of many of the theories of English discussed so far. From the eugenics of Steadfast and the British National Party (which has replaced the concept of racial blood with that of racial DNA in their modernising drive) to the cultural exclusivity of Scruton and Heffer to the slippery politics of the former imperial policeman Orwell, race and empire – by their absence as well as their presence – have shaped articulations of English identity.

These engagements and disengagements form part of the fragmented, disruptive model of imperialism and its consequences that has been one of the main outcomes of recent postcolonial studies. Instead of seeing the cultural activity of empire as an exportation of 'English values' from a centre to a periphery, a more complex pattern of challenge, resistance and reciprocity has emerged. Imperial activities, theorists such as Edward Said and Homi Bhabha have argued, constructed not only the subjects of the empire but also the imperialists themselves. In these readings the dynamic of empire becomes one of displacement rather than expansion and of hybridisation rather than confident consolidation of existing cultural values and meanings. As Ian Baucom puts it, empire 'is less a place where England exerts control than the place where England loses command of its own narrative of identity. It is the place onto which the island kingdom arrogantly displaces itself and from which a puzzled England returns as a stranger to itself' (Baucom 1999: 3).

Anxiety and puzzlement about imperialism's implications for national identity were evident from the latter part of the nineteenth century. The ideological and popular political coherence given to the imperial project as an 'expansion of England' also raised questions as to how long and with what consequences such expansion could be sustained. Elliott Mills anticipated such unsustainability in his *Decline and Fall of the British Empire* (1905), a pamphlet that influenced Robert Baden-Powell in his development of the Boy Scout movement. In a fantasy of the end of England apparently written by a representative of victorious Japanese imperialism in the year 2005, Mills writes of

> the possessions that were stripped from England because she had slumbered; of the Isle denuded of troops; of the corn-ships that never came; of the fleet that grew weary with watching; of the dark night and the crowded transports; of streets that lay sodden with the blood of those who ran because they had never learned to shoot; of the women who cursed them for cowards when the foreigner was quartered in their homes.
>
> (Mills 1905: 44)

This apocalyptic mix of economic decline, military incompetence, masculine crisis and miscegenation is a vivid concentration of a range of contemporary expressions of national unease within a vision of imperial collapse.

Even at the time of Benjamin Disraeli's elevation of Victoria as Empress, Liberal politicians like Sir Charles Dilke had been making comparisons between an ageing England and the 'young countries of Greater Britain [that is, the Dominions] . . . in which the order of society seems to be the most secure and the condition of the people the best' (Dilke 1890: 245). Another pamphleteer of the period, E. F. Chidell, anticipated the end of England as a self-sustaining industrial and economic power, imagining instead a renewal of Englishness only through 'a system of emigration on a vast scale to the great self-governing colonies'. 'Many omens warn us that the work of England in these islands is accomplished', he writes, but 'in Africa she may be girt afresh with strength and dignity' (Chidell 1903: 9, 41). Those unquestionably committed to the idea of an imperial England also revealed difficulties in defining their identity within it. Lord Alfred Milner, formerly High Commissioner in South Africa, faced the issue directly in a speech on 'Empire Citizenship' in 1912. 'But what is my country?' he asked, 'an easy question, you might think, to answer. And so it is for most members of the human race. But it is not altogether so easy for any subject of His Majesty King George V'. For Milner, the answer lay in an abdication of limited national allegiance in the service of a greater identity. 'The fine saying "the Empire is my country" is not a phrase of my coining, though it precisely expresses what I feel', he concludes, arguing for the difficult need to abolish English or even British identity in the service of a transcendent and de-nationalised global imperialism (Milner 1998: 488, 489).

Different challenges to English identity were posed by the colonised themselves. Dilke, Chidell and Milner developed their theories of emigrant England with the Dominions in mind, holding to Hall's 'great unspoken British value – "whiteness"'. The consequences of the dissemination of Englishness throughout an empire that was not white became fully evident only with the large-scale emigrations to Britain after the Second World War. However, the challenges to Englishness as a discrete identity were already apparent in the developing intellectual traditions of the 'English' Caribbean, India and Africa in the first third of the century. In his autobiography *Beyond a Boundary* (1963), the Trinidadian C. L. R. James recalled his first visit to England in 1932. 'The British intellectual was going to Britain', he writes, as neat a summary of the ideological and geographical intimacies and distances of imperialism as any later postcolonial theory (James 1963: 114).

James's work describes a complex evolution and mingling of identities, as imperial power dynamics, both political and cultural, were put to the test by new physical and ideological movements. 'If the ideas originated in the West Indies', James writes of his development towards radical anti-imperialist positions, 'it was only in England and in English life that I was able to track them down and test them' (11). In a knowing reversal of the imperial order of things, James describes the arrival of the Caribbean migrant who was coming home to England in order to change it.

The tests that James applied in his first years in England were not only to his own ideas but also to the cultural centre of Englishness. 'Londoners have had sixty years of compulsory education and all the advantages of a great modern city', he complained in a report for the *Port of Spain Gazette* in 1932. 'When you look around at the intellectual quality of the people you are astonished' (James 2003: 117–18). James quickly began the process of decolonising his relationship with English culture, differentiating aesthetic and intellectual achievements from the social and economic forces that produced them and confronting the fact that the 'average man in London is eaten up with colour prejudice' (83). The reverse imagination of the colonial migrant produces in James's work a detailed critique of the structures of imperialism and at the same time an eloquent performance of their possibilities for change. James occupied a position of 'double consciousness', in W. E. B. Du Bois's terms, but denied the pejorative connotations that Du Bois attached to that condition. For James, double consciousness was the only position from which an assured postcolonial politics could be wrought and Englishness itself could only be radically understood and radically changed by those who both shared in it and were also outside it. The cultural hybridity that James represented, explored and celebrated was an energising process for the development of new, emergent nationalisms in the Caribbean and Africa but also in England itself.

The significance of such 'double consciousness' was less clear to the English themselves, however. The rapid, disorderly and often bloody end of empire in the two decades after 1945 precluded a thorough understanding of Englishness as an imperial identity, even as the consequences of that history were becoming evident within England. This was reflected in a contemporary intellectual inattention to the implications of empire as much as by the state's reticence about that past. Cultural theorists such as Raymond Williams and Richard Hoggart who were developing their discipline of national understanding in the 1950s and 1960s might have engaged in a newly radical analysis of social class within English culture, but they were largely silent on the issues of imperialism and race. The Birmingham Centre for Contemporary Cultural Studies which Hoggart founded in the early 1960s also proved to be socially insular even if theoretically adventurous. Paul Gilroy, in the Centre's first book-length publication to engage with the questions of race, described cultural studies as 'a discipline which, in spite of itself, tends towards a morbid celebration of England and Englishness from which blacks are systematically excluded' (Gilroy 1987: 12).

Gilroy's more recent work has engaged with the consequences of that erasure of empire from English national consciousness. In *After Empire* (2004) he argues that Britain's inability to mourn its loss of empire contributes to the entrapment of popular nationalist sentiment in mythical, silently racialised unities, such as those mediated through images associated with the Second World War and by extension those predicated upon the village England of Roy Faiers and Roger Scruton. Such fantasies, Gilroy argues, express 'a desire to find a way back to the point where the national culture – operating on a more manageable scale of community and social life – was . . . both comprehensible and habitable' (Gilroy 2004: 97). The 'myth of the Blitz', as Angus Calder has called it, fills a political and emotional absence that roughly corresponds to the shape of an empire that was lost in rather less idealisable conflicts in Malaya, Kenya, Cyprus, Aden, Oman and Ulster (Calder 1991). 'Postimperial melancholia', Gilroy argues, can only be addressed by an open appraisal of the 'hidden, shameful store of imperial horrors [that] has been an unacknowledged presence in British political and cultural life during the second half of the twentieth century' (Gilroy 2004: 102). It requires a re-imagination of Englishness both within and after empire that engages with the fullness of recent histories as well as the varieties of its present cultural make-up. Without such a process, he suggests, the resources for being English can only remain restrictive and defensive. The crippling limitation, the sheer boredom of the identity perpetrated by *This England* not only continues a process of denial and passive aggression (and not always passive aggression) but limits the culturally convivial possibilities of contemporary national life (see Gilroy 2006).

Gendered England

Gender, like race and empire, has only recently been seen to be integral to the popular and academic construction of Englishness. The American historian George L. Mosse has emphasised the way classical nationalist ideologies worked through ordered and stylised codes of masculinity and heterosexual relationships. 'Nationalism adopted [an] ideal of manliness and built its national stereotypes around it', he argues (Mosse 1985: 10). It was a process that was to become grotesquely evident in post-1918 Germany, as Klaus Theweleit has shown in his *Male Fantasies* (1987), a study of the relationship between misogyny, sexual violence and the rise of National Socialism. When English nationalist rhetoric employed similar terms, however, as in the Fascist leader Oswald Mosley's appeal to the 'natural morality of British manhood' in 1932, it marked an exception rather than a rule (Mosley 1932: 40). Whilst the nationalist projects of the Edwardian period discussed in Chapter 2 were certainly informed by attempts to define and regulate gender roles, the process and outcomes of those attempts contrasted sharply with the European models described by Mosse and Theweleit. Masculinity was always the contested centre of these movements rather than a heroic model, and the development of English self-representation frequently resolved on the management of changing gender roles rather than upon their self-evident stability.

Virginia Woolf's *Three Guineas* (1938) ambivalently confirms this sense of Englishness as a site for gendered contest, even as it remains the most sustained and radical polemic against the misogyny of the English state. The refusal of English institutions to allow women full economic and social rights, whether in law or education, Woolf argues, annuls an Englishwoman's obligations within the social reciprocity implicit in nationhood. 'How much of "England" in fact belongs to her', she asks, posing as she does throughout *Three Guineas* the question of what being English means if its female subjects are placed beyond so many of the rights and the rituals of the English state (Woolf 1943: 195). Contemporary marriage laws, for example, would have certainly fulfilled the worst fears of the English supporters' song cited in the Introduction: if an Englishwoman married a foreigner she would no longer legally be English (196). Even if she did marry an Englishman, her rights to property and to divorce remained severely limited. Despite universal suffrage, Woolf argues, such restrictions of women's investment in the material and ideological substance of Englishness rendered them aliens in their 'own' land. The legal frame of English gender relations denied women 'the full stigma of nationality' as she memorably puts it (149). This condition of legalised exclusion clears the way for Woolf's celebration of another absent centre of English nationhood. 'As a woman I have no country', she asserts. 'As a woman I want no country. As a woman my country is the whole world' (197).

Woolf's polemical text needs to be read alongside other versions of the relationship between women and nationhood that are less clear-cut. Even within the exclusive social context of the 'educated man's sister' that is Woolf's stated concern, Englishwomen's relationships with national identity provided distinctive engagements with its problems rather than Woolf's rhetorical abdication (Woolf 1943: 18). The Women's Institute provides one example of these. Based on a nineteenth-century Canadian agrarian movement, its first branch was founded in 1915. Its initial purpose was to support the war effort, the very state enterprise that *Three Guineas* defines as the ultimate expression of nationalist masculinity. The Institute's organisation of domestic food production as a contribution to the Home Front certainly defined the socially conservative position that it maintained throughout the century. However, in the postwar period it engineered a political independence from the state that made that conservatism a distinctive and in many ways quite radical position. By the Second World War, the Federation of Women's Institutes had become an entirely self-financing organisation which had developed a sophisticated policy towards its own rural constituency and towards central government. As Cicely McCall put it in her account of the organisation in wartime, 'though only too willing to co-operate with government departments in national work, [the institutes] are in no way dependent on the government for their views or their policy' (McCall 1943: 11).

The independent organisational structure of the Institutes reflects the critical distance that the movement maintained from the 'male' state that Woolf analysed, though without, of course, articulating Woolf's analysis of that state. In the context of Second World War debates about a postwar settlement McCall also suggests the implicit radicalism of the WI project. 'Institutes have taught countrywomen to be articulate, they have taught citizenship and they have revived forgotten crafts', she argues. Their 'self-government has taught practical democracy [and] classes and lectures have given members an opportunity to look beyond their village and beyond English shores' (48). Whilst not quite becoming women's soviets of the shires, the Institutes on this analysis had developed a distinctively gendered politics that negotiated between conservative social structures and an implicitly radical politics of self-reliance and self-determination.

The radical conservatism of the Women's Institute is typical of the complex role that gender has played in the production of English national identity. The theoretical reticence of the organisation belied a determined and ambivalent gender politics which, though it would oppose the terms and conclusions of Woolf's feminist analysis of the state, also established its own gendered critique of English political institutions and its own independent structures. Such coding and ambivalence have come to be seen as influencing a distinctive turn in the wider representation of national identity. In *Forever England* (1991), for example, Alison Light argues that between 1920 and 1940, a period that includes *Three Guineas*, 'a revolt against, embarrassment about, and distaste for the romantic languages of national pride produced a realignment of sexual identities which was part of a redefinition of Englishness' (Light 1991: 8). Like the Women's Institutes, the writers that are Light's concern demonstrated a change in the way women experienced nationhood. That 'entry into modernity', as she terms it, was also expressed in conservative terms that reversed Woolf's self-exile from Englishness by integrating nationhood into intimate, domestic discourses of experience (10).

If it was Woolf's disavowal of national identity that was to achieve later academic celebrity, it was the processes described by Light and exemplified by the Women's Institutes that had more profound effects upon the popular experience of Englishness. As the examples in Chapter 9 suggest, the negotiations of gender with other forces of national identity formation such as class and place were in the end more significant than Woolf's actually quite specific appeal to the condition of the educated man's sister. The importance of the local and the domestic in women's experience of Englishness became important to revisions not only of institutionalised gender roles but also of influential discourses of political dissent in the last quarter of a century, just as Paul Gilroy's *'There Ain't No Black in the Union Jack'* (1987) had pointed up English cultural studies' evasions of issues of race. Beatrix Campbell's *Wigan Pier Revisited* (1984), for example, was a 'quest for the essence of England and Englishness' which revised both the class and gender assumptions of George Orwell's journey (Campbell 1984: 3). Carolyn Steedman's *Landscape for a Good Woman* (1986) posed a different challenge to postwar cultural studies' construction of the working-class family in its exploration of the meaning of her mother's material aspirations and desires. Her wanting 'a New Look skirt, a timbered country cottage, to marry a prince' problematised romantic conceptions of the working-class matriarch just as surely as it suggested the irrelevance of Woolf's idealistic politics for women implicated in the changing social and domestic structures of England (Steedman 1986: 9).

These five representative discourses about English identity suggest the variety of current political and cultural approaches to the subject. They also suggest the instability and conflicts within the field. Regressive fantasies of a unified, pastoral culture, assertions of common sense and ordinariness emerging from a period of absolute crisis, missing political and nationalist traditions, the repressed other of imperialism, and the conservative radicalism of gendered critiques of the dominant ideologies of Englishness cannot combine to form a coherent discursive model for English identity. Indeed, discourses on Englishness frequently demonstrate political and cultural contradictions and blind-spots in their implied strategies that implicate them in the very problems that they seek to describe and solve. The essentially racialised pastoralism of Scruton and Heffer, for example, has nothing to say about the complex legacies of empire that Gilroy describes. In its turn, Gilroy's attention to London's cultural encounters, dialogues and exchanges can be seen to continue a long indigenous history of metropolitan exclusivity and regional exclusion. A YouGov poll in 2005 also discovered a very Orwellian cast to England/Britain's self-perception. Its informants top four phrases describing 'Britain and what it is to be British' were 'British people's right to say what they think', 'Britain's defiance of Nazi Germany in 1940', 'British people's sense of fairness and fair play' and 'the landscape of Britain' (YouGov 2005). This studied popular anachronism cannot be explained by the kind of anti-theory that Orwell himself developed in answer to the political and personal emergencies of the 1940s.

Talking about England, as the current popular literature on the topic tells us, is never easy. The examples of England performing itself to itself that follow do not contradict that verdict, but in their variety and difficulty they also suggest the ways in which the country that has not yet spoken has also been very active in maintaining its silences and contradictions. Englishness Studies, if that potentially embarrassing fantasy is to have any foundation at all as a serious enterprise, has to begin by acknowledging the strange state of that identity without celebrating its eccentricity or falling prey to its own myths of exceptionalism and ineffability.

Chapter 2

Reviving England

The Boy Scouts, the English Folk-Dance Society and the Espérance Morris movement were all founded in the Edwardian period, a golden age of Englishness that was also a golden age for worrying about England's identity and future. Robert Baden-Powell, Cecil Sharp and Mary Neal, their respective founders, confronted what they saw as a crisis in the social fabric of England by instigating voluntary movements for the recovery of healthy national bodies, the establishment of healthy national minds and the revival of healthy national traditions. The Scouts and the two folk-dance movements provide instructive case studies of the contradictions inherent in such projects of national revival. For example, Baden-Powell, Sharp and Neal all argued that the decay of character, physique and traditional knowledge in English youth was due to the destructive effects of industrial and urban modernity, and each advocated a restorative primitivism applied through adventure, dance or song. Yet all three were also notable for their skilful exploitation of new technologies of communication. Each also confronted significant theoretical and practical problems in the foundation and conduct of their organisations which suggested the difficult roles of class, gender and race in the construction of a new Englishness. The camp grounds and village halls of the Scout troops and folk-dance groups proved to be less venues for the consolidation of English national identity than public theatres for the performance of conflicts inherent in that identity.

Scouting for Boys – and Girls

The Scouts were the product of a siege. Robert Baden-Powell was one of the few British military heroes of the Anglo-Boer Wars of 1899–1902, his canny exploitation of the fame that accrued from his conduct of the 219-day siege of the outpost of Mafeking allowing him to develop a distinctive means of dealing with the crisis that he identified in English life. That Baden-Powell's celebrity stemmed from siege not battle was significant in the period of imperial and national self-questioning which the false victory of the Boer War only intensified. Siege mentality – cunning, improvisation and paranoia – defines *Scouting for Boys* (1908), the founding text of Baden-Powell's new movement in which he invoked the perils, lessons and inspirations of the months in Mafeking as means for understanding and improving England's contemporary moral and physical condition. 'Be prepared', the Boy Scouts' motto, was a personal and a political injunction (as well as a characteristically immodest reference to the founder's initials). Scouts, he declared, must be alert to the possibility of enemy attack, 'for though [invasion] may not be probable, it is quite as possible as it was at Mafeking; and every boy in Britain should be just as ready as those boys were in Mafeking to take their share in its defence' (Baden-Powell 1908: 9). A considerable literature of invasion anxiety had been current in England since the 1870s and *Scouting for Boys* has vivid flashes of future struggles and the necessary means of repulsion. 'Peace cannot be certain', he tells his young readers with typically violent emphasis, 'unless we show that we are always fully prepared to defend ourselves in England, and that an invader would only find himself ramming his head against bayonets and well-aimed bullets if he tried landing on our shores' (313).

Whilst enemies massed around the shores, Baden-Powell identified even more serious threats lurking within the stockade of England and within the bodies of its besieged adolescents in particular. 'Fall of the Roman Empire was due to bad citizenship', reads one of the capitalised mottoes that punctuate the text (336). Bad citizenship in turn is said to result from failures in civic and personal codes of family discipline and education. '2,000,000 boys. / 270,000 under good influence' is Baden-Powell's tersely pessimistic assessment of the male youth of the nation (339). Urban life and a consequent decline in physical and psychological toughness, he suggests, resulted in a young male population ill-equipped to respond to any future crisis. He equates the behaviour of a crowd at a football match with the 'bad citizenship' of Rome's decadence and contrasts them with the imperial ideal that he himself embodied:

> thousands of boys and young men, pale, narrow-chested, hunched-up, miserable specimens, smoking endless cigarettes, numbers of them betting, all of them learning to be hysterical as they groan or cheer in panic unison with their neighbours . . . One wonders whether this can be the same nation which had gained for itself the reputation of being a stolid, pipe-sucking manhood, unmoved by panic or excitement, and reliable in the tightest of places. (338)

England was endangered, and Baden-Powell proffered his Scouting movement as a practical strategy for producing 'a nation of good God-fearing, virile citizens in the next generation' (Collis et al. 1961: 49).

What is striking about Baden-Powell's intervention is not only the popularity of his largely improvised solution to the ills of English youth but also the contradictions and anomalies that its development revealed in the national resources of his revivalism. Scouting has come to be seen as the pre-eminent modern English youth organisation, a 'character factory' as Michael Rosenthal calls it (Rosenthal 1986). However, in the early days of the movement Baden-Powell was projecting a far more idiosyncratic and at times slightly deranged sense of Englishness than subsequent accounts have allowed. *Scouting for Boys*, the book that the official history of the movement calls 'a charter for character training' and Rosenthal 'a marvellously variegated paean to the value of obedience', is a case in point (Collis et al. 1961: 27; Rosenthal 1986: 8). It first appeared in six fortnightly instalments, published by Arthur Pearson, the founding editor of both the *Daily Express* and *Tit-Bits*, two of the most innovative popular periodicals of their day. Baden-Powell's willingness to exploit the very mass culture that his book argued was most ruinous to contemporary boyhood and manhood was only the first of the quirks of a classic text that over the years was quietly withdrawn by the movement that it initiated.

Scouting for Boys is notably disorganised and very odd. One historian of the Scout movement has claimed that the incoherent structure was a deliberate strategy, imitating Pearson's success in addressing a 'semi-literate public' by using 'tit-bits' of narrative and information. A 'more solid text-book style treatment', he suggests, would have alienated its prospective readership (Reynolds 1950: 25). Given that the pricing of the instalments (4d) already limited any 'semi-literate' market, the suspicion remains that eccentricity and improvisation were endemic to Baden-Powell's approach. Idiosyncratic codes of conduct ('A Scout smiles and whistles under all circumstances') are set beside 'Camp Fire Stories' and short plays of sometimes uncompromising grimness (Baden-Powell 1908: 50). In the exemplary tale of 'Winter's Stob; or, the Elsdon Murder', for example, Scouting methods lead to the hanging of a gypsy. A drama set on the South African veldt ends in summary execution and secret burial, with earth to be energetically stamped down by the young performers as its final act (141). Training in tracking methods is interrupted by digressions that articulate undisguised personal prejudice. 'I was once accused of mistrusting men with waxed moustaches', the Chief Scout protests at one point. 'Well, so, to a certain extent, I do. It often means vanity and sometimes drink' (77). Practical advice on reading spores and first aid is combined with discussions of topics that seem outside the immediate remit of a revivalist national movement – suicide, for example. 'Most people at one time or another of their lives get a feeling that they will kill themselves', he writes off-handedly. 'As a rule they get over it in a day or two' (304). But if they don't, advice is given on dealing with cut throats, poison, hanging and other methods of self-destruction. A visit to a slaughterhouse is recommended as preparation for dealing with violent human deaths (305).

Such passages are more than appealing eccentricities. They suggest a dilemma in Baden-Powell's analysis of an English crisis and the way out that was fundamental to the future structure and practice of his organisation. *Scouting for Boys* was intended as a primer for a new kind of mass movement and he had already held his formative experimental Scout Camp on Brownsea Island, Dorset in 1907. There he explored the possibility of bringing together boys from different social backgrounds in a context of outdoor adventure. His close links with the Boys' Brigade had provided him with an example of a successful national youth organisation and his dealings with Arthur Pearson demonstrated his appreciation of the importance of modern strategies of publicity and circulation. However, despite his fascination with the imperial cultures of Germany, Japan and later Italy, which had established state organisations of youth training, Baden-Powell balked at admitting that the Scouts was an organisation at all. He emphatically denied that it was military in origin, emphasising its difference from the cadet corps already established in the public schools and distancing it from the uniformities of the Boys' Brigade. Personal development within a collective context replaced formal discipline. 'I do not believe in much *drill* for boys', he wrote, 'it does not develop their individual initiative' (Collis et al. 1961: 55). This sense of necessary individualism is a paradoxical element in what was to become the definitive English youth organisation, but from the beginning it was embedded in the movement's name. Baden-Powell was not interested in brigades but in scouts, solitary and informally organised operatives. At the beginning of *Scouting for Boys* he evokes 'British adventurers and explorers, the scouts of the nation', emphasising that national and particularly imperial history was energised by individual endeavour and risk rather than controlled by procedural formality and routine (13).

The sense of Englishness as individual rather than institutional is also apparent in Baden-Powell's mistrust of formal education. Although he considered membership of the Scouts unnecessary for public school boys, he was also sceptical of some of the prized values of that other imperial character factory, particularly sportsmanship. 'High averages and clean flannels', he asserts, are useless against the real demands of empire (23). His ideal education was closer to that described in Rudyard Kipling's *Stalky and Co.* (1899) and *Kim* (1901), books that demonstrated national and imperial schooling taking place beyond the formalities of classroom and playing field. Kim learns to be English by acting out other identities along the Khyber Pass, and Stalky learns Englishness beyond the influence of the great public schools. Both confirm Baden-Powell's view that true entrepreneurial English masculinity was necessarily shaped beyond 'the steadying influence of tradition' (181). Stalky in particular – lower-middle-class, resourceful, loyal and violent – is a Scout before his time and the alternative organisation that he establishes with his 'company' is much closer to Baden-Powell's vision of the Scout patrol than any public school cadet corps. 'The patrol is the character school for the individual' was a Scouting motto and that individual schooling was conducted outside any explicitly authoritarian system (Reynolds 1950: 36). The Scoutmaster's role, argued Baden-Powell, was 'neither that of a schoolmaster nor of a Commanding Officer, but rather that of an elder brother *among* his boys', and he was particularly proud that in the early days of the organisation boys would seek out their own Scoutmaster (Baden-Powell 1933: 284). The most striking (and most mocked) aspect of the latter's uniform, his shorts, was introduced both to demilitarise his appearance and to emphasise equality with his troop (Warren 1987: 391). Scouting was thus intended to be informal, self-motivated learning, 'a recreation in which the boy would be insensibly led to educate himself' (Baden-Powell 1933: 277–8).

This mistrust of formal structures of Englishness also led Baden-Powell into contradictions in his thinking about empire. The Boy Scouts was an imperialist organisation. Its mythical place of origin was Mafeking, a site of colonial crisis that provided the occasion for a display of English improvisation and self-reliance that the movement was intended to foster in the nation as a whole. Scouting paraphernalia and rituals were also manufactured from Baden-Powell's experiences of empire, as well as from the mythology of the American frontier which always appealed to him. The Scout hat was modelled on the stetson which he had admired in Buffalo Bill's Wild West Show and appropriated for his scouting work in the Ashanti campaign in West Africa; the left handshake was avowedly of West African origin; the Scout colours of green and yellow were those of the South African constabulary; and the inaugural Brownsea Island camp had been roused each day by the sounding of a koodoo horn, captured by Baden-Powell in Matabeleland (Reynolds 1950: 48, 49, 18). This assemblage of imperial signs was intended to bring the modern English boy in touch with an adventurous colonialist past. However, like Dilke and others, Baden-Powell was also driven to contemplate the possibility that 'real' English manhood had been lost to England, a conclusion that was drawn not only from observing the 'miserable specimens' of the proletariat, but also the incompetence of their social betters. 'Take even the captain of your cricket eleven', he wrote provocatively in *Scouting for Boys*, 'and put him down on the South African veldt alongside the young Colonial, and see which can look after himself' (23). Public school bodies, he implies, needed to absorb the outdoor lessons of the Dominions. But the most unstable aspects of Baden-Powell's imperial thinking emerge in his attitude to the lessons of 'primitive' cultures that England must absorb in order to preserve its own civilising mission.

Repeatedly, Baden-Powell was drawn to fantasies of the natural man, even as he engaged wholeheartedly with the eugenics of his time. Army scouting, he reflected late in life, was aimed at 'taking the men back as nearly as possible to the primitive', and this need for the rediscovery of a lost body's lost instincts is trailed through the theory, if not eventually the practice, of his movement (Baden-Powell 1933: 273). 'The physical attitude of the natural man, as one sees it in the savage, is the one to cultivate in the boy in mind as well as body', he writes, as stark a statement of a boyhood heart of darkness as could be imagined (Baden-Powell 1908: 361). He liked to include illustrations of exemplary savages in his books – warriors, Indian gypsies, Red Indians, trackers – and of Scouts imitating their bodies, learning the theatre of being primitive. So whilst the organisation was a product of the promotional, organisational and institutional powers of a late capitalist imperial state – a 'shrewd marriage of public service and good business', as Robert H. MacDonald describes it – Baden-Powell also insisted that abandoning some aspects of that civilisation was essential to its own survival (MacDonald 1993: 9). The paradox became particularly intense in the early years of Scouting when the loose-knit, improvised organisation that Baden-Powell envisaged began to proliferate dangerously out of control. The *Official History* quotes a critic of the liberty that was initially allowed to Scoutmasters and their troops: 'Gauntlet gloves with fringes – *à la* cowboy – silver-plated spurs, bandoliers, revolvers, bowie-knives, riding-breeches, and gaiters are common sights' (Collis et al. 1961: 65). It was a taste for violent display that was hardly discouraged by Baden-Powell's flamboyant presentation of a Maxim gun to the best troop at an early Crystal Palace rally (Collis et al. 1961: 59).

This period of Scouting also saw intense conflicts over class and gender. The redemptive ideal of an informal national organisation, which 'appeals to every class, from hooligan to high-born' foundered early upon the realities of English social hierarchy and upon Baden-Powell's own position within it (Reynolds 1950: 1). Although the inaugural Brownsea Island camp was supposed to be an experiment in social mixing, the public school contingent of the twenty-two boys were automatically appointed patrol leaders. 'The rougher boys were perceptibly levelled up in the matter of behaviour, cleanliness, etc.', the Chief Scout claimed (Rosenthal 1986: 86). Despite his optimistic conclusion, the movement's ability to redeem hysterical, narrow-chested smokers from ruin was always in doubt if the accounts of hooligan dung-throwing and abuse in response to public outings of Scouts and Guides are to be believed (see Collis et al. 1961: 41; Kerr 1932: 44–5). Baden-Powell quickly realised that ideals of the primitive body represented by the Zulu tracker or Kipling's Kim or even the Boer War hero had to negotiate with the realities of the predominantly lower-middle-class boys and families that actually supported the movement. The really wild youth of England remained on the whole unmoved or in ambush, despite the pieties of social reformers in the ranks (see Bryan 1936).

The most serious challenge to the early project of Scouting came not from imperial contradictions or rough lads, however, but from girls. In 1909, only a year after the launch of the Scouts, Baden-Powell was forced to confront this unexpected enemy within. He reported in the *Headquarters Gazette* that 'already some 6,000 girls have registered themselves without any encouragement as "Boy Scouts", and are carrying out the same games and practices' (Kerr 1932: 31). As Rose Kerr recalled, 'Baden-Powell had not been particularly keen on the idea of scouting for girls' for whilst class differences could theoretically be accommodated within the informal hierarchies of Scouting, a significant number of girls tracking, camping and coping with suicides presented quite different difficulties of management (34). One Guide's memory of the early days of the movement in Liverpool gives some idea of the problems. 'When the girls got at loggerheads with each other', she recalled, 'we made them put on boxing gloves and settle their differences in cold blood' (45). Such manifestations of the primitive female body persuaded an anxious Baden-Powell to separate Boy and Girl Scout troops and enforce a different set of national ideals for the latter before they became 'a sort of Amazon Cadet Corps' (37).

The term 'Guiding' had a purposeful ambiguity from the beginning. Kerr notes that, like the Scouts, the name had an imperial origin in 'the famous corps of Guides in India' (35). However, in his article on the question, Baden-Powell had already trailed a different implication of the term. 'If we want the future manhood of the country to be men of character', he argued, 'which is the only guarantee for safety for the nation – it is essential in the first place that the mothers, and the future wives (the guides of those men), should also be women of character' (29). Guides were thus rapidly transformed from adventurers in the Khyber Pass into future matrimonial and maternal helpmeets of Scouting Englishmen. In 1912 a new version of *Scouting for Boys* was produced under the nominal authorship of Baden-Powell's sister, Agnes. Entitled *The Handbook for Girl Guides or How Girls Can Help Build up the Empire*, it set about adapting the original text for newly gendered purposes. Surprisingly, a good deal of the rough-and-ready original material was maintained – the suicide passage (though not the slaughterhouse recommendation), dealing with mad dogs, siege missiles and 'How to secure a burglar with eight inches of cord'. However, a significant amount of new material was deployed alongside these invitations to cold-bloodedness. Agnes Baden-Powell's preface sets the tone: 'Its aim is to get girls to learn how to be women – self-helpful, happy, prosperous, and capable of keeping good homes and of bringing up good children' (Baden-Powell 1912: vii). 'One doesn't want women to be soldiers', the Chief Guide reassured her readership – or their parents – 'we none of us like women who ape men' (22). Womanliness is defined mainly by nursing, with activities such as 'planning a small hospital in your clubroom' being suggested for the new organisation (30). The camp loom was turned over to the girls and fresh adventures were devised for the kitchen store and the linen cupboard.

Baden-Powell's rapid re-organisation of spontaneously created Girl Scout troops was resented by their members. 'The new name was not received with any great enthusiasm by those who had already styled themselves "Girl Scouts"', Kerr admits, 'and many of them felt that the scheme now proposed to them, with its substitution of nursing and domestic duties for the more boyish activities, was rather a watered down edition of Scouting' (Kerr 1932: 35). They accepted it, however, in obedient Scouting or subservient Guiding spirit, 'in deference to the wishes of their Chief' (36). Agnes Baden-Powell then set to countering the fears of middle-class families that Guiding 'would deprive [girls] of every sort of maidenly modesty, and would lead to their rushing about the country with few clothes and fewer manners' (37). By the First World War, both Guiding and Scouting were centrally controlled, clearly gendered organisations which had shaped the early inconsistencies of *Scouting for Boys* into an orderly version of national character training. As Agnes Baden-Powell put it, 'scouting for boys makes for MANLINESS, but the training for Guides makes for WOMANLINESS' (Baden-Powell 1912: 22). The exemplary deaths of first-generation Scouts on the Western Front consolidated myths of national service that had begun in the different military circumstances of Mafeking and demonstrated the adaptability of Baden-Powell's initially quirky individualistic vision to the sacrificial demands of industrial warfare (see Gate 1933).

Despite the incorporation of Scouting within the norms of Edwardian and post-Edwardian society, though, the progress of Baden-Powell's redemptive project defined clearly the fault-lines in English national identity. His attempts to rescue Englishness from late imperial decadence were themselves beset by conflicts of race, gender and class. The inculcation of models of superior 'savage' health and perception implicitly questioned the capacity of empire to endure as a civilising mission and by basing the psychology of the movement on the Mafeking siege Baden-Powell emphasised defence of nation at the expense of confident expansion. Whilst class redemption was rapidly consolidated into a reinforcement of a hierarchical status quo, the unexpectedly radical emergence of Girl Scouts was a danger unanticipated by the ascetic Lieutenant-General (though to some extent foreshadowed by the stringent warnings about 'continence' which his publisher saw fit to remove from the first edition of *Scouting for Boys*) (Baden-Powell 2004: 351–2). 'All well, four hours' bombardment. One dog killed' had been Baden-Powell's characteristically plucky summary of a day under siege at Mafeking (Rosenthal 1986: 31). Such simple optimism under fire, however, was not enough to control the dangers let loose by his application of the lessons of the siege to the difficult condition of English national identity. The problems that Baden-Powell encountered, particularly those concerning gender, were also to be apparent in a parallel initiative to rescue the English body, the folk-dance movement.

The Straight Knee and the Bent Knee

Cecil Sharp's revival of English folk-dancing provides a complementary Edwardian case-study to that of Baden-Powell's Scouts. Like Baden-Powell, Sharp was oppressed by a sense of national decline, physical degeneracy and urban corruption and, like the Lieutenant-General, he sought to revive a national body-culture by an appeal to primitive values developed through sophisticated modern systems of organisation and publicity. His writings on folk-dance were as improvised, opinionated and shrewdly marketed as *Scouting for Boys*, though Sharp, unlike Baden-Powell, was also interested in establishing a scholarly as well as a performative legacy. Class and race also obtruded into his project, as did gender, a factor emphasised by a contemporary rival to Sharp. Mary Neal, now little known mostly because of Sharp's success in thwarting her influence, offered a contrasting vision of a national revival through dance. Her Espérance Girls' Club challenged the male hierarchical tendencies of Sharp's organisations, emphasising instead a process of cross-class and cross-gendered encounters in an idealistic model of modern English life. Neal and Sharp's conflict devolved into a public dispute about a detail of body-culture, the position of the knee in the morris dance. But in that question of straightness or bentness were articulated many of the arguments that underlay the Edwardian revival of English identity.

If the Scouts began at Mafeking, modern morris dancing began at Headington, Oxfordshire. It was there that Cecil Sharp first saw the Headington Quarry morris dancers during the Christmas holidays of 1899 and noted down some of their dance tunes. In the years after that performance Sharp had concentrated on promoting English traditional song as a means to national revival. But it was the experience at Headington that was to prove the more significant for the history of English nationalist organisations. Sharp was reminded of it when visiting the Espérance Girls' Club in North London to talk about folk song. Mary Neal, the founder of the organisation dedicated to the cultural development of working-class girls, also wished to introduce dance to their performance repertoire. Sharp gave Neal the name of the Headington dancer William Kimber and she, with characteristic directness, went to Oxfordshire and persuaded Kimber to come to London to teach her young seamstresses how to dance real English dances.

The encounter between the Headington dancers and the London girls in October 1905 became a revelatory moment of English identity. In Sharp's words, the folk dancers issued 'a summons never heard until now, yet instantly obeyed; because, though unfamiliar and unforeseen, it was of England and came, even though it was centuries upon the way, to kinsfolk'. 'Within half an hour of the coming of these Morris-men', he recalled, 'we saw the Bean-setting – its thumping and clashing of staves, its intricate figures and steps hitherto unknown – full swing upon a London floor' (Sharp and MacIlwaine 1907: 8–9). Mary Neal evoked this restoration of what Sharp called a 'birthright long mislaid' with comparable rapture but with sharper social analysis (9). She witnessed 'free-born laughter-loving healthy girls, who are not two generations away from the peasant class from which they sprung' being enlivened by exposure to old dances that they somehow already instinctively knew (Neal 1911a: 5). That shared moment of English revelation and restoration was also the beginning of a bitter personal and political controversy.

After Kimber's visit to the Espérance Club, folk-dance came increasingly to dominate Sharp's work. It offered more opportunities than folk-song to broaden the cultural appeal of traditional English culture, to create new social organisations and to establish control of the theory and practice of national revivalism. *The Morris Book* (1907), written with Herbert C. MacIlwaine and dedicated to 'Members of the Espérance Girls' Club', initiated a project comparable to Baden-Powell's *Scouting for Boys* in its articulation of an 'ordered expression of a national spirit' (Sharp and MacIlwaine 1907: 7). Order rather than spirit came to be Sharp's main priority in protecting and maintaining the birthright of dance and it was a discipline that he came to police strictly. He supplemented his textbooks with programmes of instruction organised first through a School of Morris Dancing established at South-Western Polytechnic in 1909 and later by the English Folk-Dance Society, which he founded in 1911. These developments signalled a radical change of perspective from that expressed in the immediate aftermath of Kimber's visit to London and a radical divergence from the policies that Mary Neal had been pursuing with the Espérance girls.

Sharp's change of mind was signalled in the revised 1912 edition of *The Morris Book*. The description of the moment at which generations, genders and urban and rural cultures met to produce a revelatory performance of the Bean-setting is gone. 'The Morris is not an easy dance', he now declared. 'Somehow or other the idea seems to have got abroad that anyone could teach, and anyone could learn, this dance. So far from being a simple dance, the Morris is technically, especially in its higher developments, an extremely difficult one' (Sharp and MacIlwaine 1912: 42). What had once been a 'birthright' had now become a highly mediated cultural process with 'higher developments'. Sharp redefines it as 'a professional dance' that 'must be executed in its every step and movement with precision and finish, and brought to the highest pitch of excellence' (43). Such descriptions reflected his increasingly institutionalised sense of English traditional performance and his deepening interest in controlling those institutions. The 'order of the feet' and the 'drill and discipline of the [morris] side as a whole' became his main concerns (45, 49). The military discourse is significant because Sharp, now unwilling to allow written transcriptions of the dances to be the main means of transmitting them, was intent on establishing a national discipline. To prevent the dances 'being practised in ways not sanctioned by tradition', his biographers note, Sharp 'realized that satisfactory results would not be obtained unless first-hand instruction were given by himself and he had direct control over his teachers' (Fox Strangways and Karpeles 1955: 78). Accredited instructors, he wrote, ensured the survival of 'only those dances . . . which are the survivals of genuine and unbroken tradition. And these, of course, are questions for the expert' (81). The expert in question was necessarily Sharp himself.

By 1909 when he had opened the South-Western Polytechnic school, Sharp had committed himself to a professionalising of English national tradition. It was a view of Englishness entirely at odds with that of Mary Neal. Neal's work with Espérance emphasised immediacy of contact with 'tradition' and the essential instinctiveness of the dancing itself. Her *Espérance Morris Books* (1910, 1912) implicitly dissent from the ideology of Sharp's dance texts and stress the importance of unmediated dialogue between residual rural body-cultures and the deracinated but vibrant urban adolescent. 'There must be nothing in this revival which cannot be done by the average boy and girl', she stressed. 'It must be kept, in the true sense of the word, a "vulgar" movement, understanded of the common people' (Neal 1911a: 5). Espérance was intended to renegotiate forgotten links in the English population, to 'bring a little of this serene and joyous [rural] life into the hurried, keen and vivid life of city dwellers, and to return it once more to the new generation of country folk with some of the added charm of this vivid life' (1). The emphasis on dialogue and reciprocity – a redemptive relationship between only recently separated rural and urban English cultures – is typical of Neal. So is the scepticism about the possibility – and even more the desirability – of establishing an 'order of the feet'. 'One can lay down no laws [about the morris step]', she writes, 'for I have known the same men change the step on three consecutive visits to London, so that at the end one could scarcely recognise it as the same step'. Her response was to encourage 'the spirit of the traditional way' because that was the way that she observed the tradition to work (6). Sharp also acknowledged the changeable steps of traditional dancers but set himself with zeal to replacing Neal's spirit with his own letter.

The English Folk-Dance Society aspired to a rigour in traditional dance that surpassed surviving traditional practice. 'The authority of tradition is respected with a strictness unknown to tradition itself', as a retrospective survey of the organisation's activities put it after Sharp's death (Croft 1927: 15). It was one aspect of this revisionary attention to detail that came to represent the ideological dispute between Sharp and Neal, the question of the straight leg and the bent leg. 'The free leg should swing naturally and easily from the hip-joint', Sharp instructed, 'not more than fifteen to eighteen inches, the heel of the free foot at the furthest point of the swing being some three inches, roughly, from the ground, and four to six inches in front of the toe of the supporting foot' (Sharp and MacIlwaine 1912: 50–1). For Neal, such obsessive attempts to regularise movements of a traditional body challenged the very purpose of the revival, marking the difference between 'the form and the life, the bookman and the workman, between the pedant and those in touch with actual life itself', as she put it at the height of their public dispute in 1910 (Fox Strangways and Karpeles 1955: 82). In Neal's view, variation and amateurism rather than prescription and professionalism were precisely the features of the morris that made it valuable as a popular force in modern England. Neal's vulgar dancing and celebration of the 'bent leg' was a challenge to Sharp's new traditional orthodoxy as serious and as gendered as that posed by Amazon girls to Baden-Powell's Scouts.

The 1911 Shakespeare Festival Summer School, held on the hallowed English ground of Stratford-upon-Avon, was the site for the decisive contest between these two versions of Englishness. The festival, in Neal's words, was part of 'those regenerative forces which were helping to restore to the English people their inheritance of joy and of strength, so long held in abeyance through the invading evils of over-crowded city life'. Through its celebration of old English song and dance, a new England could emerge as 'dancers and singers from a factory in Hull, children from London, country folk from the immediate neighbourhood, and county school children' came together (Neal 1911b: 202, 208). Neal's presence as an adjudicator of dance at the Festival was an impediment to Sharp's growing authority as national arbiter of traditional standards. He conducted an astute campaign to displace her, appealing to his own concern with authenticity and rigorous standards. In a debate in the *Morning Post* Neal's view that it 'seems as unreasonable to talk about an expert in morris dance as to talk about an expert in making people happy' was set against Sharp's assertion of the need to 'appraise the traditional value of the revived dance, to detect the faked dance, [and] to exercise a wise discrimination with regard to corrupt dances' (Fox Strangways and Karpeles 1955: 82). His insistence on the right kind of English tradition won through as he exploited the Festival committee's unease about the scholarship needed to underpin a national revival. As Sharp's follower Maud Karpeles put it, the Board members 'were impressed by Miss Neal's organizing ability, but they feared that the inaccuracy with which her dancers had been charged might sully the reputation of the Festival' (Karpeles 1967: 81). Sharp, more frankly, wrote on 11 May 1911, 'I have got Stratford', as the rigour of the straight knee overcame the expressiveness of the bent (Judge 1989: 567).

'Getting Stratford' was part of Sharp's wider campaign to re-imagine England through its dances and songs and to control the dissemination of that re-imagining through his organisations and his publications. His folk-song collecting had been largely confined to the South West, but the

Headington connection allowed him to establish a national geography of traditional England which encompassed the south-west Midlands and the North East where he recorded sword dances which, like the morris, were quickly edited and published. These journeys parallel those of the popular English topographers discussed in Chapter 4 and he made his ley-lines of tradition with comparable discretion and ideological purpose, omissions being as important as enthusiasms. As Georgina Boyes notes, 'north-western morris was excluded from the English Folk Dance Society syllabus as a matter of conscious policy' because it was viewed as 'degenerate', a judgement also applied to the vibrant step-dancing and clog-dancing styles of northern England. The complicating presence of modern industrial England in a movement committed to peasant essentialism seems to have determined Sharp's 'wise discrimination' here, as did difficulties in notating, and therefore publishing, the dances (Boyes 1993: 101).

Sharp's determined attempt to become a national dancing master in the manner of his admired (and decidedly non-traditional) John Playford faced significant political and practical challenges despite the 'defeat' of Mary Neal in 1911. Like Baden-Powell, Sharp was forced to confront contradictions generated by his own theories of Englishness and by the very success of his organisation. These also devolved upon questions of race and gender. Neal's dissenting theory of traditional dance and its role in modern national revival was based upon her sense of its potential for both social and gendered democracy. The Espérance movement that stimulated Sharp's interest in folk-dance in the first place was directed at working-class girls and Neal's idiosyncratic feminism led her to act on the committee of the Suffrage movement at the same time that she made the connection with the Headington dancers (Neal 1940: 149). Her celebration of the 'freedom, cleanness, sturdy vigour, robust jollity [and] total lack of self-conscious posturing, of anything finicking or dainty' in the dances that Kimber brought to the club registered a gendered as well as a social equality that was essential to her politics (Neal 1911a: 3). Kimber taught the girls male dances and the girls then became teachers of male dances to both boys and girls. In this way tradition allowed freedoms that the strict gender roles of contemporary social dance denied. For Sharp, though, as for Baden-Powell when he witnessed outbreaks of Girl Scouting, such freedoms were problems to be controlled rather than outcomes to be celebrated.

Part of the theoretical project that Sharp developed after the first *Morris Book* was to establish English traditional dance as a gendered hierarchy. The morris became an explicitly male dance, requiring movements that were 'forceful, masculine and strong' (Sharp and MacIlwaine

1912: 43). Even in the period in which he and Mary Neal worked together, the femininity of Neal's environment was a source of unease for Sharp. The first *Morris Book*'s description of the Espérance dancers' recovery of their birthright is immediately qualified by the comment that 'the feminine temperament inevitably robs the dance of something of its sturdiness' (Sharp and MacIlwaine 1907: 9). Sturdiness became central to Sharp's polemics on the dancing English body and formed part of the barely suppressed sexual politics of his arguments with Neal – she noted later that both Sharp and his collaborator Herbert MacIlwaine 'were bitterly opposed to the whole Votes for Women campaign' (Neal 1940: 149). The second edition of *The Morris Book* addresses the issue of sturdiness more directly in its attempt to manage women's dancing. 'None but the pedant . . . would . . . debar women from participation in a dance as wholesome and beautiful as the Morris', he writes. 'Women, however, would be wise to avoid those dances in which such essentially masculine movements as the "Gallery", the "Kick-jump," &c., occur'. Women's morris, he concludes, was a 'free translation' of tradition, but it could not be the tradition itself (Sharp and MacIlwaine 1912: 42).

Having established this principle, however, Sharp faced the difficulty that a significant number of the members of the English Folk-Dance Society were female. His strictures on the gendering of traditional dance posed problems for some of his women followers who were attracted to folk-dancing precisely because of the freedoms it offered in movement and social identity. Florence Golding, for example, a contributor to the *English Folk-Dance Society's Journal*, attacked the issue through the question of dress. 'Every woman who really cares for Folk Art must feel the call of the Morris, and glory in its disciplined vigour and restraint', she writes, adopting orthodox Sharpean discourse. But, she confesses, 'the flick of a woman's skirt only intensifies that indefinable something in her temperament which always robs the Morris of its predominant feature, viz. the portrayal of strong emotions under absolute control combined with manly vigour and easy dignity' (Golding 1914: 14). Whilst not pursuing the brisk pragmatism of Mary Neal ('the skirts should well clear the ankles, and the dancers should be encouraged to have very little starch in frocks or petticoats'), Golding nevertheless presses the question in Sharp's own house journal (Neal 1911a: 14). 'What Shall We Wear?' she asks in the title of her article, not 'Shall We Dance?' By weight of their membership and their social presence at dances, the limits of Sharp's gendered nationalism were tested even by his loyal followers.

Race also became an issue in Sharp's theories of the relationship between dance and Englishness. Folk-song, he had argued, was determined by the 'racial characteristics of the community', but the more complex body-culture of dance provoked more difficult questions (Sharp 1907: 29). In the first edition of *The Morris Book* he accepts quite readily the non-English origins of the 'moorish dance':

> the weight of testimony must be held to show Morocco as the fount and origin [of the dance], no matter if the genius of our own folk – so very far removed from anything native to Africa – has, in the process of the centuries, altered it until it bears, in spirit, little resemblance to the parent stock.
> (Sharp and MacIlwaine 1907: 13)

Even if 'the spirit has been Anglicised', he admits, 'the [Moorish] steps remain' (14). This acknowledgement of cultural hybridity in the heart of English tradition did not survive revisions impelled by the demands of Sharp's rapid institutionalising of national dance. The second edition of *The Morris Book* rubbishes the Moorish theory, replacing it with a pan-European, religious account of its origins. Noting the blackened faces of some morris traditions, Sharp explains away his previous interpretation as merely an inherited verbal reference: 'this would at the present day lead to the dance being called a "nigger dance" ', he claims. 'To our forefathers, for whom the typical black man was the Moor, not the nigger, the natural equivalent would have been a "Moorish" or "Morris" dance' (Sharp and MacIlwaine 1912: 10–11). By such logic were English traditional dancers rescued from the fate of dancing black dances.

The abrupt, lightly argued change of opinion on the origins of morris is at once characteristic of Sharp's scholarship and a sign of his developing cultural politics. The victory over Mary Neal at Stratford was achieved through his establishment of a command of the purity and authority of tradition. Just as the bent leg needed to be straightened, so moorishness had to be excised from the essential English national dance. Neal's social and cultural project, whilst accepting the importance of a revived 'folk-art' to the development of an English 'race-consciousness', as she termed it, also stressed the hybridity and reciprocity of national tradition (Neal 1911b: 204). Her own insistence on the unmediated encounter between traditional dancers and the Espérance girls was intended to encourage just such spontaneous exchanges. Ironically, Neal's most dangerous weapon in her battle with Sharp was her knowledge that the Headington morris team, Sharp's *locus classicus* of traditional revelation, had been 'invented' in a way that fitted much more easily with her model of cultural revival than it did with his. The Headington side was not traditional at all in the purist sense that Sharp cultivated. It had been revived by a local historian for a civic celebration in Oxford, the performance being recreated from recollections of a local morris side that had stopped performing in 1887 (Kidson and Neal 1972: 160; Grant 1999). The performance that Sharp witnessed on Boxing Day 1899 also lay outside the strict prescriptions of tradition favoured by Sharp. The Headington team danced Whitsuntide dances, an untraditional conflation of seasonal rituals motivated by the need to generate some ready cash, a contemporary social and economic reality outside of Sharp's developing primitivist theories of tradition.

The Headington dancers were also not expressive of a living Oxfordshire dance tradition, a fact that Sharp uneasily admitted in the second edition of *The Morris Book* (Sharp and MacIlwaine 1912: 76). In 1907 Kimber told Sharp that Headington Quarry had only performed twice in the previous two years and even then had used a very small repertoire of dances (Grant 1999: 653). Such inconsistency was unimportant to Neal who emphasised the spirit and physical presence of the morris rather than any objectively defined authenticity. 'Any average person of intelligence can collect a morris dance', she pointedly told the *Morning Post* in 1910, noting favourably the dancers' indifference to questions of technique (Fox Strangways and Karpeles 1955: 82). Neal also acknowledged the musical promiscuity of English tradition. The Headington side, she observed, 'took any tune which was popular at the time and adapted it to the dances, so that the tunes are not by any means all traditional'. They danced to 'Buffalo Girls', for example, a nineteenth-century American blackface minstrel tune, a fact that Sharp, excluding as he did 'Nigger Songs of the Christy Minstrel type' from his traditional notice, did not mention (Kidson and Neal 1972: 131; Schofield 2004: 497).

By abandoning the Espérance Club's practice in favour of the 'professionalising' of English dance, Sharp also abandoned any popular national purpose. His success in promoting a morris revival was largely institutional, developing formal links between the Folk-Dance Society and Women's Institutes, the Workers' Educational Association, Girl Guides and Boy Scouts, as well as army convalescent camps during the First World War, where 'folk-dancing became part of the process of "hardening"' (Croft 1927: 9). There is, though, little evidence that the folk-dance movement touched working-class constituencies in either the country or the city. M. Sturge Gretton, writing in the first issue of the *English Folk-Dance Society's Journal* in May 1914, claimed some success in persuading 'peasants' to cycle nine or ten miles each way to dances at Kelmscott, Oxfordshire (Sturge Gretton 1914). However, Margery Howe's account of an English Folk-Dance and Song Society Summer School in the Lake District in the 1930s is probably more representative of the popular response to Sharp's national project. 'The farming community always gave us a wide berth', she recalled, 'neither could we enlist any of the many artisans, labourers, gardeners or the domestic staff . . . Most of these people danced traditionally, but could not be persuaded to become "folk dancers" ' (Boyes 1993: 109). The distinction between 'dancing traditionally' and being a 'folk dancer' might be thought a fine one. In fact it articulates a key distinction between social usage, custom and tradition and the institutionalised definition and preservation of such practices.

The history of the national revivalism of Sharp, Baden-Powell and Mary Neal is, in the end, one of failure, at least on the terms that they set out their vision of reconstituted English body-cultures. Sharp moved ever further into the institutionalised modernity of his invented English traditions – Director of the Folk-Song and Dance Society, Inspector of Training Colleges in Folk-Song and Dance, Honorary Master of Music at the University of Cambridge. The capital letters swamped the demotic sources that were the base of his movement. Baden-Powell became a benevolent Chief Scout for an organisation that burgeoned in the empire and later the Commonwealth, and which quickly lost the urgent, often violent, sense of national peril and degeneration that *Scouting for Boys* initially expressed. Mary Neal, in many ways the most culturally radical of the three, abandoned Espérance activity during the First World War. Towards the end of her life she wrote a strange confessional essay that expressed regret for teaching the girls male dances. 'I had quite innocently and ignorantly broken a law of cosmic ritual', she concluded, 'and stirred up disharmony which became active as time went on'. The 'bitter estrangement' between herself and Sharp was because she forced women to live on a 'masculine rhythm' (Neal 1940: 149, 150).

All three Edwardian national organisations expressed both the intensity of a national-cultural imperative in England and the contests and fault-lines that such projects provoked and exposed. The Scouts and the dance organisations of Sharp and Neal were not state-sponsored enterprises, nor did they work through any established ideological apparatus of university or political party. They were in many ways individualised, improvised projects provoked by a sense of the destructive effects of urban living, mass consumption, imperial exhaustion and nostalgia for expressive cultures of the past. Baden-Powell's construction of the Scout's uniform and body-culture from fragments of his colonial experience was a striking embodiment of this process in action, as was Neal's belief in the almost magical power of the encounter of rural dancer and urban girl. The lack of popular resources – material and ideological – for these initiatives was both an unacknowledged symptom of the problem of national identity that they were tackling and a significant barrier to the success of the organisations, at least in terms of establishing a mass movement. Nevertheless, the histories of Scouting and folk-dancing suggest the powerfully covert modernity of their discourses of Englishness. Primitive England was exalted through processes that relied upon mass communication, universal education and the effective lobbying of government, publishers and social elites. They were compromised projects, neither popular, national, nor successful on the terms that they set themselves. Hunched adolescent smokers went to professional football games in greater numbers despite *Scouting for Boys* and traditional dancers continued dancing traditionally, bending their knees when they felt like it. Nevertheless, the theatre of the Boy Scouts, the English Folk-Dance Society and the Espérance Morris performed vividly the problems of establishing a national identity when there was no national common ground to dance or camp upon.

Chapter 3

Festivals

Every so often, the British state, impelled by coincidence of calendar or an anniversary that cannot easily be ignored, organises a public performance of national identity. The Festival of Britain in 1951 and the Millennium Experience of 2000 were the two main attempts in the second half of the twentieth century to re-articulate Englishness or Britishness. Unlike the Edwardian revivalist movements described in the previous chapter, these projections of identity were static, monumental and official, allowing for little of the personal idiosyncrasy and improvisation that characterised the movements of Baden-Powell, Sharp and Neal. Nevertheless, the need to present the nation in a tangible form that its citizens could visit and understand pressed the question of the available resources for describing and envisioning its future. As with the Scouts and the folk-dancers, the decisions taken about the location, content and style of the performances suggest continuities in the struggles to define Englishness as well as changes determined by the different historical and cultural circumstances of the events.

Framed by these two national celebrations, the 1984–5 Miners' Strike provides a disorderly, unofficial commentary on the festivals' national politics, cultural geographies and performances. The strike was the last great industrial conflict of twentieth-century Britain, but it also dramatised arguments about national identity and cohesion, most particularly, perhaps, about the legacies and fate of a postwar social and political settlement that the Festival of Britain had worked hard to establish and the Millennium Experience tried tentatively to revive. Its political theatre – violent, divisive and intensely localised – took place far away from customary places of English self-representation and posed questions about the construction and integrity of late twentieth-century nationhood that went beyond the immediate issues of the contraction of the coal industry. Uniquely, the strike came to be represented and to represent itself as a struggle about heritage, about the maintenance of established ways of life rather than economic betterment. The performances and expressions of this struggle drew upon definitions of and conflicts between tradition and modernity that had long been at the centre of arguments about Englishness. And the meanings of heritage were later to be tested against other contemporary cultural usages of the term as the strike itself came to be represented and re-staged in popular film and performance art in the late 1990s. Mark Herman's *Brassed Off* (1996), Stephen Daldry's *Billy Elliot* (2000) and Jeremy Deller's *The Battle of Orgreave* (2001) all posed the problems of recording and memorialising a period of complex political and historical division.

Exhibiting England

In many ways the Festival of Britain was an exercise in putting George Orwell's theories of Englishness into state practice. It was initiated by Herbert Morrison, the architect of the Labour Party's postwar planned economy, both to mark the centenary of the Great Exhibition of 1851 and to articulate a revived sense of nationhood six years after the end of the Second World War. Its projection of the social virtues and tentative pleasures of a new England was expressed most fully in the South Bank Exhibition housed in a set of temporary pavilions erected on a 27-acre site on the South Bank of the Thames. The exhibition set out to re-articulate the relationship of postwar nationhood against an Englishness represented by its great nineteenth-century predecessor. Sir Joseph Paxton's Crystal Palace, the definitive symbol of Victorian innovation and national ambition, was referred to directly only in a 'miniature display' outside the main circuits of the site where a scale model of the building could be seen. This scaling down and marginalising of 1851's architecture was part of the Festival's policy of emphasising a common contemporary experience of nationhood at the expense of celebrations of national and imperial grandeur. The lion and the unicorn, those heraldic emblems of the English state that Orwell had evoked as symbols of the distance between state nationalism and popular patriotism in his 1941 essay, were displayed on the South Bank as bizarre large corn dollies. It was a whimsical sign of the Festival's intention to present a nation busy redefining its history and its iconography.

The South Bank Exhibition also saw its mission as distinct from previous exercises in national self-promotion, 'neither a museum of British culture nor a trade show of British wares', as its souvenir guide puts it (Cox 1951: 8). The official handbook of the Festival of Britain described its project as an 'autobiography of a nation', a phrase that marked an explicitly subjective turn in its representation of nationhood (*The Festival of Britain 1951*: 3). Instead of national and imperial achievement, it displayed what Michael Frayn recalled as 'a modest and informal complex of interlocking neighbourhoods, each with its own character' (Frayn 1963: 329–30). The exhibition concentrated upon the spaces where postwar nationhood was being constructed in ordinary English lives. Taking seriously Orwell's wartime observation of the instinctive 'privateness of English life', it set out to recast the narrative of Englishness as small-scale, personal and modern (Orwell 1970a: 77).

Like Orwell's essays, though, the Festival's interest in ordinary England disguised a more determined and more contradictory politics than it admitted. If the 1851 Crystal Palace had housed a promiscuous display of the commodities of international capitalist modernity for visitors to wonder at and wander within, the South Bank's 'autobiography' was shaped by a more conservative and more tendentious national narrative. Whilst the Crystal Palace guide had merely recommended its visitors to 'follow as much as possible the course of the sun', on the South Bank visitors were managed and persuaded (Gibbs-Smith 1950: 27). 'This is a free country', the official exhibition guide admits, 'and any visitors who, from habit or inclination, feel impelled to start with the last chapter of the whole narrative and zig-zag their way backwards to the first chapter, will be as welcome as anyone else. But such visitors may find that some of the chapters will appear mystifying and inconsequent' (Cox 1951: 8). And the days of England being celebrated as inherently 'mystifying' were over on the South Bank.

The emphasis on guidance, sequence and order in the main exhibition site (the guide provides route maps for each pavilion as well as for the overall site) suggests the prescriptive programme that underlay the project. Visitors were involved in a working exhibition of a postwar national-corporatist venture, what Becky Conekin describes as 'simultaneously a public celebration, an educational undertaking, and a constructed vision of a new, democratic national community' (Conekin 2003: 9). The glamour of capitalist production, evident in the very nickname of the Crystal Palace, was replaced by an emphasis on purposeful control of the means of production and orderly, moderate and occasionally pleasurable consumption. It was a staged performance of a postwar managed economy where inventiveness, adventure and efficiency were shown to lead towards definable national goals of coherent and unified social progress. Even those parts of the Festival officially sanctioned for enjoyment alone implicitly contributed to the narrative of improvement. Visiting the Battersea Pleasure Gardens – a cautious revival of the notoriously pleasurable early nineteenth-century venues – Frank Frost reported enthusiastically in *Britain Today* that he 'had the impression that Planning and Private Enterprise had really co-operated' (Frost 1951: 14–15). It was a response that would have warmed Herbert Morrison's corporatist heart.

Part of the 'educational undertaking' of the South Bank exhibition was a thoroughgoing revision of discourses of national representation aimed at removing problematic reference points and reshaping traditional materials. So, whilst visitors were encouraged to begin their 'narrative' with exhibits on the 'The Land', 'The Natural Scene' and 'The Country', all of which suggested familiar locations of Englishness as ancient, traditional and essentially rural, the contents of the pavilions were designed to readjust such expectations. 'Yearly, the farmer's confidence in the scientist is growing', the exhibition guide claims, 'while the scientist is learning to accept those vagaries in nature that have always been reality to the farmer' (Cox 1951: 17). The farmer becomes in this account 'a technician putting to everyday use the results of five hundred years of development and of science', just as that old pastoral symbol the village forge, recreated in 'The Country Pavilion', became 'the village engineer's workshop' with a real 'modern blacksmith' displaying his engineering skills (19).

The determination of the exhibition to 'modernise' Englishness involved both this discursive adjustment and other strategic evasions. Housing, perhaps the most pressing social issue of the postwar period, was literally placed out of bounds. The ' "live" architecture' exhibition was located in East London's Poplar district with the claim that it represented new communities emerging from 'blitzed ruins and from the slums and chaotic planning of the past' (*The Festival of Britain 1951*: 13). The 'Homes and Garden' pavilion of the South Bank meanwhile concentrated on evoking domestic lives lived out in planned environments without obvious class or local affiliations. The 'contemporary role of the bed-sitting room' was the nearest it came to acknowledging the social problems caused by a devastated urban housing stock (Cox 1951: 71).

Other absences were indicative of longer-term trends in national self-perception and representation. Despite Harry Hopkins' sense of the 'strange "un-English" atmosphere of space and light and sparkle' to be found on the South Bank where the pavilions were open until an un-English 11.30 pm, the Festival as a whole suggested a new national introversion (Hopkins 1963: 272). Empire, embedded in the titles of all previous twentieth-century state exhibitions, was hardly mentioned in 1951. Four years after Indian independence, the Dome of Discovery rendered empire, now recast as the Commonwealth of Nations, merely as a product of 'this desire of ours to discover and explore' (Cox 1951: 45). Ethnicity and race were similarly effaced. There were no displays of imperial diversity or colonial success. 'The People of Britain' pavilion set out to tell the story of 'one of the most-mixed people in the world', though despite the beginning of large-scale Caribbean migrations three years previously, the mixing is said to end with the Normans (63). This early evidence of Paul Gilroy's theory of determined imperial forgetting was complemented by other silences. The South Bank Exhibition made little or no reference to emergent postwar Europe, for example, or to the dominant cultural presence of America. However, this retreat into modest insularity also exacerbated older tensions in the construction of nationhood itself.

Whilst visitors to the South Bank were invited to experience a new style of British festival – guardedly modern, carefully playful and remarkably unimperial – they also experienced an older English hegemony and a reasserted metropolitan emphasis. For this was emphatically an *English* experience, and a London experience. The 'turning inward' that Conekin identifies was not just away from the global interests that had been the main features of the 1911, 1922 and 1938 exhibitions but also towards a notable lack of any enthusiastic devolution of the Festival style or funds beyond the South Bank (Conekin 2003: 198). Other British nations saw little of the 'colour, femininity, lightness [and] extravagance' that Alan Powers identifies in the Festival's pavilions (Powers 2001: 55). Glasgow hosted a display on 'Industrial Power'; Wales held an 'Agricultural Land Reclamation Event'; and a 'Farm and the Factory' exhibition was organised in Belfast. A small-scale travelling exhibition brought a taste of metropolitan delights to the provinces, but, in an enforcement of the old regional hierarchy, to experience fully the new national vision the visitor had to come to London.

Issues of modernity, region and nationhood were also played out in Trowell, the hamlet on the Nottinghamshire-Derbyshire border selected as the Festival of Britain village. Trowell was conveniently in the very centre of England (though not, of course, in the centre of Britain, a further indication of the unacknowledged Anglocentrism of the Festival as a whole). However, it was an atypical 'typical English village'. A *Times* editorial on the choice noted that 'when the House of Commons was told that industry had been "superimposed" on this village the truth was stated mildly. Vast ironworks to the west of the village dominate the landscape and it is against their distant array of chimney stacks and slag heaps that the church tower of Trowell is first seen by the traveller.' 'There is no village green, nor is there even a single public house', it concludes (*The Times* 22 February 1951: 3). Like the blacksmith-cum-engineer in the

South Bank pavilion, Trowell was intended to revise perceptions of England and its traditions.

'The object of this selection is to encourage places which are not conventionally beautiful to seize the opportunity of Festival year and to have a go at improving their amenities', Herbert Morrison responded to hostile parliamentary questioning about the choice:

> it is the type of English village where the old rural life is passing away and where an industrial community has been superimposed [An HON. MEMBER: 'This is a funeral, not a Festival'] . . . the parish council is struggling . . . to prevent the village from being spoiled. It was chosen merely as an example of modern social problems in a village.

Morrison's uneasy acknowledgement that the award was made on the basis of village problems rather than village beauties was indicative of the modernising impulse of his festival. He was rescued by another member's smoother summary of Trowell's value to the project through its combination of 'the strength of modern industry with the peaceful beauty of the English countryside' (*Hansard* 19 February 1951: 882). But Morrison's was a more accurate summary. For even beyond the aesthetic challenges of 'ribbon building, slag tips and open-cast workings' to which Trowell's own festival programme uneasily admitted, the Festival Village represented accurately the cultural discrepancies between regional and metropolitan England in 1951 (Trowell Festival of Britain Committee 1951: 5).

Whilst Trowell may have been a modern English village, its response to its elevation to national status made no obvious contribution to the revisionary national experiment on the South Bank. Children's sports, a cricket match played in Victorian costumes, the Gardening Association's awards for best front and best back gardens (local values were certainly active in that distinction) and the Scouts' cleaning of the church clock were quintessentially provincial English celebrations (*The Festival of Britain 1951*: 67). It was a style of civic performance that was replicated nationally, providing a sharp contrast to the aesthetics and cultural politics of the London exhibition. John Kirby's index of national Festival events confirms that by far the most popular was the historical pageant, a staple performance of pre-First World War imperial exhibitions and village festivals alike. Trowell, like Burnley, Tunbridge Wells, Clitheroe and Hereford, presented a performance of Sir Edward German's Edwardian light operatic warhorse, *Merrie England* (1902), and maypoles and the odd cavalcade contributed to the essentially conservative forms of national self-expression, even in the larger English cities. 'Chipping Campden en fete [*sic*]' seems an isolated embrace of the continental style that Harry Hopkins experienced on the South Bank, but the repertoire of English national imagery in the wider reaches of the festival proved remarkably resistant to any adjustment in national self-perception (Kirby 1993: 15).

The responses of the English regions described by Kirby can be set beside popular innovations elsewhere in Britain. There was no English equivalent of the Edinburgh People's Festival, for example, an alternative to the Edinburgh International Festival, which was funded by the city Labour Party and Trades Council. The People's Festival used the frame of British festivity to develop new, specifically Scottish cultural encounters between past and present. Hamish Henderson describes its *ceilidh* as bringing together for the first time in the capital Lowland and Highland traditional singers and Scots writers like Hugh MacDiarmid in front of a young urban audience (Henderson 1992: 164–5). Traditions performed in a new context and supported both by the academic resources of the new School for Scottish Studies and radical political groupings formed a coherent cultural challenge to the official discourses of British modernity represented by the International Festival. English regional dissent from metropolitan modernism, however, was expressed through a continued allegiance to the older invented traditions of the maypole and *Merrie England*.

The Festival of Britain, then, advertised a postwar national settlement committed to social planning, the virtues of moderate consumption, social partnerships of capitalist enterprise and selective nationalisation, and the abandonment of the discourse of imperial grandeur. In its metropolitan centre-piece, the South Bank Exhibition, it also experimented with what Bryan Appleyard calls 'an uncertain, hedged modernist optimism' (Appleyard 1989: 93). The pavilions on the South Bank, the architecture of the Royal Festival Hall and the ostentatiously 'modern' Skylon represented a tentative 'English way' in design, architecture and social thinking that offset European modernist practice with self-consciously native idioms. However, the Festival also confirmed limiting continuities of national representation even as it suppressed the imperial rhetoric that had previously dominated such state events. The failure to extend the type of project inaugurated on the South Bank to the rest of England, let alone the rest of Britain, reaffirmed old economic and cultural differences between the metropolis and the regions. Non-metropolitan responses to the Festival also pointed up the paucity of cultural resources to present a postwar revision of national identity with an event like the Edinburgh People's Festival emphasising the difference between those resources and the dissenting nationalist projects elsewhere in Britain.

Dividing England

Arthur Scargill once nominated a visit to the South Bank Exhibition in 1951 as one of his life's three 'magic moments' (Crick 1985a: 52). However, as leader of the National Union of Mineworkers during the 1984–5 strike, Scargill also participated in the ending of the post-war social and economic compacts that the Festival of Britain had celebrated. Herbert Morrison, the Labour politician most closely associated with the Festival, had also drafted the 1945 Labour government's nationalisation programme and the two initiatives were complementary. Morrison's concept of the 'public corporation', a nationalised industry working within broader capitalist structures, was implicit in the rhetoric and design of the South Bank Exhibition. Just as science and technology were shown to be integrated in traditional English life, so responsible social planning was argued to be compatible with responsible capitalist enterprise. An advertisement in the South Bank Exhibition guide for the Standard Motor Company put the policy concisely: 'all that's best of the Past joining with, and giving authority to, the needs of the Present' (Cox 1951: xxi). 1984–5 marked the ending of this social and economic compromise and to its public cultural expression.

The Miners' Strike aimed to secure the existing economic and social structures of miners and mining communities, and, by extension, a culture of labour that was embedded in settlement of place rather than left exposed to the contingencies of the market. In this sense, the strike was a uniquely historicised industrial dispute, what Raphael Samuel called 'a war of ghosts in which the living actors were dwarfed by the shadows they had conjured up' (Samuel et al. 1986: 6). Samuel's recurring use of theatrical metaphors in his writing on the strike also suggests its strongly performative elements. It was both a ritualised and improvised display of competing national and regional representations of Englishness and Britishness played out on an unprecedented scale as an expanding and increasingly politicised news media came to shape public perceptions of the strike. The first and very likely the last heritage strike came to dramatise the two competing meanings of heritage at the end of the century, that of a living social tradition and that of a created historical image.

In one sense, the public theatre of the Miners' Strike was remarkable for the clarity of the oppositions that were proposed as postwar economic and social compromises foundered. The 'versuses', as Tony Harrison called them in his contemporary poem *v.*, were stark (Harrison 1987: 238). Margaret Thatcher was able to deploy a reactivated nationalist rhetoric after a 'moment of imperial atavism', as E. P. Thompson termed the Falklands War of 1982 (Williamson 1988: 169). She defined the miners as an 'enemy within' equated with the 'enemy without', the defeated Argentine military junta (Young 1991: 372). Scargill, a highly localised international socialist, also worked in binaries. His rhetoric re-articulated the political analysis that he had laid out for *New Left Review* in 1975. 'It is *them* and it is *us*', he argued, 'it is a class battle, it is a class war', and it remained so in 1984 (Scargill 1975: 26). Old oppositions of English metropolitan and regional cultures were also re-articulated in the dispute. The Channel 4 journalist and biographer of Scargill, Michael Crick, recalled going to Grimethorpe colliery in South Yorkshire at the beginning of the strike because 'we [had] heard something about a brass band, but above all the name sounds just right'. Arriving there he duly met with 'the southerner's idea of a mining community' (Crick 1985b: 244). Such re-treading of Orwell's road to Wigan Pier after fifty years was to be characteristic of much contemporary reporting of the strike and of its subsequent passage into the cinema fictions of *Brassed Off* and *Billy Elliot*. However, such strategies and discourses disguised less tractable histories of nationhood and region that were played out in the anti-festival of the dispute.

As Crick's reference to the geographical and cultural remoteness of Grimethorpe indicates, the main events of 1984–5 took place in little-known parts of England. The cultural geography of mining that was pushed to prominence by the strike was one that had been shaped outside of the main trajectories of industrialisation. The locations of the coal measures and the intensity of labour required to exploit them had produced uneven patterns of development and settlement over a century of the expansion and contraction of the industry. They were patterns that largely worked against a dominant model of an urbanising working class. For whilst there were relatively large conurbations in larger and older coalfields such as South Yorkshire, there were also many small 'pit villages' that remained relatively isolated and, in most ways, culturally homogeneous. Some of these, like Grimethorpe itself, were well established. Others were much more recent. Villages in north-east Nottinghamshire which were at the centre of some of the most violent and most intensely reported conflicts of the dispute – Ollerton, Harworth, Bilsthorpe – had been constructed only in the 1920s, for example. Robert J. Waller notes that these pits were 'situated in open countryside previously untouched by coal-mining, isolated by poor bus services and a lack of private transport, and with traditions and customs far removed from those usually associated with established coalfields' (Waller 1983: 12–13). The long history of the relocation of substantial groups of workers and their families from other regions also created complex patterns of migration which in turn produced communities that were anything but homogeneous. Malcolm Pitt's study *The World On Our Backs* (1979) evokes east Kent, where the 'composite language of regional dialects, industrial working-class phraseology, and the diverse vocabularies of the coalfields is [*sic*] virtually a foreign tongue to the aboriginal population' (Pitt 1979: 67).

The coalfields, then, presented an alternative map of England, outside the domestic tourist routes of the south and west established in the early twentieth century and also outside the simplicities of the North/South divide that Crick evoked. Whilst the slogans of the strike emphasised binary oppositions – 'Which side are you on?' – its cultural realities were never that simple. 'It was a national strike but not a national strike', concluded Huw Benyon, noting that the primary loyalties of those involved concerned neither class nor country but '*our* pit and *our* village' (Benyon 1985: 2). This localism was embedded in an industry that maintained a distinctively regional and customary character, something reflected in the National Union of Mineworkers itself. The NUM retained a federal structure even after the nationalisation of the industry in 1947. Its federal units were also determined by county boundaries, normally a fairly weak marker for an English working class that tended to find identity in the towns, cities and areas of the cities in which they lived. For a largely non-urban workforce of miners, though, the county area expressed local cultural differences shaped around the different geological conditions and associated working practices of the county coalfields. 'When the officials returned to their own Areas [from national union meetings]', writes Vic Allen, 'it was as if they were crossing frontiers' (Allen 1981: 187). Those frontiers marked long-held political and cultural rivalries as well as solidarities, both of which defined the historical and political theatre of 1984–5.

Even the county union organisations were expressive of diversity rather than unity. Allen notes that the four 'panels' that made up the Yorkshire area, South Yorkshire, North Yorkshire, Barnsley and Doncaster, 'reflected local loyalties and were competitive in their relationships' (135). Historical anomalies persisted, untransformed by the postwar national consolidation of industry and union. Bolsover colliery, for example, was geographically in Derbyshire but because of legacies of the 1926 strike retained membership of the Nottinghamshire area of the NUM. During the strike, competing demands of local allegiance and national solidarity proved both an imperative to action and a point of weakness. 'Hundreds of Yorkshire pickets streamed joyously across the [Nottinghamshire] border', Martin Adeney and John Lloyd reported of the early days of the strike, again marking the unusual political importance of the county boundary in the long and tense history between the two federated unions (Adeney and Lloyd 1986: 88). The same rivalries of history shaped the Nottinghamshire miners' resistance to such aggressive expressions of federalism, and their own localised interpretation of which side they were on. Andrew Richards notes the case of a Nottinghamshire village that was sealed off against the 'infiltration' of pickets from outside coalfields, with police allowing people in and out by making a judgement on the 'localness' of their accent. It was a striking example of the significance of old local shibboleths in the definitive civil conflict of the late twentieth century (Richards 1996: 130).

'The animating spirit of the 1984–5 strike', Raphael Samuel argues, 'was that of *radical conservatism*' (Samuel et al. 1986: 22). It was a spirit that united even the conflicting Area Unions in an assertion of local customary rights both to labour and to dwell, a claim that recalled more the nineteenth-century combinations that opposed rural enclosure than any conventional labour dispute of modern industry. This traditional element was emphasised by an accompanying assertion of what Samuel calls 'the hereditary principle in relation to the union, in relation to the village, and above all in relation to the miner's job' (23). The inheritance of labour, the striking miners argued, determined the viability of local economies and historical networks of family and community. A comparable appeal to heritage and tradition was also made by those miners who opposed the strike. Andrew Richards cites a Nottinghamshire miner's analysis of the NUM Executive's rejection of demands for a national ballot on the strike in apparent contravention of union rules as a betrayal of a hereditary principle. The NUM regulations, the miner argued, were not 'rules written by any Tory or landowner [but] were written by our forefathers for us, for our generation' (Richards 1996: 190). Like the employee–work relationship amongst the striking miners, the legal frame of the union becomes in this statement an issue of generational continuity, a fixed traditional principle to be defended against new practices – and new betrayals.

Interpretations of the most serious British industrial dispute of modern times as a contest defined by threats to heritage and tradition drew upon concepts of and arguments about national identity that had a broader currency in cultural studies and social history during the 1980s. Martin J. Wiener's *English Culture and the Decline of the Industrial Spirit 1850–1980* (1981), Patrick Wright's *On Living in an Old Country* (1985) and Robert Hewison's *The Heritage Industry: Britain in a Climate of Decline* (1987) all provided critiques of Englishness which the authors represented as variously stunted and foreclosed by its relationship with an imaginary past. Anticipating the modernising rhetoric of the government in the Miners' Strike, Wiener noted England's continuing fascination with itself as a place of tradition rather than innovation. A stalled and compromised nineteenth-century industrial revolution, he argued, had been consolidated rather than transformed in the postwar period, perpetuating a 'pattern of industrial behavior suspicious of change, reluctant to innovate, energetic only in maintaining the status quo' (Wiener 1981: 154). Wright and Hewison, though less obviously party political, depicted an English cultural landscape dominated by ahistorical representations of history rather than a living culture that perpetuates historical change. They argued that the emergence of institutional and civic practices of heritage – working museums, designated historical areas in towns and cities where industry had disappeared, re-enactments of battles, crafts and traditions – rendered history merely a spectacle 'purged of political tension' (Wright 1985: 69). The very act of restoring and celebrating 'English heritage', they suggested, was a denial of history as an active force that informed contemporary life. To live in a heritage culture is to be in the grip of what Wright, referring to the National Trust, termed 'an ethereal . . . holding company for the dead spirit of the nation' (56).

Such critiques of late twentieth-century English historical culture were countered by other arguments about the significance of such invented or maintained traditions. Raphael Samuel, who took a sustained and active interest in the strike, also mounted a defence of the development of heritage. For Samuel, the proliferation of heritage sites did not mark the foreclosure of an active social history but rather offered a means of pursuing its civic and communal ideals in a period shaped by the individualist logic of neo-liberal economic theories. Heritage projects, he argued, represented 'one of the few areas of national life in which it is possible to invoke an idea of the common good without provoking suspicion of party interest . . . one of the few where notions of ancestry and posterity can be invoked without embarrassment or bad faith' (Samuel 1994: 292). For Samuel, heritage culture allowed historians to pursue performatively the democratising principles of postwar social historiography. It also allowed non-specialists to participate in what he terms the 'theatres of memory', the active process of establishing and analysing the past (Samuel 1994).

Samuel's argument was tested in the years after the defeat of the miners in 1985, for the strike itself came to pass from active English political memory into English heritage. It is a passage that can be dated to October 1992, when the NUM marched in London in protest at a further round of pit closures. The notable public sympathy expressed for their performance and their cause in such unlikely areas as Kensington and Chelsea with 'the upper middle classes rattling their jewellery . . . and posh London suburbia hanging out the banners', as the Yorkshire NUM official Dave Douglass remembered it, reflected one aspect of this enclosure of heritage (Douglass 2002: 5). Unlike the confrontations of 1984–5, the NUM march was perceived as an orderly, even a nostalgic carnival, something very different from the insurrectionary political display of the picket lines and the battle of Orgreave eight years earlier. The miners appeared in the capital as reminders of an increasingly distant point of crisis, rather than as actors in a continuing national conflict. It was a metropolitan journey reproduced as the sentimental finale of *Brassed Off* a few years later, as the miners' brass band is shown to celebrate collective identity in the face of defeat. Saving the remaining pits in the context of the failure of the 1984–5 strike could be rendered by now sympathetic viewers of the march as an act of historical preservation rather than as a political decision about national identity.

Jeremy Deller's 'time-based artwork', *The Battle of Orgreave* (2001) pressed the questions of memory, heritage and politics in the Miners' Strike in other ways. Using some of its original participants, mainly miners but also some police, it sought to recreate the strike's most notorious encounter of pickets and police on 18 June 1984 as the miners sought to close the coke and coal depot that was supplying Scunthorpe steel works. The unprecedented paramilitary tactics of the police, including the use of cavalry charges, produced some of the most startling television images of the strike and focused contemporary debates on the politicising of its policing, the causes and meaning of violence in the dispute, and the coverage of the strike by rival news media. Deller's performance project was intended to replicate the events of the day and to restore what Len Masterman termed the 'absences' in the original television coverage (Masterman 1988: 99). The re-enactment also sought to restore the significance of Orgreave and the Miners' Strike as a whole in a broader historical context, re-defining Orgreave as 'part of the lineage of decisive battles in English History', as Deller (2002: 7) put it.

The Battle of Orgreave is heritage culture at its most ambitious, asserting the potential of such events to restore the cultural memory of a historical moment preserved only in the individual memories of those that took part and in the incoherent and politically weighted images of contemporary media reports. In this way the project claimed Samuel's argument for the social democratic potential of historical performances that recovered local memory and established a record of popular history. Careful re-enactment, Deller argued, could achieve a sharper historical perspective upon 'something that was essentially chaos' at the time (Deller 2002: 7). More significantly, it allowed its original protagonists to participate in that act of historical revision. However, *The Battle of Orgreave* also revived the objections to heritage projects made by Wright and Hewison in the 1980s.

Whilst some of the actors were former miners and policemen, by far the majority were recruited from battle re-enactment societies whose normal range of historical reference tended to end with the English Civil War. The implicit inclusion of Orgreave in this largely apolitical gaming of military manoeuvre arguably displaced the politics of heritage and struggle onto a heritage of spectacle, shaping it instead as a modern version of that most stylised of English national performances, the historical pageant. The strike thus became part of a tradition of aesthetic memorialism that began on the streets of Kensington and Chelsea a decade before. 'A commentary explaining what was happening and pop hits from 1984 were played over loudspeakers', notes Alice Correia, 'fashions of that year were revisited and participants were dressed in costumes appropriate to the time and place' and 'miners' threw 'foam-rocks' (Correia 2006: 97, 98).

The Miners' Strike of 1984–5 still remains a contested performance of English identity as it becomes itself a test of historical memory and heritage. Deller's project to restore 'the English Civil War Part II' to national historical significance only served to sharpen that contest. The radical conservatism of the strike itself contrived to make highly localised and traditional conceptions of community and heritage a national political challenge to neo-conservative economic and social policies. How such a moment is remembered inevitably represents contradictions embedded in the anti-festival of the strike itself. Deller's project was funded by a public art company, 'with the majority of its funding coming from corporate sponsors and private donors', as Alice Correia notes, a sign of the passage of the theatre of memory from public to corporate institutions (Correia 2006: 107). At the same time the debates and recollections of the strike and the issues of re-enactment presented in Mike Figgis's film of Deller's piece suggest the significance of its memorialising to those participants. Whilst the process of *The Battle of Orgreave* is a controversial one, it needs to be set against a more general repression and forgetting of the events of 1984–5. Twenty-five years later there is still no authoritative written history of the Miners' Strike.

Forgetting England

The Festival of Britain sought to affirm a new settlement of Anglo-Britishness beyond empire and within a social contract of centrally planned development, and the Miners' Strike was a desperate political theatre that marked the dissolution of that contract. The Millennium Experience in Greenwich which opened on 1 January 2000, seemed to have no such discernible meanings or purpose. 'The message is no message', wrote Iain Sinclair, poet and sceptical witness to the construction of the Dome, 'look and wonder' (Sinclair 1999: 21). Yet the rhetoric that filled it in the final years of the century – and, as one glossy account of its construction noted, 'the structure itself weighs less than the air inside' – has come to provide a canny guide to the struggles with English national identity over the previous century (Power 2000: 176). For despite the best efforts of its designers, its publicists and its political and commercial masters, historical and cultural meanings did leak from beneath the Dome's Teflon sheeting.

Initiated by a Conservative government in terminal decline, the Experience's purpose was defined blandly by its first champion, Michael Heseltine, as one of making 'a statement of great confidence and pride in ourselves' (Heseltine 2000: 509). A new Prime Minister, Tony Blair, whose government rather reluctantly inherited and carried through the project, tempered this old-fashioned view of a national festival. In language that recalled the measured statement of national stocktaking that was typical of the Festival of Britain's publicity material, Blair described it in his Foreword to Elizabeth Wilhide's sympathetic account of the evolution of the Greenwich project as an opportunity to say 'who we are, what we do, and what the future may have in store for us' (Wilhide 1999: np). How this project of self-representation was to be achieved, however, remained a difficulty right to the end. Wilhide's *The Millennium Dome* (1999) is also a compendium of late twentieth-century discourses of English identity in serious trouble. Alex Madina of the New Millennium Experience Company, for example, is quoted as saying that the Dome was not 'a graspable structure'. 'The genius of it', he suggests, 'is that actually the meaning keeps eluding you'. 'The Dome is unique in the sense that the way the spaces have been developed has been entirely content-led', he went on. 'The Experience is a comment and it's asking you to engage and complete that circle' (9, 156). At the time such evasions of the central questions of a hugely expensive and ambitious national enterprise – who we are, what we do and what the future might have in store for us – seemed uncomfortably close to panicky improvisation under pressure of Greenwich Mean Time. But they confirmed a lack of even the revisionary rhetorical resources of planning and responsible consumption that the Festival of Britain deployed. The Dome really did seem to be about an absent centre of nationhood with appeals to participatory democracy disguising a lack of any clear idea of what England or Britain might mean.

The slipperiness of such rhetoric had a purpose beyond disguising puzzlement about national identity, however. For though it could not acknowledge it, the Dome was being forced to manage some old contradictions in English identity that had been given new form by the new government. Drumming up commercial sponsorship at a 'business breakfast' in 1998, the new Prime Minister declared that the Greenwich project would 'bring the nation together in a common purpose' (Blair 2004: 182). It was a tentative admission of a national disunity that was implicitly blamed on previous Conservative administrations (and the nearest the project came to acknowledging the social consequences of the Miners' Strike), but it was also relevant to the constitutional condition of the United Kingdom a year into his own. Devolution legislation in Scotland, Wales and Northern Ireland in 1998 had posed again the question of the nature of England's relationship with its partner nations and principalities, and implicitly at least raised that of its own constitutional future. To celebrate nationhood whilst the nation was in the midst of renegotiating the terms of that nationhood was always going to test the resources of politicians, designers and national theorists alike. As one marketing analysis of the failure of the Millennium Experience to attract its projected audiences concluded, 'the desire to reflect Britain during a time of shifting national loyalties [was] fraught with branding and communications difficulties' (Trueman et al. 2001: 11). And Britain was always hard to brand even at the best of times.

The studied vagueness about what the Millennium Experience actually was tended to disguise the ways in which the Dome was firmly in the tradition of English/British public representation. Its initial planning, for example, paid even less attention to its being an inclusively British celebration than the Festival of Britain. Stripped of its postmodern rhetoric, the Dome was an old-fashioned English metropolitan exhibition even though no one really knew what they wanted to exhibit there. An early proposal for smaller scale 'Millennium Spheres' to be constructed throughout the nation had been quickly rejected – 'no latent understanding of product' was the Millennium Commission's verdict (Nicolson 1999: 65). Discussion of two proposed regional locations for the Experience – Birmingham and Derby – had been cursory under Heseltine's chairmanship. 'London was the capital', is his exasperated explanation of the decision, and that was that (Heseltine 2000: 510).

Adam Nicolson also suggests that some old regional prejudices were at work against Birmingham's bid. 'The very name seemed to the pro-London members of the government . . . to bring with it a pall of functional mediocrity', he comments. It would be 'struggling for beauty', the Commissioners concluded (Nicolson 1999: 69, 71).

The problem of filling the vast space of the Greenwich Dome also led to the postmodern vision of the project increasingly relying on the history it attempted to exclude. Not that the engagement was immediately evident in the endless evasions of its marketing. 'The Experience is not a curated collection of exhibits for passive inspection and appreciation', Alex Madina noted with due acknowledgement of current theories of the necessary relativism of cultural display, 'people aren't trying to give a monolithic view about where we are the moment' (Wilhide 1999: 156). But with the tent standing empty something had to be there, monolithic or not. In the end a model that was not that dissimilar to that of the pavilions of the South Bank Exhibition was agreed. 'All you need to do, to make people love it and own it', declared the designer, 'is to make it a village fête, but a fête for the nation' (Nicolson 1999: 68). Given the much-advertised revolutionary modernity of its covering, such a retreat to the village green was surprising, but it was one part of the largely incoherent negotiation with English national discourses that marked the project.

The tentative return to the model of the Festival of Britain was confirmed by the appointment of Peter Mandelson, Herbert Morrison's grandson, as the 'single shareholder' of the New Millennium Experience Company, the new 'public corporation' managing the project. Under Mandelson's control, the Dome, willingly or not, represented the continuities and changes in the fifty years between it and the Festival of Britain. The Experience, as its name suggests, intensified the discourse of subjectivity that was already central to the 1951 strategy of renegotiating post-imperial nationhood. In 1951, however, the visitor was a citizen there to be playfully educated into his or her new role in the nation. In 2000 the visitor was conceived primarily as a consumer. Morrison's desire to 'do something jolly' was transformed into an 'experience' anticipated by Tony Blair, in his most populist mode, as 'exhilarating like Disney World – yet different. Educational and interactive like the Science Museum – yet different. Emotional and uplifting like a West End musical – yet different. It will be shaped by the people' (Donoghue and Jones 2001: 493; Blair 2004: 193). More accurately, it was shaped by private companies as the Experience, underwritten by public funds, projected its 'core values' through commercially sponsored zones. Readjusting the careful calibration of corporate and state enterprise visible in the South Bank Exhibition, Mandelson delivered a Dome in which The Body Zone was sponsored by Boots, L'Oréal and Roche, Self Portrait by Marks & Spencer, Learning by Tesco and Journey by Ford.

The nation was not convinced by the story about itself that was told to it in Greenwich. Unlike its two main precursors, the Great Exhibition and the Festival of Britain, the Millennium Experience was a popular and commercial failure, with only 6,517,000 of the targeted 12 million visitors appearing (of whom 1,000,000 did not pay) (Hewison 2001: 547). However, the struggles of the Dome to articulate its purpose, the insecurities of its civic and commercial identity, its thoughtless metropolitanism and its uneasy relationship to its precursor on the South Bank made it an apt, if costly representation of contemporary nationhood. Jennie Page, the Chief Executive of the New Millennium Experience Company during the planning and building of the Dome, was always prone to revealing obfuscations about the enterprise that she oversaw. The 'structure expresses what the project itself is', she claimed, 'which is a great overarching complicated knitted web holding down something vast and semi-opaque' (Wilhide 1999: 18). As a definition of Englishness at the end of the twentieth century it could hardly be bettered.

The Anglo-British state's two attempts to represent officially what it thought its country meant in the last sixty years have been ones of readjustment and negotiation rather than a confident assertion. Withdrawal from global self-projection was the unstated theme of the Festival of Britain with its calculated revision of the imperial rhetoric of its predecessors. At the same time its celebration of orderly, insular progress instituted a comparable revision of domestic discourses of tradition. England, at least its symbolic exhibition on the South Bank, tried to show itself as sensibly modern. The Millennium Dome's desperate attempts to avoid saying anything at all about Anglo-British identity suggested the serious dilemmas of a nation-state struggling for a rhetoric to manage the consequences of domestic devolution, European integration and multiculturalism. The tortuous abstractions of its policy statements and the blandness of its exhibitions expressed a national discourse floating free of the conflicts that the Dome was apparently engaged in resolving.

At the absent centre of the Dome was not only the progressive social democracy that the South Bank Exhibition had articulated in 1951, but also the noisy and dissenting political theatre of the Miners' Strike that took place in the years between the two national celebrations. The 'gigantic mirror of the nation', as Peter Mandelson called it, did accurately reflect the absences and confusions of a nationhood that found it difficult to represent itself in the terms of monument or narrative (Hewison 2001: 548). 'What you see in the Dome was shaped by the opinions and wishes of thousands of people across the UK who told researchers what they wanted in the millennium celebrations', the official guide claimed (*Millennium Experience: The Guide*: 8). If that claim was accurate, it bespoke an abandonment of class, race, empire, politics and history as national descriptors and the acceptance of the topography of the shopping mall as an accurate representation of national identity. The fate of London's other millennial attraction suggested an alternative interpretation, however. As the Dome began its symbolic progress to bankruptcy, David Marks and Julia Barfield's London Eye continued to turn and became England's most popular tourist attraction. The 135m, slow-turning ferris wheel sited on Herbert Morrison's South Bank would not have been out of place in his 1951 exhibition with its tentative grafting of technological and stylistic innovation, educational purpose and national fun. As its 3.5 million annual riders are instructed (gently and slowly) about the landscape of metropolitan England and look down river to Greenwich, they also participate in the historical problem of memory and forgetting that English modernity set itself at the end of the twentieth century.

Chapter 4

Journeys

In the early 1920s, S. P. B. Mais was travelling near Plumpton. 'We swept round a corner of the Downs', he writes, 'at our feet lay the green and golden carpet of the Sussex weald. Suddenly out of a hidden lane right across our bows came the South Downs hounds, homing after cubbing'. ' "My God!" ' says his companion, ' "England!" ' . . . We were silent: we had all seen a holy thing: we had seen England. None of us will ever be able to communicate what we saw: none of us will ever forget it' (Mais 1922: 311–12). Mais's English journey, his sudden vision of nationhood and his expression of inexpressible Englishness, embody both the aspirations and the strategies of a popular genre of English travel writing produced in the period around and between the two world wars. Only J. B. Priestley's *English Journey* (1934) and H. V. Morton's *In Search of England* (1927) have retained any popular currency, but they are a tiny part of the hundreds of books and essays that recorded journeys by car, bus, horse, foot and bicycle 'in search of England'. These accounts formed substantial sections of some publishers' lists, whether formalised as a series such as B. T. Batsford's 'The British Heritage' or as part of the more informal preoccupations of a company like J. M. Dent. Some writers, including Mais and Morton, made a long career out of finding England. Others, like Edward Thomas, C. E. Montague, H. J. Massingham and the film-makers Michael Powell and Emeric Pressburger, used the narrative conventions of the genre to develop a more challenging enquiry into the nature of English modernity.

Rural Travels

The literature of national travel between the wars was founded upon two basic premises, both of which relate to the theories of nationalism and identity discussed in Chapter 1 and the Edwardian revivalism of Baden-Powell, Sharp and Neal described in Chapter 2. The first was the idea that England was a lost or neglected place in need of rediscovery. 'Never before have so many people been searching for England', wrote H. V. Morton, and the theme of loss and recovery was taken up by many other travellers (Morton 1927: vii). M. V. Hughes's *About England* (1927) begins 'England is not well known to the English people' (Hughes 1927: 3); the romantic imperialist historian Arthur Mee in his bizarre *Enchanted Land* (1936), a 'New Domesday Book of 10,000 towns and villages', suggests that England 'which had opened the gates of the world, [was] largely unknown to her own people' (Mee 1936: 5); and W. J. Blyton's concern in *English Cavalcade* (1937) was with 'this unknown, secret England' (Blyton 1937: 8). National travel and the books it produced were consequently devoted to unearthing the secret. In order to do so, however, the travellers were unanimous on one thing: they should set out with no strategy or timetable.

This was the second premise: English journeys must lack any premise. 'My plan of travel was to have no plan', one early twentieth-century traveller writes, and this became a commonplace (Hissey 1917: viii). Morton claimed to have written *In Search of England* 'without deliberation by the roadside, on farmyard walls, in cathedrals, in little churchyards, on the washstands of country inns, and in many another inconvenient place'. 'It was a moody holiday, and I followed the roads', he declared (vii). And so did everybody else. A. F. Tschiffely's recommendation is to 'find a good horse, ride afar, in any direction, just jog along, anyhow and anywhere, canter over quiet country lanes, over hills and through dales – sunshine or rain – alone with a horse to see the real England!' (Tschiffely 1936: 7). A. G. Street, another professional England-seeker, praised Dorothy Hartley's *The Countryman's England* (1935) for a similar waywardness: 'one just meanders, and that is the only way to enjoy a journey through the English countryside. Nothing in the book appears to be planned . . . yet everything is there' (Hartley 1935: v–vi). Such celebrations of the qualities of what Edmund Blunden calls 'the watchful wanderer' were routine in a literature that claimed to value the haphazard, the accidental and the chance encounter (Turner 1945: 8). These English travel books articulated a kind of anti-theory of Englishness, celebrating the very evasiveness they were avowedly seeking to define. They affirm a nation that is uncomfortable with the certainties of the guidebook and which, though it might be glimpsed by chance as in Mais's moment by Plumpton, is ultimately unenclosable. The discovery that England could not be definitively discovered merely invited more journeys and more searching, of course, and such was the volume of travel and publication that the idea of the unpredictability of English journeys became very predictable indeed.

The 'wanderings' of the writers committed to discovering 'unknown England' actually conformed to a fairly limited set of routes. Most of the journeys began with a ritual leaving of London, the place of production for the publishers of the books, newspapers and magazines through which accounts of the unknown nation were made known to mass audiences. For the travellers, though, despite the fact that most of them lived in or near London, national reality was always located elsewhere, 'not the Fleet Street where I work', as Mais puts it, 'but the country-side to which I belong' (Mais 1922: 9). Nevertheless, the same writer's *It Isn't Far From London* (1930) reassures his metropolitan readership that the 'spiritual exaltation' of that countryside is available, at a pinch, on day-trips from the capital (Mais 1930: 12). Haphazard wandering, once London had been left behind, had a marked tendency to keep south and head west. Morton's route in *In Search of England* – the New Forest, Weymouth, Exeter, Cornwall, Glastonbury, Hereford and Worcester – traced a well-worn path of mid-century England-seekers whose travels avoided the complications of the industrial, the urban and the suburban and kept them securely 'between the two North roads', as one traveller of 'quiet roads and sleepy villages' puts it (Fea 1913: 9). At times, when transit through ugly industrial areas was unavoidable, English travellers found uses for the modern technologies they normally deplored. Tschiffely, for example, after wandering alone with his horse in the real England of the New Forest, Hampshire, Salisbury Plain, Chipping Norton, Worcester, Ludlow and the Lake District (always the acceptable hills of Northernness), suddenly found himself in 'the midst of gloomy industrial parts' near Warrington. Immediately, he hired a truck to transport himself and the horse to more English places. 'The region we sped through', he noted, 'is not fit for innocent animals to live in . . . As we drove past long rows of dismal smelly dens, which serve as human habitations, even the thought of living in them made me shudder' (Tschiffely 1936: 133).

Such avoidance of the places of industry is entirely typical of the genre, as is Tschiffely's willingness to use the products of that industry to avoid the odours and ugliness of those parts of England incapable of providing the searcher with revelation. While he is beguilingly brazen in his expediency, other writers suggest the pliancy of the rhetoric of popular English topography when it confronted its own implication in English modernity and was forced to manage its celebrations of the rural in contexts of industrialism and mass production. Some set rules and limits to the conveniences of modern transport. Mais, for example, tells

Londoners, 'by all means avail yourself of the train or the motor-bus to avoid the suburbs going out and coming back, but the only part of the day that matters is the part you spend in the saddle or on foot' (Mais 1930: 12–13). Others who were more reliant on the internal combustion engine were also more inventive in their absorption of motoring within an historical continuity of Englishness. James John Hissey, for example, describes himself as 'a contemplative motorist', boasting of a car 'conveniently small for exploring byways and lanes' and hence fully integrated into the rural scene (1917: 2, vii). Morton, whose *In Search of England* and its sequels were entirely dependent upon car journeys, presents driving as a return to the older ways of road transport that had been eclipsed by the defining nineteenth-century modernity of railways. 'The King's highway is once more a place for adventures and explorations', he writes, continuing optimistically, 'I would venture to prophesy that within the next few years we shall see a decline in the popularity of the seaside resort . . . and a revival of the country inn' (viii).

More ecologically-minded travellers perceived the contradictions inherent in a mechanised search for premodern nationhood. 'There is scarcely a by-road left in England', noted C. E. M. Joad in *A Charter for Ramblers* (1934), 'whose praises have not been sung, and to which, because it is praiseworthy, motorists have not been elaborately guided' (Joad 1934: 41). However, by lamenting the fact that he could not 'lose myself in reverie of the past, nor daydream about the future, nor sink into that delicious coma in which from being *in* the country I become *of* the country', Joad missed the point about the contradiction that he deplored (43). For the genre of 'finding England' was predicated upon the rhetorical management of such contradictory positions. If the motor-car could be said to revive the turnpike, so could the eye of the trained beholder perceive and sustain English tradition in English modernity. The genre of English travel was not a project of observation and description but one of rhetorical and topographical transformation.

Morton's *In Search of England* includes only one encounter with the industrial North that so offended Tschiffely, but his visit to Wigan, ten years later to be made England's archetypal proletarian place by George Orwell, suggests the revisionary strategy of English journeying. Morton restores Wigan from a mining town to 'an old-fashioned country town' (Morton 1927: 153). It was not 'a mushroom town that grew up over night on a coalfield', he concludes. 'It has history, and behind it the traditions of centuries of loyalty to the Crown' and consequently remained part of the 'real' England that its superficial (and repellent) modernity appeared to have destroyed (154). Morton's sequel to *In Search of England*, *The Call of England* (1928), claimed to confront the 'shirked realities' of the earlier book through a sustained visit to the North (Morton 1928: vii). It deploys this strategy of national reintegration on a wider scale as industrial England is re-absorbed into a still-dominant rural aesthetic and historical continuum. 'It is only when we go there', he writes, with a characteristic imputation that the reader as well as the writer is not 'of the North', 'that we realize how very slightly the age of coal and steel has deformed the green beauty of England. Our manufacturing districts, vast as they are, form merely a scratch on the map in comparison with those miles of wild and romantic country, whose history and beauty rival anything the south can boast' (vii–viii). 'The streets of Hull are full of Vikings', he asserts, an imaginative re-ordering of the port's citizens which restores them to the inclusive national narrative that the English travel genre always implied (17).

Morton's rendering of Hull as a Viking settlement was typical of the English travel narrative's general avoidance of any engagement with the overt modernity of industrialism and the social and political conflicts that it implied. Just as Morton could recast Wigan, on the brink of severe economic depression, as a traditional English market town, so were whole histories of urban and rural struggle effaced by a genre that found national identity in the aesthetics of rural topography alone. The England that was 'found' in these journeys was both limited and evasive as the genre's codes were deployed to repress the ideological contradiction of tradition defined and rescued by the products of the modernity that it was set up to oppose. Yet in some examples of the genre it is this very contradiction in English representation that is itself the main concern. In the work of Edward Thomas, C. E. Montague and H. J. Massingham the defining narrative codes of journeying and haphazard discovery are still strongly present, but they become means of exploring the political and social tensions of Englishness rather than achieving its strategic redemption.

Edward Thomas was a jobbing journalist and his travel writing never departed far from the structures and typical locations of the commercial travel narratives. However, two of his works of English topography, *The Heart of England* (1906) and *The Icknield Way* (1913), both participate in conventional celebrations of essential rural Englishness and articulate an interior critique of the common assumptions of the genre. They present a far more troubled sense of the implications of twentieth-century wanderings than the travel writers referred to earlier in the chapter. The essays in *The Heart of England* quickly establish familiar narrative codes of leaving London and finding an essential Englishness in the countryside. Thomas is initially 'entrapped in a town where I had once known nothing but fields' (Thomas 1982: 8). There follows the ritual journey out of London and chance encounters with iconic rural characters such as tramps and watercress sellers. Typically enough, he makes an explicitly anti-modern journey in 'tracts of country which are discovered by few except such as study the railway maps of England in order to know what to avoid' and evokes the villages and inns that he finds there (57). But his attempt to find 'the old, roomy England' is never completed in a revelation like that of Mais at Plumpton or resolved by any personal security in a rural national identity (38). Places are nameless and routes dreamlike; the tramp who defines that 'old, roomy England' for him is revealed as a murderer; a folk-song session in the archetypal English inn begins with the pastoral lyricism of 'The First Daffodils' but ends with 'Poor Old Horse', a song of economic distress and personal suffering. Ultimately, his journey is irresolute and irresolvable. A lane that in other examples of the genre might lead to the essential England he seeks is too complex for the traveller. It has 'many windings and turnings back, as if it were a humble, diffident enquirer, fortunately creeping on, aiming at some kind of truth and not success, yet without knowing what truth is when he starts' (57). In a rhetorical turn that both uses and inverts the familiar convention, the English landscape is shown to be itself in search of England and can offer no certainties for its travellers.

The Icknield Way, published on the eve of the First World War, maintains this approach to English identity. In some ways its account of the walking of an ancient route suggests Hilaire Belloc's influential travel book, *The Old Road* (1904), a journey of national pilgrimage from England's ancient capital Winchester to its medieval sacred centre, Canterbury. For Belloc, such roads were 'the humblest and the most subtle, but [also] the greatest and the most original of the spells which we inherit from the earliest pioneers of our race' (Belloc 1910: 4). To walk them was to reconstitute that old racial identity and to fend off the threatening modernity of technology and American culture that by the end of his journey he found to intrude even into Canterbury itself. Thomas's journey is also a national pilgrimage of sorts, but one that is altogether more obscure and desperate than that of Belloc's attempt to reconstitute medieval Catholic English identities. Far from being a means of recovering such securities, the road, like the lane in *The Heart of England*, is expressive of the problem itself. 'I could not find a beginning or an end of the Icknield Way', he confesses (Thomas 1913: vii). Evasion, indeterminacy, fragmentation and irresolution compose this Englishness, disallowing accurate description or joyful possession. The book contains detailed and loving evocations of its places, but these are clouded by a sense of the impenetrability of the land and of the walker's inevitable isolation from it. 'To-day I know there is nothing beyond the farthest of far ridges except a signpost to unknown places', he writes.

> The end is in the means – in the sight of that beautiful long straight line of the Downs in which a curve is latent – in the houses we shall never enter, with their dark secret windows and quiet hearth smoke, or their ruins friendly only to elders and nettle – in the people passing whom we shall never know though we may love them. (vi)

Thomas's point of contact with essential England is here also the point of a realisation of his distance from it.

In Thomas's work the land resists the enclosures of experience and meaning that the genre of the English travel book established whilst exploiting their conventions of haphazardness and intuition to achieve a much darker vision of nationhood. Instead of the chance encounter and the momentary vision establishing an essential national identity for the wanderer as they did for Mais and Morton, for Thomas they confirm only the disturbing incoherence of the experience of modern England. For him, being English was a condition of withdrawal rather than revelation, of strangeness rather than knowledge, of passing through rather than dwelling and of encounters with ghosts and ruins rather than with people and places. This ambivalent version of the trope of the English wanderer anticipates developments in the genre in the years after the war in which he was killed.

The proliferation of the literature of rural wanderings in the 1920s and 1930s was in part a continuation of the powerful imaginative resource of pastoral Englishness that, as Paul Fussell has shown, developed in First World War writing (Fussell 1976: 231–69). However, Thomas's strategy of using journeys and landscapes to question rather than affirm the meaning of England was continued by C. E. Montague, an anti-war leader writer on the *Manchester Guardian* who volunteered in 1914 and served on the Western Front. Montague's *Disenchantment* (1922) provided an early assessment of the ruinous social consequences of the war and this theme was continued in his English travel book, *The Right Place: A Book of Pleasures* (1924). *The Right Place* uses the journey to problematise postwar national identity whilst deploying the conventions and locations of the genre – one chapter is entitled 'Along an English Road', for example, another 'Country Houses'. In a letter to the travel writer H. M. Tomlinson in 1923, Montague described the strategy of the book in terms that would not be out of place in Mais's writing. It was intended, he claimed, as an expression of an 'authentic irrational affection for England – not the prime cuts of her only, but the delectable boiling pieces and the endearing offal too' (Elton 1929: 259).

But *The Right Place* is a book that is haunted by the same difficult questioning of the resources for such celebration that characterises Edward Thomas's dark pre-war journeys.

The 'rich, living knowledge of sensuous contact' with England to which Montague aspires is sought not through the haphazard rambling that the genre normally celebrates but through strange, obsessive travel – a 24-hour cycle ride from Manchester to London that begins in the middle of the night, for example (Montague 1924: 135). Like those of that less fortunate veteran, the poet Ivor Gurney, another compulsive walker on postwar rural roads, Montague's journeys reveal a nation in which the constituent elements of Morton's and Mais's Englishness are distorted and damaged. 'The old feudal England, beautiful and somewhat naughty in her day as some old women have been in their prime, died of malnutrition during the war', he writes in the chapter on country houses (169). What remains is the 'sinister, sequestered beauty of this solitude islanded in the midst of crowds' (171). The cathedral cities familiar from the itineraries of inter-war English journeys – Norwich, Lincoln, Canterbury, York, Rochester, Chester, Exeter – are recast by Montague as exhausted historical resources. 'Nearly all of them wear something now of that Chelsea pensioner look', he comments. 'More or less, the world has passed them by – a world they partly envy and partly disdain, feeling it ugly and raw as compared with their fair, mellow selves, and yet ruefully feeling, besides, that it seems in these vulgar times to have more of a function than they' (175). Timeless England, in Montague's disenchanted journeys, has aged badly.

The Right Place also revokes the customary geographical order of the English journey. Instead of the south-westward trajectory between the north roads, Montague takes on the north roads themselves. Northern landscapes come to articulate the difficult postwar politics of national identity in the book, as England becomes emphatically regionalised rather than integrated. In the chapter entitled 'Across the Pennine' he sets 'the bony hardness of England's North-western soil and the persistent hardness of man's work upon it' against 'some pleasant parts of the south [in which] you may reasonably tremble for England' (146, 147). Returning to his wartime experience, Montague writes of the 'working north' that its 'effect on your spirits resembles that of a front line in war, in contrast with that of a base' (148). Such a 'front line' requires a new peripatetic aesthetics of Englishness quite different from that of the typical travel book and its celebration of the comforts of the southern 'base'. In the chapter entitled 'Joys of the Street', Montague examines in detail the subtle architectural cultures of places avoided by the more conventional wanderers within unknown England. 'If by the

grace of God or the help of a friend you have escaped mal-education',
he suggests wryly in a discussion of the local differences between
Liverpool and Manchester, 'you will observe that in each city a ware-
house means a different thing' (190–1). A similar discrimination is
applied to the bank buildings of those cities, as well as to the architecture most despised by inter-war journeyers, the suburban villa.

The Right Place works against the grain of its genre. The orienta-
tion of its travel on the north roads, its celebration of the provincial
and the urban and its persistent sense of the First World War's disturbance of the means of national representation are all foreign to the routines of English travel. Like Edward Thomas, though, Montague does
not revoke the connection between the pastoral English landscape and
national identity. Recalling the outbreak of war in 1914, he affirms
that soldiers' attraction to natural landscapes was 'not any mere intellectual definition of England . . . even the autumn mists over flat
lowland meadows, to which soldiers awoke in their camps, became
movingly English' (112). However, he is also acutely aware that this
pathetic fallacy could not be sustained through the disenchantments of
the peace. His travelling in the 1920s was concerned with tracing the
very fault-lines and borders within England that Morton, Mais and the
rest were intent on effacing.

Political Walks

The troubled journeys of Thomas and Montague were followed in the
1930s by more explicitly political revisions of the preoccupations and
geographies of the classic searchers after England. Jack Hilton's *English
Ways* (1940), for example, is an account of a walk from Bolton to
Epsom. Unlike the solitary male wanderers, and these include Thomas
and Montague, he travels with his wife, pushing their belongings in a
pram. This is a sign of an intention to reverse the gentlemen travellers'
reticence about the economics of their English journeying. By contrast,
Hilton is attentive to the cost as well as to the landscape of England and
he provides detailed financial accounts. The places they visit are also just
the kind of towns through which T. S. Tschiffely would have sought
mechanical passage for himself and his horse: Sheffield, Chesterfield,
Mansfield, Derby, Nottingham, Leicester, Northampton, Reading. His
rendering of this 'fluid and almost chaotic England', as John Middleton
Murry calls it in his introduction, is a downbeat narrative in which
descriptions of working practices and analyses of industrial relations
replace evocations of crafts, heritage and rural inns (Hilton 1940: 16).

Rejecting the persona of the amateur wanderer, Hilton appears as a 'semi-skilled working-man who', according to Murry, 'spends more than he ought on beer' (11).

English Ways is an explicitly political revision of the travel genre and Hilton's book is not just a critique of the strategies of an H. V. Morton. As Andy Croft has argued, it is also a critique of the most famous political journey of the 1930s, one that will be discussed in the next chapter. Hilton had been involved in organising George Orwell's visit to the industrial North which resulted in *The Road to Wigan Pier* (1937), an involvement that he apparently regretted on reading Orwell's disparaging and evasive account of working-class life. His redemptive journey south, Croft suggests, is a 'hard-working apology for a book about which Hilton felt partly responsible' (Croft 1990: 250). Rejecting the geographical and cultural trajectory of both Morton and Orwell, Hilton uses the form of the travel narrative to reassert the ability of working-class subjects to represent themselves and to challenge their erasure or parody in the most celebrated examples of the genre.

English Ways needs be read beside other political journeys in the 1930s and the Second World War which, in their different ways, point to the imminent dissolution of the genre as a workable mode of popular national definition. H. J. Massingham's *Through the Wilderness* (1935), for example, includes an account of a walk that returns to the troubled landscape of Edward Thomas's pre-First World War journey on the Icknield Way. Massingham's narrative, though, whilst sharing Thomas's unease, articulates much more explicitly the political and social catastrophe of Englishness that he sees revealed there. 'The country I traversed', he writes of a walk from Henley to Guildford, 'might have been anywhere . . . I got lost four times in this country, but I was really lost all the time, because I was travelling on and on without getting anywhere, without passing anything and leaving anything behind. I was awake but in a nightmare' (Massingham 1935: 109). Massingham's nightmare is more material than Thomas's disturbing conviction of the evasiveness of pre-war England. Like the work of other English rural polemicists of the decade such as Joad and G. M. Trevelyan, *Through the Wilderness* presents a vision of the despoliation of the 'England to save which the young men went to die in the Great War', as Trevelyan puts it (Trevelyan 1929: 15). Joad and Trevelyan put their faith in new national institutions founded for the preservation of that England – the Ramblers' Association, the National Trust and the Youth Hostel Association. But Massingham's critique of urbanisation and suburbanisation is a far bleaker meditation upon the contradictions inherent in the proposition of the countryside as the essential resource for an Englishness imperilled by modernity.

Through the Wilderness evokes Edward Thomas's 'old, roomy England', rooted and culturally distinct, only to see it invaded by its *alter-ego*, a new postwar nation that is 'adrift from landmarks, set in the void, an expressionless mask' (109). This self-invasion is also a 'flow of escape', as he calls it, an instinctive national urge to dwell in the natural world (112). The suburbanisation of England is peculiarly difficult to resist, he argues, because it is shaped by the positive desire to make contact with an essential nationhood that can exist only outside of the cities and towns. 'It is love which moves him', says Massingham of the ruinous impulse of the urban English dweller to travel to the country-side and thereby destroy the very England that is most cherished (115). Such a polemic, as its author uneasily recognises, is made more difficult to sustain by that fact that Massingham was himself a recent urban emi-grant who had built a house on a hillside overlooking the Icknield Way. However, this apparent weakness in his position allows him to define a crucial distinction between the unthinking, desperate and destructive urban escapee and the self-conscious restorer of English identity. 'As things are at present', he writes, 'no town-dweller has any right to colonise the country unless he is able to establish some kind of rhythm and ritual between himself and the place where he chooses to live, the community to which he is exotic and the countryside which can only resent his presence by witness of the violence he does it'. The incomer must make 'his own individual contribution to an organic tradition he is otherwise disturbing' (2).

Massingham's own contribution is rather unconvincingly described as being 'to carve out something under an acre from a bare pasture and construct a house and garden out of it' (2). An accompanying photo-graph shows a gaunt, ugly, mock-Georgian house surrounded by what seems to be a suburban rockery, but it acts as a national and political symbol for its dweller. 'While I was building my house', he writes, 'I had come to realise that my business was to draw up a kind of covenant between myself and the land and that this was what the land itself demanded of me, the alien' (280). The covenant, 'first established on our islands by the megalith-builders', could also be confirmed by walking the landscape of old England. Massingham describes two walks in *Through the Wilderness*, one along the Icknield Way, the other along the Ridgeway. Both are seen as restorative of national and individual iden-tity. To walk the old roads, Massingham suggests, is to experience the 'suspension of the tyranny of time' and to reconnect the walker with an ancient and still potentially active history (184). Such 'land-conscience,' as he calls it, is a quasi-political force that can channel the desire for 'true' contact with the land and nation (278). Without such discipline, urban and suburban emigrations into the countryside could only be destructive. 'Land-conscience', he argues, offers a means by which the chthonic urge of a people to establish an identity through contact with its 'real places' could be achieved without the occupation and subsequent destruction of that land.

Seven years later Massingham reflected on 'the fiasco of my attempt to become part of the organism of place in my own village and to discover by participation in it the spirit of local community'. 'Who was I . . . to come butting in from outside, disturbing the established disorder?' he asks (Massingham 1942: 86–7). But his commitment to 'earth-scholarship' remained (87). As late as 1950 he was asserting that 'it is time for the whole nation to move into pastures new, to base itself firmly once more upon its own countryside', an injunction that his admirer, Roger Scruton, was to take literally at the beginning of the next century (Massingham 1950: 11; Scruton 2004). But even by the time of *Through the Wilderness* such 'covenants of the field' were uneasily situated between the conservative pastoral nationalism of Stanley Baldwin, fascist discourses of *volk* and soil, and radical working-class movements such as the Ramblers' Association – 'the hikers who try to reopen the old rights of way off the Icknield Way, they are fulfilling the covenant', he affirmed (Massingham 1935: 292). This contradictory politics of the English travel narratives persisted into the Second World War where it was explored in the only English feature film to engage fully with the genre. Michael Powell and Emeric Pressburger's *A Canterbury Tale* (1944) came to mark both the first translation of the popular literary genre into popular cinema and that genre's effective end as a means of English self-definition.

Wartime Journeys

A Canterbury Tale was the third in a sequence of six wartime films made by Powell and Pressburger – it was preceded by *49th Parallel* (1941), *One of Our Aircraft is Missing* (1941) and *The Life and Death of Colonel Blimp* (1943) and followed by *I Know Where I'm Going!* (1945) and *A Matter of Life and Death* (1946). All of these were produced within the political constraints of wartime propaganda. However, instead of setting out to assert a known Englishness, Powell and Pressburger used the context of wartime disorder and change to explore that identity. The films set up provocative dialogues with other nationalities – German, American, Scottish – and evoked unsettling aspects of English identity that frequently went beyond the cinematic conventions established by the Ministry of Information. Of the six films, *A Canterbury Tale* is both the most explicit in its engagement with questions of Englishness and the most difficult to interpret.

Beginning with a short sequence that evokes the Chaucerian pilgrimage alluded to in the title, the film tells the story of three young wartime 'pilgrims' to Canterbury just before the D-Day landings: Bob Johnson, an American soldier, Peter Gibbs, an English soldier, and Alison Smith, an English Land Girl. They meet by chance at night in the village of Chillingbourne, a few miles from their destination, and are immediately pitched into a strange plot involving the mysterious 'Glueman', a figure who assaults young women by pouring glue on their hair. The slight narrative of solving the mystery is counterpointed by scenes of village life that celebrate rural crafts, architecture, archaeology, landscape and custom, as the local magistrate (and, as it turns out, the Glueman himself) Thomas Colpeper guides the young pilgrims to a true sense of English values. He eventually helps complete their pilgrimage to Canterbury where in Powell's words, they 'receive their blessings' (Powell 1986: 448).

Formally, *A Canterbury Tale* is one of Powell and Pressburger's simpler films. It limits the epic narrative and the complex editing of its precursor, *The Life and Death of Colonel Blimp*, replacing that film's playful cultural contrast of Hollywood production values and conservative English social values with an austere black-and-white cinematography and detailed evocations of Powell's native Kent. The propagandist purpose is also much more evident than in *Blimp* as the young American soldier is shown learning the realities of England and finding previously unacknowledged cultural continuities between the Allies. The *Press Book* for *A Canterbury Tale*, which suggested strategies for local cinemas to market the film, was emphatic about its message of transatlantic entente. 'Run a 'Get-Together-As-You-Please' Party on Stage Each Night with U. S. and British soldiers', it suggested, ' and don't forget the Ladies!' (*Press Book: A Canterbury Tale*: 12). This is a curious recommendation for a film in which the main protagonist attacks women with the avowed intention of preventing them from abandoning their local partners for exotic wartime lovers. However, it suggests the way in which *A Canterbury Tale* functioned adequately within the Ministry of Information remit to encourage transatlantic understanding whilst presenting an Englishness that is always complex and at times plain odd.

In his autobiography Powell describes himself as 'English to the core, English as a Cox's Orange Pippin' and recalls the making of *A Canterbury Tale* in terms that would not have been out of place in a book by Mais (Powell 1986: 232). 'I was looking forward to the great swags of the laden hop-vines', he writes, 'to the dusty lanes with the dogrose in the hedges, to the sharp Kentish voices'. But, as he goes on to suggest, the film that he made there 'looked on the surface conventional, but . . . was filled with subversive material' (438). The English topographical conventions are clear enough, from the frolicsome Chaucerian pilgrims of the opening sequence through the old rural traditions preserved in Chillingbourne to the unifying forces of church and history displayed in Canterbury Cathedral in the final sequence. However, these are set against other aspects of Englishness which led one critic to call it 'the kinkiest film of the war' (Wright 1974: 197). Just as Edward Thomas complicated his traditional England with images of social distress and intractable lanes, so Powell and Pressburger's film challenges its own propagandist discourse through a witty, self-conscious cinematic style and a disturbing sexual narrative.

The film begins with an image of historical continuity, as a falcon released by one of the Chaucerian pilgrims is transformed into a Spitfire watched by the same actor now in a contemporary military uniform. However, the first scenes of the narrative proper disturb this sense of English heritage. The stranding of the three modern pilgrims in Chillingbourne is shot in a style that recalls a contemporary Hollywood thriller. Erwin Hillier's expressionist cinematography, the American accent of the actor John Sweet and the immediate threat of sexual attack displace the stereotyped England of the prologue. Although Charles Hawtrey's eccentric stationmaster attempts to offer some comic reassurance when he describes Chillingbourne as 'the kind of place where people sleep at night', he couldn't be more wrong. Even as the film begins, its magistrate and English nationalist ideologue is on the prowl with a gluepot, looking for women.

This tension of genre and tone is maintained throughout the film even though its main emphasis turns to the evocation of rural Chillingbourne. Hollywood conventions of narrative and editing are abandoned just as Bob, Alison and Peter abandon their railway timetables and enter an old world of horses and walking. Bob finds common ground with the wheelwright who articulates the film's pastoral philosophy in his saying 'you can't hurry an elm', and Alison finds herself hearing the music and voices of Chaucer's pilgrims as she lies by the old road of medieval pilgrimage. At this juncture the film treats directly with the literature of English journeys discussed earlier. Emeric Pressburger, its scholarly scriptwriter, adjusts the Southwark origin of the Canterbury pilgrims to emphasise that other medieval pilgrimage route from Winchester, the journey that Hilaire Belloc had made in *The Old Road*. London, the stated destination of the American soldier, is never reached and is deliberately absent from the film, except in fading memories of Alison's pre-war job as a salesgirl and Peter's as a cinema organist. Belloc's redemptive journey is relevant to the film in several ways. Chilham, the equivalent of Chillingbourne in Belloc's book, is a place of uncertainty and transition where the old road disappears and where Canterbury first becomes visible to the pilgrim (Belloc 1910: 270–3). It is an ambivalence that is maintained in the film, for although Chillingbourne represents English tradition, it is not an idyllic place. The threats and disturbances of the film's beginning are never far away.

In one of Powell and Pressburger's self-referential jokes, the magistrate Colpeper warns the avid cinema-goer Bob against the corrupting modernity of film, recommending his own educational lectures on archaeology instead. *A Canterbury Tale* redeems itself from its protagonist's strictures by celebrating those same English cultural continuities and showing them being revealed rather than destroyed by the hazards of war and film, with two Londoners and an American receiving the blessings of its traditions. In their other wartime works, conflicts of national and cultural identity tended to be worked out through the constructive tension between an older Englishman – played by Roger Livesey in *The Life and Death of Colonel Blimp, I Know Where I'm Going!* (in which he is a very English Scot) and *A Matter of Life and Death* – and a younger female lead. Their difficult but mutually enriching dialogues of English past and English present establish the political trajectory through which a postwar national identity could be envisioned as a flexible negotiation between the two. In *A Canterbury Tale*, however, the dialogue is a particularly strange one and is determined not by the male protagonist but by his *alter-ego*, the Glueman.

Colpeper, like Livesey's characters in the other films, is prone to lecture formally and informally on the nature of England, and Alison, like the other women, is young and liberated from the confines of job and role by the circumstances of war. But whilst the magistrate shares the others' sense of tradition, his oddness is not redeemable in the ways that the eccentricities of Livesey's roles allowed – significantly, perhaps, he turned down the part (Howard 1996: 47). If Colpeper can be seen as local law-giver and national healer, borrowing his name from the celebrated sixteenth-century herbalist, he is also, in the words of a contemporary reviewer, 'plainly a crackpot of a rather unpleasant type, with bees in the bonnet and blue-bottles in the belfry' (LeJeune 1947: 121). His peculiar sexual aggression is part of this. Although Pressburger had reportedly toned down an earlier version of the script in which Colpeper slit women's skirts with a knife, the glue in the hair adds a perversely intimate stickiness to the actions of an otherwise notably untactile and ascetic intellectual who lives with his mother and mows his meadow with a scythe (MacDonald 1994: 236).

The audience of the film is set the problem of squaring Colpeper's nationalist theories with his other life as a messy sexual predator apparently impelled in his aggression by anxieties about English miscegenation. Eric Portman, an actor who had played the Nazi anti-hero in the first of Powell and Pressburger's wartime sequence, has none of the avuncular charm of Livesey, and while Colpeper's doctrine of sexual exclusivity is affirmed in the blessings granted to Alison and Bob in Canterbury as their lost lovers are returned to them, its troubling expression in quirky assault remains at issue throughout the film. Against his rigid sexual codes, other characters articulate an alternative assessment of the times. Another victim of the Glueman ponders the risks of going out in the English darkness and concludes with sexual pragmatism that 'a girl must live' and it is worth the risk. Alison herself provides an obliquely sexual narrative in her meditations on the old road and, in a reference that it is hard to think accidental in the work of a writer like Pressburger, bears the name of the most sexually astute of Chaucer's Canterbury pilgrims, The Wife of Bath. An audience is hard pressed, therefore, to accept Colpeper as an unproblematic spokesman of English values and must make difficult judgements about the national identity that he projects.

A Canterbury Tale brought to the cinema many of the preoccupations of the English literary journeys that were recorded in the first half of the century, but it also marks their limits as means of postwar English self-representation. Colpeper, in the end, is a limited spokesman of the nationalism he so passionately affirms, a limitation that is both gendered and cultural. His explicit distaste for women and for cinema is part of this, particularly for Powell who found it impossible to dislike either. When Alison gazes at a village house and describes it as 'a perfect place . . . what wouldn't I give to grow old in a place like that', she is shocked to find Colpeper there, sharpening his scythe. The moment is eerie. Though it initiates her sense that she has misjudged the moral and political seriousness of the magistrate, it also establishes the fault-lines in Colpeper's beliefs. His obsessive celibacy and his aversion to modernity are flaws that cannot be redeemed by pilgrimage. Whilst he might be an earnest articulator of English tradition and values in wartime, the future of England lies elsewhere – notably in the reckless marriages depicted in Powell and Pressburger's next two films in which a head-strong Englishwoman abandons her wealthy fiancé for a laird, and a fighter pilot is brought back from death to marry an American. The traditional, rural Englishness of *A Canterbury Tale* is finally in tension with what Powell always considered to be the necessary cosmopolitanism of film. And its writer, who said of the film 'this is the only one of them that is entirely mine', was a Hungarian émigré (MacDonald 1994: 234).

Postwar Journeys

The act of travelling in England during the first half of the twentieth century provided a means of describing the nation to itself in a popular literary genre that emphasised haphazard revelation and an identity defined through rural, southern landscapes and communities. This peripatetic genre also generated critiques of its own as the contradictions of an English modernity defined by such assertions of rural tradition and social continuity become evident. Edward Thomas's description of isolation within a nation that is indefinable, C. E. Montague's reversal of the itineraries and preconceptions of English journeying, H. J. Massingham's attempt to consolidate rural Englishness in a context of urban change, and the perversity of England's theorist in Powell and Pressburger's *A Canterbury Tale* all contributed to this.

Whilst the Second World War, like the Great War before it, encouraged a temporary intensification of the nostalgic English travelogue in works like Harry Batsford's *How to See the Country* (1940), M. D. Anderson's *Design for a Journey* (1940), S. P. B. Mais's *'There'll Always Be an England'* (1940), H. V. Morton's *I Saw Two Englands* (1942), Edward Seago's *Peace and War* (1943) and W. J. Turner's *The Englishman's Country* (1945), it also marked its effective end. People still travelled the nation after the war and wrote books about their journeys, but the density of the genre, its capacity to assert the eternal verities of Englishness as well as to mark the contradictions in such assertions, had weakened. Mais, the man who had experienced that moment of national revelation on the South Downs in 1922, continued his career as a popular topographer after the Second World War, but his *Round Britain Coach Tour* (1964) promised few opportunities for such national revelation as the routines of mass travel replaced the haphazard wanderings of an earlier period.

English travel at the end of the century was largely abandoned to the foreigner, the artist and the photographer, the rural circuits of Mais and Morton replaced by expeditions into national otherness that evoked more the strategies of George Orwell's road to Wigan. The 1980s and 1990s saw the development of a masochistic popular taste for ironic travelogues of declining England by urbane Americans such as Paul Theroux's *The Kingdom by the Sea* (1983) and Bill Bryson's *Notes from a Small Island* (1995), a strategy taken up with rather less urbanity in the Scot A. A. Gill's *The Angry Island* (2005) a decade later. The photographers Ian Berry, Don McCullin and Chris Killip also presented bleak revisions of the English journey genre in their respective collections *The English* (1978), *Homecoming* (1979) and *In Flagrante* (1988). They display a fragmented, embattled Englishness trapped in decaying nineteenth-century modernity of mill-towns, seaside resorts and inner cities, using an iconography barely changed from the 1930s social documentary of Bert Hardy and Bill Brandt in *Picture Post*. Even the English landscape photographs resisted interpretations of national continuity and moral resource that the early twentieth-century wanderers had made. McCullin, the celebrated photographer of wars in Vietnam and the Congo, saw continuities only with those conflicts. 'I do tend to turn my landscapes into battlegrounds', he remarked of his English pictures. 'They almost come out looking like the First World War image of the Somme and Flanders' (McCullin 1987: 8).

Peripatetic Englishness, if it now exists at all, has retreated to the work of performance artists like Richard Long, whose articulations of the English South West have much in common with the popular genre discussed in this chapter. However, what one critic has called his 'understanding of the rhythms of nature, the power of movement and time and [a] love of walking, cycling and camping' make no claims to national meaning (Seymour 1991: 32). In Long's obsessive circling of territory, it is as if the walks of Edward Thomas and H. J. Massingham and the rides of C. E. Montague have survived in form alone, with their cultural politics abandoned to an earlier England.

Chapter 5

The North

The journeys in search of England described in the previous chapter were performances of both national identification and national exclusion. Travelling provided a means of establishing a cultural and political sense of the territory of Englishness but this was achieved through the consolidation of only a particular part of that territory as possessing essential national values. The consensus that real England lay somewhere on the Downs near Plumpton or in any number of other such places on the southern and westward trajectory from London merely reinforced the power of an already-existing economic and cultural hegemony. In this sense the often-repeated opposition of London and real England was a false one, for these journeys proved the reciprocity of the capital and its surrounding countryside. One of S. P. B. Mais's travel books is called *It Isn't Far from London* (1930) and the title tells a cultural as well as a geographical truth. The interrelation of the cultural industries of the metropolis and the southern rural signifiers of Englishness is confirmed in the discourse of many of the writers discussed in the previous chapter, who moved easily between the oppositions of metropolis and pastoral sanctuaries of nationhood. It is a dynamic that might go some way to explaining why H. J. Massingham and Roger Scruton made their covenants with the land in Oxfordshire and Wiltshire rather than, say, on a hill-farm in north Derbyshire.

'All English regionalism', Tom Nairn argues, 'has to face the dilemma of one overwhelming region, the "Great Wen" of tradition now swollen to irreversible centrality as a multicultural city-state eclipsing all others' (Nairn 2002: 111). It is a dilemma that is experienced and expressed most overtly in that vaguely defined area known as the English North. Northernness is, of course, as much an imagined identity as an Englishness constructed from the metropolitan and rural resources of the South, and one exploited and parodied as much by Northerners as by others. Nevertheless, the fragmented and under-researched histories of Northernness suggest some of the ways that modern English identity has both needed and controlled a domestic cultural 'other'. The dissenting narratives and performances that have emerged from the distinctive political and cultural histories of the North also offer a parallel identity to that of a dominant south-eastern Englishness. They provide not only critical perspectives upon the formation of a nationhood founded and funded in the 'overwhelming region', but also alternative trajectories for thinking about English modernity itself.

The popular literature of travel discussed in the previous chapter tended to erase the North or transform it into acceptable forms. A. F. Tschiffely's rapid detour around Warrington is an example of the former; H. V. Morton's restoration of Wigan as an English country town an example of the latter. The southern cultural hegemony also operated in other ways. At times the territories north of the Trent are rendered a binary opposite to the achieved identity of real England, both a necessarily abject resource and a dire warning of the consequences of modernity. As early as 1893 Robert Blatchford had spelled out the hierarchies and perils of national progress by reference to the social geography of the great English territorial divide. 'As a practical man', he asks an Oldham weaver in his influential collection of socialist essays, *Merrie England* (1893), 'would you of your own choice convert a healthy and beautiful country like Surrey into an unhealthy and hideous country like Wigan or Cradley, just for the sake of being able once a year to go to Blackpool, and once a night to listen to a cracked piano? (Blatchford 1976: 8). Even for a socialist like Blatchford, Surrey, or at least an aesthetic ideal of the 'Home Counties', was representative of the 'Merrie England' that needed to be defended and extended. Wigan and Cradley (in the West Midlands), on the other hand, formed an awful warning of what capitalism, industrialism and its concomitant materialism of cracked pianos could lead to if left unchecked.

This chapter will examine the ways in which the North has been constructed as an English other and the ways in which it constructed itself as a distinctive expression of English modernity. The first section will consider two more journeys, those of George Orwell from London to Wigan and of Tom Harrisson from London to Bolton. Orwell's account of his time in Wigan and the North, *The Road to Wigan Pier* (1937), became a definitively misleading picture of the region, displaying a repertoire of imagery and judgements that remained influential throughout the century. Harrisson's work in Bolton with his anthropological project Mass-Observation produced a much more nuanced interpretation of the town, though it maintained Orwell's – and Blatchford's – sense of the North as being the 'other' place in the national psyche, an

English unconscious to be carefully observed and analysed, but not lived in. Orwell's and Harrisson's journeys are offset by those of two other visitors to Lancashire in the 1930s who found very different cultural and political meanings in the region. Mohandâs Gandhi's visit to Darwen in 1931 and C. L. R. James's residence in Nelson in 1932 revealed the distinctive radical and progressive traditions of the area that both influenced and hosted the contrasting anti-colonial initiatives of the Indian nationalist and the Trinidadian pan-Africanist.

Another kind of modernity is apparent in the place that Robert Blatchford dismissed as capitalism's sop to those that laboured and lived in places like Wigan. Blackpool provided what Bill Schwarz has called a 'provincial modernist experience' and one that was unique in Europe (Schwarz 1987: 152). Yet it was a modernity that was wrought from cultures, traditions and labour patterns that were specifically regional and that expressed a distinctive amalgam of premodern custom and industrial disciplines. Blackpool's transformation of local culture into national meaning was also evident in the work of two popular Lancashire comedians of the 1930s and 1940s. Gracie Fields became Britain's highest-paid performer of the 1930s, developing a distinctively northern stage and film persona into a stardom that offered one of the few distinctively English challenges to the dominant American musical and cinematic culture of the period. Her contemporary, Frank Randle, shaped a northern performance that was in often militant contrast to the codes of metropolitan popular theatre with which Fields negotiated. Nevertheless, his exploitation of the independent local economies, technologies and performance styles of his native Lancashire pointed to the potential for an alternative English modernity beyond the economic and cultural control of the 'Great Wen'.

Northern Journeys

George Orwell's *The Road to Wigan Pier* and the anthropological reports of Mass-Observation from Bolton, or 'Worktown' as it was termed, provide complementary contributions to a specialised genre of English topographical writing. Both represent the North as an unknown England, though one very different from that conceived by Morton and the rest. For Orwell, Wigan is a place of previously unwitnessed social abjection; for Mass-Observation Bolton is a place of strange rituals and customs more usually associated with the colonial 'other' of classical anthropology. Both towns, however, are used to affirm a national-cultural norm that belongs to the metropolis rather than the working-class North.

The first part of *The Road to Wigan Pier* deploys the techniques that Orwell was to use in his essays on national identity a few years later, with vivid images detached from social contexts replacing argued political points. Reporting back from what, in his most Conradian vein, he calls 'the filthy heart of civilization', Orwell presents the North as a defamiliarised England – a kind of primitive colony within the borders of the mother country (Orwell 1962: 18). The tripe shop-cum-boarding house where he lodges, the image of a woman poking a stick up a drain-pipe in a slum backyard and the evocation of '*lower-class* sweat' combine to form an inversion of Mais's Plumpton vision (125). Instead of revealing essential Englishness, Orwell displays English modernity. The people that live in the slums of Wigan, Sheffield and other northern industrial centres are 'characteristic by-products of the modern world'. 'It is a kind of duty to see and smell such places now and again', he tells his readers, 'especially smell them, lest you should forget that they exist; though perhaps it is better not to stay there too long' (16).

Orwell took his own advice, making a rapid tour of Wigan, Barnsley, Sheffield and Leeds during February and March 1936 and never returning. *The Road to Wigan Pier*, although published by Victor Gollancz's Left Book Club imprint, is notable for its omission of any acknowledgement of what Raymond Williams calls the 'actual social and political network' that allowed him access to the places of work and unemployment that he describes so vividly (Williams 1971: 51). His silence about the socialist groups and trade unions that helped him was indicative of Orwell's always cautious dealings with political organisations, but it seems also to have been determined by the primitivist anthropology that shaped his approach. 'When you go to the industrial North you are conscious . . . of entering a strange country', he writes, and the evocation of that strangeness was a stronger motive than any recognition of that same North's active participation in local and international political change (Orwell 1962: 98). If, as Richard Hoggart suggests, 'the North of England was stranger to Orwell than Burma', Orwell was also intent on maintaining and exaggerating that strangeness (Hoggart 1974: 40).

The contemporary reports of Mass-Observation, which were based on observations in Bolton, a few miles north-east of Wigan, provide a different, but no less idiosyncratic account of Northernness. Founded in 1937 by the amateur anthropologist Tom Harrisson and the poet Charles Madge, Mass-Observation began as a loose-knit organisation that set out to study 'the beliefs and behaviour of the British Islanders . . . to get written down the unwritten laws and to make the invisible forces visible' (Madge and Harrisson 1938: 8). Their methods involved both the detailed study by full-time 'observers' of a representative English town and the recruitment of volunteer diarists and observers from around the country who were willing to record the minutiae of English experience. The research had a broadly political purpose. Harrisson, anticipating Tom Nairn in some ways, saw England as an incompletely modernised state. A distant elite in an outmoded Parliament and a commercial popular press, he argued, neither recognised nor represented the popular opinions and feelings of the nation. Mass-Observation set out to initiate a new national discourse. Its reports, rapidly disseminated via the new budget publishing venture of Penguin paperbacks, would challenge 'the ignorance of one section of society about how other sections live and what they say and think' (Mass-Observation 1986: 142).

This project of rationalising national communication systems was complicated by the idiosyncracies of the organisation, however. Harrisson and Madge were particularly interested in the ways in which Englishness was lived beyond the principles that their organisation sought to propagate. The popular response to the abdication of Edward VIII in 1936 and reactions to the crisis with Germany in 1938 led them to develop comparisons between England and the 'primitive' cultures that had been the subject of *Savage Civilisation* (1937), Harrisson's study of New Hebridean tribal society. In moments of unprecedented national trauma, they argued, residual, premodern forms of behaviour and understanding challenged the apparent securities of the secular state. The section on the Munich crisis in *Britain* (1939), for example, evokes the 'personality-magic of Hitler and Chamberlain, the blood-thirsty bogey and the Old Man Who Goes Up in the Sky' (Mass-Observation 1986: 57). In England ' "when things get too bad" ', they conclude, 'there are many who turn to magic' (22).

What remains so appealing about Mass-Observation, and where its work differs markedly from Orwell's, is its willing acceptance of the magical, the odd, the random and the trivial as constitutive of English identity. It encouraged a self-consciously eccentric range of popular anthropological study that quite went against its stated national purpose: 'Behaviour of people at war memorials, Shouts and gestures of motorists, The aspidistra cult, Anthropology of football pools, Bathroom behaviour, Beards, armpits, eyebrows' (Calder and Sheridan 1984: 4). Such a list both advertised and parodied the organisation's sense of the endless expressiveness of modern popular culture. Whilst Orwell used lists and details to create a calculated effect of 'common sense', Mass-Observation flaunted modernist disjunctions of discourse and narrative. It set out to celebrate a nationhood of social diversity, setting itself against 'the invention of unanimous feelings for a "country", which in fact can only have such apparent unity in Fascism' (Mass-Observation 1986: 235).

Despite this engaging liberality, though, Mass-Observation was not free of the limiting ideologies of the Englishness that it sought to expand. This was particularly evident in its use of Bolton as an anthropological site for the investigation of Englishness. In many ways its selection maintained Orwell's sense of the North as an English 'other', an unknown region within to be explored, recorded and analysed rather than as an integral part of the nation. Harrisson made explicit comparisons of Bolton and the New Hebrides, claiming in a letter that his research was 'proving as exciting and extraordinary, as unhealthy and uncomfortable, as any in Malekula' (Heimann 1997: 126). 'The investigators 'penetrated every part of local life', he asserts in his introduction to the study of Bolton leisure, *The Pub and the People* (1943), unselfconsciously using a characteristic metaphor of colonial exploration (Mass-Observation 1987: xiv). Basil D. Nicholson was even more explicit in his introductory note to the first edition. 'It represents . . . the diary of some travellers on perhaps the last excursion-trip made intelligently to a Lost World', he comments (Mass-Observation 1987: xii). 'Worktown' thus became a strange and exotic place of wonders which, like Orwell's Wigan, is denied the political and historical contexts of its making. It acts as kind of colonial outpost from which information useful to the centre of power could be sent downriver.

Postcolonial North

Embedded in the images of the English North that Orwell and Mass-Observation provided in the 1930s was a thwarted political and cultural geography. What they represented as otherness was, as Patrick Joyce points out, the '*locus classicus* of a new urban industrial civilization' (Joyce 1991: 19). Northern cities like Manchester and Leeds and towns like Bolton and Wigan were not primitive settlements beyond the imaginary frontier of the Trent, but what modern Englishness actually was. The real 'other' of modernity, in fact, was made up of the feudal survivals experienced with such irrational awe by Mais at Plumpton and Enoch Powell at the Old Berkeley East meet. A cultural process that 'entrenched premodern elements within the new society, and gave legitimacy to anti-modern sentiments', as Martin J. Wiener puts it, also disguised an actually existing modernity (Wiener 1981: 7). Two anti-imperialists and two comedians of the 1930s also recognised this and provide the means for exploring the hidden modernity of the English North.

Mohandâs Gandhi came to England in September 1931 as Congress Party representative at the London Round Table Conference on Indian constitutional reform. He spent a week of his visit in the cotton districts of Lancashire and in West Yorkshire explaining the meaning of his anti-colonialist strategy of *khaddar* to those who were likely to be most affected by it. *Khaddar* was his campaign to resist the importation of non-Indian goods, particularly the cotton that Gandhi argued should be produced in the impoverished Indian villages which were his main political focus. He used his meetings with industrialists, cottonworkers and the unemployed to initiate a debate about the relationship between local industries, imperialism and global economics. The encounters produced extraordinary expositions of emergent postcolonial politics away from government negotiations and within the English industrial communities that were also shaped by imperial policy that controlled those markets.

'Pray tell me', he asked at a meeting with unemployed cottonworkers, 'what I am to do with a fifth of the human race living on the verge of starvation and devoid of all sense of self-respect. It should occupy the attention even of unemployed Lancashire' (Rajagopalachar and Kumarappa 1932: 284). Gandhi's insistence upon placing the issues of English class struggles within a colonial context produced a sharp analysis of relative economic positions. 'This . . . is a fortune', he remarked of the 17 shilling dole, 'and for you, a resourceful race, it should not be difficult to hit upon other industries and occupations. For my starving crores, I have no other occupation' (287). It is hard to imagine this discussion of the relationship between the enmeshed economies and class and national identities within imperialism taking place elsewhere in England, particularly given the response that Gandhi received to his uncompromising arguments. 'The warmth of reception could only be equalled by what Gandhiji has been familiar with in the towns and villages of India', reported his secretary, Mahadev Desai, a judgement supported by a photograph of Gandhi amongst cheering cottonworkers which was carried by the *Northern Daily Telegraph* (279).

A year after Gandhi's visit another colonial journey was made which again suggested the particular significance of northern culture and politics for developing anti-colonial struggles. The Trinidadian Learie Constantine had played professional cricket in Nelson since 1929 and invited C. L. R. James to join him in Lancashire. Constantine's presence was itself ambivalent testimony to English racial and imperial politics. Despite being the finest all-rounder of his generation and a West Indian Test player, no first-class county team would employ a black Caribbean player. Instead, Constantine became a professional player for the Lancashire League side. James always represented their journeys north as political journeys. In his final article for the *Port of Spain Gazette* in August 1932, he contrasted his disappointment in the intellectual life of the imperial capital with an account of an industrial dispute in Nelson during which the cottonworkers boycotted the town's cinemas in support of striking projectionists who had been threatened with a wage cut. The 'nucleus of a great civilisation', as the article is called, is relocated from the cultural failures of London to this instance of local radicalism and cultural solidarity. 'I could forgive England all the vulgarity and all the depressing disappointment of London for the magnificent spirit of these north country working people', he concludes (James 2003: 124).

James's stay in Lancashire established the trajectory for his intellectual and political career. His anti-colonial polemic *The Case for West Indian Self-Government* (1933) was first published by a Nelson firm in 1932, the history of the San Domingo revolution, *Black Jacobins* (1938), was begun there and his commitment to an understanding of popular culture – especially cricket – as a complex expression of class struggle and change was established in the town. Like Constantine himself, James came to read the pragmatic disciplines of Northern League cricket as a paradigm for broader changes in the imperial game and the social systems that it embodied. At the same time, like Gandhi in his briefer visit, James and Constantine were in dialogue with northern political traditions and they established their own political identities through social and cultural organisations that worked at a remove from the 'nucleus' of empire. 'We were educating thousands, including ourselves', James remarked with characteristic inclusiveness (James 1963: 121).

In their northern journeys James and Gandhi emphasised political networks and interests that the more celebrated visits of Orwell and Mass-Observation effectively suppressed. The particular congruence of north-western cultural and political traditions and emergent postcolonial ideas depended upon a shared divergence from metropolitan models of nationhood. The distinctive local radical traditions that James and Gandhi encountered there had been shaped through the legacies of nineteenth-century liberalism and the particular modernities of northern industrial development. Their dissenting models of political activity and discourse offered common ground with the emergent postcolonialism of the pre-Second World War period, just as it had with European nationalist movements of the previous century. It was a meeting formally expressed at the Fifth Pan-African Congress held in Chorlton Town Hall, Manchester in October 1945. This gathering of anti-colonial activists, Pan-Africanists and black radicals, which included Kwame

Nkrumah, Hastings Banda, Jomo Kenyatta, George Padmore, W. E. B. Du Bois and Amy Ashwood Garvey, anticipated the intensification of the postcolonial and civil rights struggles in Africa and beyond in the decade that followed. Welcoming the Lord Mayor of Manchester as representative of 'the most liberal city in England', the conference also confirmed Gandhi's and James's sense of the relevance of the North West's particular political traditions to the emergent politics of postcolonialism (Padmore 1963: 29).

Northern Modernities

The complementary relationship of local northern cultural traditions and emergent national and international movements was also notable in the very different context of English popular culture. Gracie Fields and Frank Randle, two Lancashire comedians of the mid-twentieth century, suggest contrasting versions of the dissenting modernity of expression that northern culture set against dominant forms of Englishness. Fields' performance style and persona, characterised by gauche, sexless energy, sentimentality and broad northern pastiche, has not worn well, but in the 1930s she was the only English star who could consistently compete with Hollywood at English box offices whilst pursuing a highly successful and lucrative stage career. She was perhaps the shrewdest negotiator of the changes taking place in English mass entertainment in the interwar period brought about by talking pictures, the increasing dominance of American song and dance forms, and the gradual decline of music hall and variety theatre. It was a negotiation pursued through her Northernness rather than despite it, and it set a pattern for other later northern performers.

On playing the London Palladium for the first time in 1928, Gracie Fields reportedly began her act by saying, 'Eee, by gum. It's all too grand for me!' a comment that confirmed her persona as a Rochdale mill girl who, by embarrassing accident, found herself on the pre-eminent London variety stage (Pilton 1976: 25). At the Holborn Empire in 1933 she was asking her audience to 'imagine we're in our front room and we're having a bit of a "do". We've had a nice tea – some boiled ham and lettuce, and a tin of salmon, and we're all right now' (Moules 1983: 65). Such self-presentation as an ordinary northern working-class woman was integral to her popularity but it was also part of a complex staging of class and region. By 1931 Fields was the highest-paid performer of her time, developing a career of unprecedented mobility that exploited new developments in the technology, performance venues and marketing of mass entertainment. Her performative power, though, depended upon a denial of that mobility and upon her assertion, on stage and off, of the continuity of her fame with her humble origins. Paradoxically, she became England's greatest modern star by appearing to stay provincial and ordinary.

Fields' representation of what might be called a nationalisable Northernness was at the centre of her success and it was a construction of identity that was demonstrated in her well-publicised and carefully organised returns to her hometown of Rochdale. The visits celebrated her stardom through concerts, receptions and charity functions, but they were also intended to demonstrate her social intimacy with the town. Rather than stay in a hotel, for example, she lodged above an off-licence. Her visit was both real – the off-licence was owned by her mother's friend Bertha Schofield – and performed – she had her photograph taken there for the national press to show that she was home. Her stardom was demonstrated in the context of her ordinariness, a process described in a local newspaper report of her performance at the Rochdale Hippodrome. 'Over her dress she wore a lovely cloak of silver brocade against which the effect of her Titian hair was extremely beautiful', it notes. 'The cloak, by the way, was soon discarded when she "got going" and her hair looked lovelier still when she had rumpled it by running her fingers through it once or twice in a characteristic gesture' (*Rochdale Observer* 5 December 1934: 4). The signs of glamour and stardom – silver brocade, Titian hair – are appreciated by the local reviewer, but so is the way in which they are subsequently discarded as our Gracie forgets – or rather remembers – herself in a performance for her own northern community.

Fields, then, reversed the process of 'othering' evident in Orwell's and Harrisson's northern journeys and created an identity through a calculated negotiation between both regional and national identities. It was a process that defined all aspects of her professional career. A lunch hosted by her record company EMI at the Trocadero cabaret to mark the release of her four millionth record in 1933, for example, was transformed into a 'Lancashire do'. Waitresses dressed in clogs and shawls served fish and chips, hot pot, beer and tea to an audience that included industry executives, her parents, the Mayor of Rochdale and her first clog-maker. But it was a performance of Northernness that was set beside the markers of her success within the contemporary entertainment industry – tables with 'a large facsimile of [her] four millionth record for covering' and souvenir place-mats also in the shape of records (*The Stage* 16 February 1933: 4). Such oscillations between ordinariness and stardom, working-class prudence and metropolitan extravagance, and

London and Rochdale temporarily suspended the cultural divisions that they implied. It also allowed Fields to establish a distinctively English stardom that diverged significantly from the dominant American model.

Hollywood, Richard Dyer notes, insisted on distancing its stars from the industrial processes of cinema. To be a star it was necessary to be perceived as beyond the demands of daily work (Dyer 1979: 44). Fields, though, always talked about her films as products of her labour and drew analogies with her youthful employment in the Rochdale mills. She told *Film Pictorial* in 1934, 'I ought to feel at home, by rights, because here I am back in the mill again – right where I started. I have to get up at six o'clock, only instead of knocking off at 5.00, as I did in Rochdale, I work till 8; and instead of cotton fluff, it's incandescent carbons and dust and grease-paint'. Even her considerable wealth was presented in terms of wage-labour rather than capital – 'instead of a shilling a week it's two pounds a minute – or so they tell me', she commented (Breen 1934: 8). Yet Fields' presentation of film as northern mill labour disguised an astute and thoroughgoing engagement with what American popular culture meant in 1930s England.

The self-composed 'Lancashire Blues' (1930) is a characteristic expression of Fields' celebration of the northern local against all that America represented. 'I've tasted their waffles and corn on the cob', she sang, 'but give me a hot pot straight off the hob'. However, despite its relish of provincial cuisine the song was an example of the way Fields integrated American popular culture rather than opposed it within her performance. Her success was based on the oppositions that the title of 'Lancashire Blues' suggests, an ability to initiate and maintain a cultural dialogue with American mass culture without forgoing her Englishness and whilst projecting her Northernness. Her act was a sophisticated statement of cultural competence and one that allowed a range of responses to the shifting identities that were on display. This strategy could never be openly acknowledged, only performed; her skills were necessarily contained within and silenced by a persona of guileless Lancashire plain-speaking. When the success of her film *Sing as We Go* (1934) started rumours of a move to Hollywood, a sceptical editorial in the *Era* noted a 'local appeal which she has nationalised'. 'No one outside this country would quite understand that', it concluded (*The Era* 12 August 1936: 1). It was an argument that persisted even when Fields finally did go to America in 1937. The response of English film magazines to the publicity-shots of her in an evening gown reflected the distinctive regional-national stardom that she had developed. 'To British filmgoers', *Film Weekly* commented, 'Gracie Fields is the spirit of homeliness, the girl who was just born for clogs and shawl and untidy hair.

Hollywood, which doesn't properly know her yet, seems to have other ideas . . . Gracie has gone right through the grooming mill and come out the other side like this. Eee! She looks like a film star' (*Film Weekly*, 24 April 1937: 4).

Fields, then, offered the most complex and most successful English response to the challenge of American popular culture in the 1930s. Hers was a definedly northern modernity that exploited such a potentially limiting repertoire of representation to create instead a supple performance that integrated the genres and styles of transatlantic popular culture whilst still projecting an image of local, wholesome simplicity. Frank Randle, Fields' near-contemporary, represented a contrasting version of her national-regional politics. Instead of the good-natured, common-sensical 'essence of Lancastrian femininity', as J. B. Priestley described her, Randle veered between the belching, lecherous old man of his stage act and an ostentatiously successful Blackpool resident with his yacht and Bentley (Priestley 1968: 253). And whilst Fields articulated a national inclusiveness, moving easily from the Rochdale Hippodrome to the London Palladium, Randle stayed in Blackpool, playing northern theatres and appearing in a series of low-budget films produced in Manchester. However, although Randle aggressively celebrated the cultural oppositions that Fields succeeded in negotiating, like Fields he understood the distinctively modern resources that the history and politics of the North West provided and he exploited them in an extraordinary, if chaotic, career.

Randle was born the bastard son of a domestic servant in Wigan in 1901, origins that informed his popular theatre of deprivation and excess. Though he had moved from Wigan to the luxury of Blackpool by the time that George Orwell arrived there, Randle's stage act formed a virtual commentary on Orwell's influential report on the 'filthy heart of civilization'. This was not, however, a critique like that of Raymond Williams in the 1970s. Randle was quite content with filth and any other of the images of abasement in *The Road to Wigan Pier*; in fact his performance was a delighted display of them. It revelled in drunkenness, toothlessness, belching, dirty feet and resolute, if hopeless, randiness. From his early thirties, Randle was performing old men – bald, decrepit, squalid in body and mind, but resilient. If Orwell made it a duty to see and smell the Wigan slums, Randle made comedy from the bodies of their inhabitants and offered it to the working-class audiences that Orwell admitted he could not address. His was a cunning, abrasive act, uninterested in Fields' national resolution or in Orwell's politics of change. Instead, he performed a distinctively regional cultural resistance and territorial knowledge, emphasising his own grotesque body whilst at the same time showing how it contributed to the distinctive modernity of what he referred to as his 'own midden' of the North (Williams and Williams 2006: 110).

The only existing recording of Randle on a stage seems to be one made at the Feldman Theatre, Blackpool in 1938. Then aged 37, he performed his long-standing character sketch, 'The Old Hiker': 'eighty-two and as full of vim as a butcher's dog'. 'I'll take anybody on of me age and weight, dead or alive', he gurgles, 'and I'll run 'em, walk 'em, jump 'em, fight 'em . . . aye . . . and I'll play 'em dominoes'. It is at once an innocent and a scornful challenge to Orwell's presentation of northern working-class fatalism. The bathetic domino-playing only points up the omitted alliterative 'fuck 'em', an inevitable reference point in a monologue that lasciviously reports his unlikely encounter with a couple of 'hot 'uns' on his rambles. No other comedian explored so resolutely the condition of the ageing proletarian body that repelled Orwell, and no other comedian celebrated that body's capacity to resist its afflictions of labour, mortality and morality. The hiker, an emblem of the organised, healthy, aspirational working class of the 1930s, is made by Randle into an aged, drunken lecher, unnaturally proud of and still fascinated by his decrepit body (at one point he celebrates the discovery of hair still growing on his knee). A few years later Ewan MacColl's earnest socialist rambler was to declare himself 'a free man on Sunday', but Randle's hiker asserted unlimited comic freedom. It is a performance of solidarity and opposition beyond the political terms of either Orwell or Williams, but as precisely directed as Fields' recovery of the process of her filmmaking as factory labour. Randle's old men performed a redemptive display of resistance and celebration in the face of the physical depredations of industrial working conditions that are never mentioned but always implied. It was a politics that was vividly demonstrated by Randle's performative interest in teeth.

In *The Road to Wigan Pier* Orwell reported that 'various people gave me their opinion that it is best to "get shut of" your teeth as early in life as possible. "Teeth is just a misery", one woman said to me' (Orwell 1962: 87). Whatever the truth of the story that he had healthy teeth removed to enhance his act, Randle knew all about their cultural significance for his audiences. Whilst their absence contributed to the collapse of the body and the premature ageing that so disgusted Orwell (and which Randle performed with such relish), the miseries of pre-National Health Service dentistry were avoided. These miseries formed part of a scene in Randle's film *Somewhere in Camp* (1942) in which terrified recruits are bullied and brutalised by an army dentist. Like the woman in Orwell's anecdote, the toothless Randle believes himself immune from the torment, but he is nevertheless summoned to the chair. During the inevitable slapstick battle that ensues, the dentist exclaims delightedly, 'Just as I thought, deep, deep down embedded in the gum there's a stump of a tooth. It'll have to come out!' (the 'tooth' is later revealed to be a piece of dirt embedded in the gum and capped by a collar stud). This is visceral, rough comedy which displayed the intimate dreads and actual pain of northern working-class audiences in ways no other performer contemplated.

The comic debasement of toothlessness, however, was always balanced by Randle's recognition of the cultural value of a full set. At some point in both stage act and film he would appear with gleaming dentures extravagantly on display. At the end of *When You Come Home* (1947), for example, an amply betoothed Randle enters his wealthy patron's sitting-room, the teeth signifying his character's transformation from oppressed factotum to confident protagonist. The transition marked Randle's own insistence on his competence in both 'civilised' and 'uncivilised' performances. His appearance as the old hiker had to be set beside that of the wealthy performer who was paid £1000 a week to play the old hiker. But the teeth also stressed the mobility and artifice of social and cultural difference, their removal and insertion displaying an arbitrariness of respectability and class that Randle was always keen to affirm. He would occasionally – and in appropriate contexts – reverse the trick. Arthur Askey recalled him beginning a show in London's West End with teeth in and dress-suit on. An elegant woman came from the wings with a velvet cushion. Randle reached into his mouth, removed his dentures and carefully placed them on the cushion to the disgust of the metropolitan audience. It was a deliberate and aggressive act of social and cultural debasement and insult, and a reminder to his audience of the contingencies of the markers of English class and culture (*The Emperor of Lancashire* 1989).

Randle's midden was a limited one. It centred on Blackpool, his home and place of summer work, and extended east through the cities and mill towns of the North West's industrial belt into West Yorkshire. His performance was bound up with the distinctive economy and culture that those places created in the late nineteenth and early twentieth centuries. However, its modernity, even more than that of Gracie Fields, was subordinated to the distinctive regional identities of voice and culture to which Randle appealed. This was also the case with Blackpool. From relatively early in the century, Blackpool had come to be represented as a place of nostalgia, a representation of an older North. When J. B. Priestley went there in 1934, the period of Randle's rise to local fame, he immediately thought about the past. 'The Blackpool that sang about

Charlie Brown and the girls with their curly curls was the Mecca of a vulgar but alert and virile democracy', he mused. 'I am not so sure about the new Blackpool of the weary negroid ditties' (Priestley 1968: 268). Scripting Gracie Fields' *Sing As We Go* the same year, Priestley reasserted that 'old' Blackpool, making it the place where Gracie finds both work and pleasure, and where national social and economic strife is resolved through the actions of a newly benevolent capitalism. Such nostalgic celebration, however, disguised the town's real significance for a study of English representations of tradition and modernity. For Blackpool, like Randle and Fields, represented the transformation of the conflicts of northern traditional custom and industrial discipline into a distinctive kind of English mass culture.

In the last thirty years of the nineteenth century Blackpool developed into a new type of tourist resort. As John K. Walton has argued, it was a development dependent upon the prosperity of Lancashire cotton towns as they benefited from the deflation of the period and an export market, the imperial consequences of which Gandhi came to Lancashire to explain in the 1930s (Walton 1998: 53). Theirs was also an economy that contained an unusually large female labour force, a factor that increased the disposable income of families in times of prosperity, something significantly lacking in that other area of English regional and cultural independence, the North East. However, Blackpool's modernity was also dependent upon the way the industrial work and leisure of the North West had been shaped by accommodations of local premodern customs, particularly that of the Wakes Week within the disciplines of work. The Wakes were week-long festivals, originally associated with individual parish celebrations, fairs and festivals of the pre-industrial agricultural-religious calendar. Struggles to maintain the cultural practices of the northern wakes formed part of the popular politics of resistance and customary radicalism in the region during the nineteenth century. The successful retention of the extended festivals even within new industrial structures of time and labour allowed Blackpool to develop its innovative mass culture. 'August bank holiday was irrelevant in Lancashire', note John Walton and Robert Poole, 'the nation's first working-class holiday industry came to centre on the traditional wakes, with the variations in timing from town to town ensuring a season of adequate length' (Walton and Poole 1982: 114).

The maintenance of extended communal holidays within the new work patterns of the industrial North allowed Blackpool to develop the first independent economy of working-class leisure. Festivities moved away from their traditional local sites to the seaside with the development of railway links, but that movement was collective, not individualised. Whole towns came to Blackpool and the varying dates of the wakes weeks of different industrial towns maintained a steady flow of visitors and a steady income for the small businesses, hoteliers and boarding houses and for the shareholders of the main attractions. Wakes holidays allowed a more extended stay in Blackpool than the excursion which was the norm at other English seaside resorts. The wholesale transplantation of industrial communities also helped shape Blackpool as a regulated industry catering for an industrial population that was not being industrious. Mass-Observation characterised it as 'the most moral town in England' in the 1930s precisely because it maintained its communal disciplines of social life and work even when it was transplanted to the place of pleasure (Calder and Sheridan 1984: 62). This late nineteenth-century fusion of traditional custom and the work and leisure patterns of intensive factory systems brought about what Tony Bennett argues was a 'rearticulation of the discourse of modernity' in the unlikely environment of the Fylde coast (Bennett 1986: 154).

The expansion of Blackpool from a small seaside village in the 1860s to an industrial tourist resort catering for four million visitors by the First World War was unparalleled in Europe. Only Coney Island and Atlantic City surpassed it in scale and those American points of reference are significant. For it was Blackpool that was able to capitalise on the importation of the technological innovations, rides and novelties that were manufactured for the American resorts. Blackpool also asserted its national significance in modern design when in 1894 it erected its own version of the Eiffel Tower (the Blackpool Tower was at that time Britain's highest building). The Corporation introduced electricity to the town in 1879, an innovation that allowed electric trams as early as 1885 and in 1912 the vast Illuminations, an initiative to extend the summer season well into the autumn (Shaw 1990: 7). This entrepreneurial Blackpool, what John Walton calls 'a freehold town whose rulers were unwilling to interfere with private property rights under most circumstances', went against that current of national compromise and traditional representation that Martin Wiener identifies in the Englishness in this period (Walton 1998: 58). Its self-proclaimed 'Progressive Corporation' allowed capitalist development in a previously remote part of Lancashire that was consequently unconstrained by the conservative landed interests of other seaside resorts or by the nonconformist progressive civic politics of some of the larger manufacturing towns and cities to the east (Shaw 1990: 10). Blackpool was consequently able to produce England's most emphatic and extravagant expressions of modern leisure and consumption: the Tower with its ballroom and circus, the Pleasure Beach with its Coney Island rides, the Golden Mile and its Illuminations – and Frank Randle.

Randle, for all that later cultural historians have come to cast him as an anarchist, Lancashire shaman or working-class hero, was essentially a Blackpool entrepreneur. His career was intimately involved in a local economy which by strange English irony produced the most advanced model of capitalism in the country in the early part of the twentieth century. Blackpool's visitors sustained his summer pier shows and allowed him the independence to tour his self-promoted revue, Randle's Scandals, throughout the North, largely evading the metropolitan variety circuits that had consolidated much of the English popular entertainment industry since the 1890s. Randle also became a star of Mancunian Films, the only regional commercial film-makers England ever produced and a company in which he later became a leading shareholder. Like Randle's often ramshackle stage act, the films made by John E. Blakeley in a studio on Dickenson Road, Manchester were not obviously innovative (or even competent in many cases) but, again, they represented the possibility of a distinctive modern cultural form being produced outside metropolitan economic control. Blakeley once remarked of the Rank Organisation, 'how can anyone in London judge a film of mine when they don't know the first thing about the people for whom I cater?' (Williams and Williams 2001: 105). That confident sense of distinctive local cultures mirrored Randle's handling of the particular experiences of labour and community in his act, and together Blakeley and Randle spoke eloquently to that culture. Philip Martin Williams and David L. Williams have noted that in 1942 Randle's *Somewhere in Camp* was outgrossed in one northern cinema only by *Mrs Miniver*, and in the following year only *Holiday Inn* was more popular than his *Somewhere on Leave* (Williams and Williams 2006: 134–5).

The legacies of Gracie Fields and Frank Randle are as contrasting as their acts. Seven years after Frank Randle's death in 1957, the Beatles' manager Brian Epstein announced the relocation of his offices from Liverpool to London. 'The artists perform often in London and they make their records in London', he argued, 'so . . . I was forced into it' (Geller 2000: 81). It was a sign that the journey made by Gracie Fields was established as the main popular cultural trajectory for a new generation of performers. Whilst Fields' deceptively homely legacy of song and film might seem to have little in common with the unprecedented success of the Beatles, their early career followed precisely her path. A year later Epstein presented a list of the 'ultimates' in the Beatles' career so far that could have been given by Fields' manager in the 1930s: an EMI contract, the first appearances at the London Palladium and on the Royal Variety

Show and their first trip to America (Epstein 1965: 14). Like Fields, too, the Beatles developed a sophisticated cultural negotiation which placed a projected North West as a distinctive local identity at the core of their ordinary stardom whilst simultaneously appealing to a unified Englishness through the popular performance styles of America.

Frank Randle had no such legacy. Although Trevor Griffiths attempted to make him a transitional figure between traditional variety theatre and proto-punk political performance in his play *Comedians* (1978), Randle was always ill-suited to such cross-cultural renderings. Nevertheless, the grotesque body of his performances as the old hiker, the vulgar boatman and the anarchic private soldier did represent an alternative conception of Englishness, albeit one that was never finally fulfilled. He confidently negotiated between a tradition of performance rooted in local dialect, local custom and local audiences, and the economic and technological contexts of modernity that Blackpool represented. Whereas Fields went south, Randle stayed where he was and held to the possibility that alternative modernities of expression and commerce were sustainable outside a South East that increasingly held to itself the means of national self-expression through domestic popular theatre and popular film. Frank Randle and John Blakeley established the possibility of a northern performance in both media which were independent, self-sustaining and unobsequious.

The place of regions in general and the North in particular in constructions of Englishness, then, has been a difficult and contested one in twentieth-century popular culture. The North was represented as an England beyond Englishness in the topographies described in Chapter 4, in George Orwell's journey to Wigan and in the reports that came from Mass-Observation's residency in Bolton. 'Deep England' lay elsewhere, somewhere south in the fields, but more significantly in the economic and ideological power of metropolitan cultural industries. The postcolonial journeys of Gandhi and C. L. R. James revealed the distinctive civic and labour traditions of the North which had shaped an alternative Englishness to that of the imperial centre and one that proved sympathetic to the emergent postcolonialism of the two activists. Gracie Fields' remarkable career in the 1930s suggested the ways in which regional identities could be used to develop a national popular culture that could engage and compete with the dominance of transatlantic performers. The Blackpool of Frank Randle, on the other hand, demonstrated the persistence of a distinctive and independent northern modernity. The construction of a working-class resort on the Fylde coast at the turn of the twentieth century remains an emphatic rebuttal of the presentations of a contemporary Englishness wholly in thrall to an imaginary past or to a real America. Randle, like the town he lived and performed in, remained committed to the innovative English performance styles that were allowed only by his distinctive occupation of the cultural consequences of northern industrial labour.

Chapter 6

Race

The death of the Jamaican activist Marcus Garvey in West Kensington in May 1940 marked the end of a formative period of black politics in England and its empire. Garvey, leader of the Universal Negro Improvement Association, editor and publisher of *Negro World* and *Black Man* and erstwhile Provisional President of Africa, had been a declining political force for some years before his death. His greatest influence had been exerted in the years after the First World War, particularly in the United States, where his populist activism and organisational skills had been influential in an African-America radicalised by the formation of politically articulate black communities in the northern cities and by the return of war veterans. Garvey's global organisation did not survive intact his imprisonment in the 1920s or the changed politics of the 1930s in which aspirations to an African empire seemed less relevant to a new generation of anti-colonial activists. Nevertheless, his presence in London at the beginning of the Second World War and his legacies of radical racial philosophy, a transnational black political organisation and an engagement with political structures of metropolitan England heralded a new relationship between English identity, colonialism and race.

Garvey and younger anti-colonial activists like C. L. R. James established geographical and intellectual networks that contributed to the transition of England from an imperial power to a postcolonial nation in the period after the Second World War. Their physical movements between London, the Caribbean, African-America and (in James's case) West Africa provided channels of political communication between the key locations of the diaspora, and their presence in England prepared for changes in indigenous attitudes to issues of empire and race. Eighteen years after his death, the part of West London where Garvey had settled experienced violent evidence of these transitions. The Notting Hill riots defined what Stuart Hall and Paul Gilroy have argued to be a racialising of English national identity in the postwar period, a process that was paralleled by changes in the self-perception of a growing emigrant population in London. These developments were also registered in the English regions as two contrasting case studies from the West Midlands illustrate. The Wolverhampton MP Enoch Powell supplied influential if idiosyncratic theory and rhetoric to the vision of an embattled and racially divided urban England moving helplessly to the violent condition of American race relations. The career of the black middleweight boxer Randolph Turpin suggests other ways in which English and American racial discourse and performance shaped regional England in the 1950s and 1960s. Turpin's troubled, inarticulate life provides a critique not only of the development of Powellite English nationalism but also of the tendency to cast the history of postcolonial England solely in terms of migrancy and emergent metropolitan identities.

Colonial England

Marcus Garvey died a British subject in the imperial capital, his presence in London an example of what Bill Schwarz has called 'the cultural proximity and dissonance of colony and metropolis' (Schwarz 2002: 89). In Garvey's case, this intimacy entailed an ambivalent but intense engagement with the culture of Anglo-British imperialism. Whilst he opposed the racial supremacy implicit in its history and ideology, the modernity of empire – its global structures, its technologies and its commitment to development and expansion – became a model for Garvey's own projects of diasporic reintegration and the revival of an Ethiopian empire. 'Let [the African] show the world a duplicate in Africa of what exist[s] in Europe', he declared in 1935 (Hill 1983: lii). This fascination with imperialism's home territory was present from the beginning of his career as a radical. The 'doom . . . of being a race leader dawned upon me in London', Garvey claimed, and there is no stranger conjunction in colonial history, perhaps, than that of a young Garvey sitting in the audience at Birkbeck College, London in 1912 listening to a lecture by that gloomiest of imperial prognosticators, A. J. Balfour (Clarke 1974: 73; Miller 1975: 16). Garvey relished the symbols and sites of the imperialist state that his political movements set out to change. When he returned to London in 1928, it was the Royal Albert Hall that he booked for a meeting intended to revive his movement, and in his old age he was to be found on Sunday afternoons at that most English site of free speech, Speakers' Corner in Hyde Park. At the same time, though, Garvey was engaged in establishing a new political geography that reconfigured

England not as an imperial centre, but as a part of a fluid continuum of diasporic political and cultural life. He made his final choice to come to London in 1934 because, he claimed, it was 'the best place for establishing links between Africa and the United States' (Miller 1975: 132). In his fantasies of a liberated and re-integrated Africa Garvey changed the imperial project from one of the global dissemination of Anglo-British cultural identity to the development of a modern transnational structure through which new identities and new civilisations could be made.

The peripatetic life of Marcus Garvey was partly a conscious performance of this imperial re-imagining, partly a lifelong review of the condition of the African diaspora and partly a result of the political persecution entailed by his being the first truly modern colonial radical. His politics was conceived through the discourses and the material realities of movement and it is no coincidence that his imprisonment in the US in the 1920s concerned an ill-conceived attempt to found a shipping line. As C. L. R. James argued, Garvey's importance lay not in the details of his frequently bizarre politics, improvised from African-American social philosophy, Masonic beliefs and imperial fantasy, but in the process and places of such improvisation. James celebrated the older man's implicit understanding of the essential modernity of empire and its human products, and of the role of the latent postcolonial population in transforming and re-directing that modernity. English imperialism, for James as for Garvey, was something to be understood and used by those intellectuals and revolutionaries attuned to the possibilities of being postcolonial. Such a condition, James argued, would be neither a return to an essential identity ('African') nor the maintenance of a deferential status quo ('Anglo-British colonial'), but would be openly heterogeneous, drawing upon the fullness of a modernity of which it was the most advanced representation.

James's indulgence of Garvey's more visionary politics ('when Garvey said "Back to Africa" I don't think he was too certain about that', he remarked in 1981) was conditioned by his sense of the Jamaican as a pioneer in understanding the need to displace but not to deny Anglo-British culture (James 1984: 58). He did not have the gaudy tastes of Garvey but he did share the older man's strategy of shaping radical politics through the resources of imperialism. The 'Caribbeanness' that James and Garvey (though less self-consciously) embodied was not a rejection of English modernity, though it actively opposed its colonial and racial ideologies. In the Caribbean, James argued, England had produced the conditions for its own transformation, a process predicated upon the social structures that had emerged there. But that transformation depended upon the recognition of the condition of modernity as one of change not of consolidation. It also demanded acceptance of the role of the colonised in effecting that change, for it was they who would provide a dynamic model of a new Englishness as yet unknown to England.

For James, being a migrant living in England was a dialectical process of mutual progress rather than one of acculturation or exile. In a beguilingly reasonable rebuttal of W. E. B. Du Bois's assertion of the destructive effects of the 'double-consciousness' of African-Americans, James suggested an alternative political practice for the colonial emigrant to England. 'You have to be able to find out something about the country you are living in now and you have to be able to report the state of the colonial territory you come from', he argued in one of the lectures to mark his eightieth birthday (James 1984: 49). The migrant will change the social formation in which he or she is participating, just as he or she is changed in turn by that place. Identity in a period of postcolonial transition is to be negotiated and re-made, not maintained, imposed or restricted by the imperatives of essentialist nationhood – James, like Garvey, always favoured federal or transnational political structures over nation-states. It was an internationalism that James found implicit in English colonialism, if not in England itself.

'I was British', writes James in *Beyond a Boundary*, 'I knew best the British way of life, not merely in historical facts but in the instinctive responses' (James 1963: 152). This acceptance of his own implication within the deep structures of English culture was not a confession of colonial indoctrination, however; one of the various boundaries that his autobiography goes beyond is that of the limiting circumference of English identity and nationhood. Cricket, the central metaphor and performance of English national and imperial culture in the book, is important because its history was that of a game penetrated and transformed by the colonial subjects who came to play it. It was evidence not of the fixture of colonial values but of their lability and of the potential of the Caribbean and other colonies to shape their own identities by actively changing their circumstances. Cricket was permeated by the developing culture of the place to which it had been taken and in turn contributed to the changes in the colonies and in the imperial centre. Written during the period of the great migrations, first from the Caribbean, then from South Asia, *Beyond a Boundary* uses the history and the metaphor of the game to celebrate the reformation of that English modernity by the only people capable of enacting that change, the colonial subjects themselves. Their arrival in England, like James's arrival twenty years earlier, becomes not a return to 'the Mother Country' but the arrival of a new postcolonial future. To be truly English, that is to be English at its potential rather than within its insular boundaries, James argued, required the abolition of precisely those limits of definition. It demanded that the English go beyond the boundary of nationhood and recognise the necessary Caribbeanness of their modernity, just as it demanded the migrant's participation in that post-imperial Englishness.

Such challenging analyses of the English condition and the English future formed part of what Bill Schwarz has called 'the intellectual disorder of decolonization' (Schwarz 2002: 81). As Paul Gilroy has argued, that improvised, untheorised and still largely unarticulated historical passage continues to limit and distort the discourse and experience of English national identity. A 'postcolonial melancholia', as he terms it, was shaped in the 1950s and 1960s, periods of ragged and bloody colonial conflicts in places as diverse as Malaya, Kenya, Egypt, Cyprus, Aden and ultimately Ulster, and of Commonwealth migration (Gilroy 2006: 27). In England these changes also brought about a newly racialised discourse of national identity, something expressed in the tortuous history of immigration legislation that began in 1948, as well as in the unprecedented violence in West London in August and September 1958. They were conflicts and changes inscribed in performances of the boxer Randolph Turpin and provided with a new rhetorical force by the oratory and skilful populism of Enoch Powell, the first English politician since Oswald Mosley to make race central to his political project and popular appeal.

The British Nationality Act, passed in the year of the arrival of the *Empire Windrush*, initiated what Kathleen Paul has termed 'an adventure involving citizenship, subjecthood, national identity and migration from which [its legislators] have not yet extricated themselves' (Paul 1997: 10). The 1948 Act attempted to address the constitutional consequences of the independence of India and Pakistan in 1947. In doing so it necessarily challenged the old, unlegislated assumption of shared imperial identity beneath the Crown. The Barbadian George Lamming wrote in 1960 of his being 'condemned . . . fortunately to the rights of full citizenship' in England by his colonial status and it was just such a paradoxical condition of disenfranchised equality that had allowed the passage of Marcus Garvey and C. L. R. James in and out of Britain (Lamming 1984: 212). The British Nationality Act set a precedent for restrictive categories of national identity and limitations of movement and dwelling by discriminating between British 'subjecthood' and British 'citizenship'. As the empire disintegrated, emigration increased and further laws were introduced. Newly-defined Commonwealth residents who had previously held common rights of citizenship and movement within a global empire found themselves circumscribed as to who they now were and where they might go. Many found that, in Ruth Landes' words, they 'belong[ed] . . . vaguely, if beautifully, to the Crown [but] never, unhappily, to the country' (Banton 1955: 200).

Opposition to the British Nationality Act, a Labour government policy, came initially from Conservative positions. Lord Colyton, for example, spoke of national pride 'in the fact that a man can say *Civis Britannicus Sum* whatever his colour may be and we take pride in the fact that he wants and can come to the Mother Country' (Foot 1969: 31). Enoch Powell also opposed the legislation on the grounds that were to contribute significantly to what Stuart Hall has called a 'historical amnesia [and] a decisive mental repression' in postwar England (Hall 1978: 25). Powell's youthful ambition to be Viceroy of India had been transformed by the circumstances of the secession of India and Pakistan in 1947 into a radical critique of the whole imperial adventure. He came instead to characterise empire as a 'strange and brief juncture' in English history developed through the political expediency of Benjamin Disraeli and Joseph Chamberlain in the late nineteenth century (Powell 1969: 255). Since then it had become a dangerous distraction from the properly national concerns of national politics. To legislate in response to the perceived consequences of such an illusory moment, he argued, was to threaten the innate compact of subject and Crown which truly defined that nation. Nationhood, for Powell, was not a question of law but one of birth and belonging.

The process of national definition that the British Nationality Act initiated was complicated and intensified by the development of Commonwealth migration during the 1950s and 1960s. Growing urban settlements of Caribbean and later South-East Asian migrants posed a visible and emotive presence of imperial consequences to successive governments at the very time that discourses of empire were being challenged or suppressed. As the Festival of Britain had demonstrated, there was no postwar political appetite for developing a coherent analysis of its history or its active legacies while its aftermath was being chaotically experienced. Powell's determination to convert the Conservative Party from imperialism to a more focused patriotism was a sign of a broader political realignment that emerged after the Suez Crisis of 1956. One effect of this rapid 'forgetting', however, was that the formation of a postcolonial England was not understood as the socio-political consequence of imperial history but was experienced as a question of race. Whilst legislators continued the task of framing 'non-discriminatory immigration legislation that would apply only to black people', as Edward Pilkington puts it, former imperial citizens had to confront the consequences of their becoming 'immigrants' (Pilkington 1988: 73). At the same time, Englishness began to be articulated explicitly as whiteness. These processes found violent expression in what came to be known as the Notting Hill riots.

The sustained mob violence in West London between 31 August and 3 September 1958 directed against the persons and property of those perceived to be 'immigrants' was the most serious civil disorder in England since the Second World War. Like the Miners' Strike twenty-five years later, the events in Notting Dale, Shepherd's Bush and Paddington can be interpreted as a performance of a moment of change in the politics of English identity, particularly English urban identity. It was part of the process by which definitions of race were being invented anew outside of older imperial frames in order to analyse and express new experiences of social change in working-class areas of English cities. Race in these circumstances was not the issue itself, but in Stuart Hall's terms 'a lens through which people [came] to perceive that a crisis [was] developing' (Hall 1978: 31). The disorders in West London in 1958 both represented and shaped new forms of English identity expressed in explicitly racial (and racist) terms. It also intensified a counter-discourse of emigrant and immigrant identities as imperial histories fell away and a new relationship with England was demanded.

This 're-racialisation' of the 'syntax' of Englishness, as Bill Schwarz has termed it, was also noted at the time of the riots (Schwarz 1996: 74). The sociologist Ruth Glass, writing in 1960, argued that the popular framing of the violence in Notting Hill as 'race rioting' and the description of it as taking place in an 'immigrant area' were simplifications of the true social – and racial – contexts. The riots, she noted, occurred in places where 'actual concrete frictions between white and coloured were not most intense. It is the friction between white and white which is symbolised in these districts and for which outlets have to be found' (Glass 1960: 146). Notting Dale in particular, a poor district within Notting Hill and a source for the violence, was a white working-class area. It both disguised and expressed its own earlier history of migration – that of Irish and gypsies – in its projection of itself as a 'settled and closed community, virulently hostile to "foreigners"', as Pilkington describes it (Pilkington 1988: 83). Its youths' policing of the borders of their own social exclusion was in Glass's and Pilkington's analyses not a defence of long-standing racial values, but a sign of the making of a new postwar urban Englishness in response to the insecurities of changing class and family structures. Whiteness was the code for such assertions and the means of forgetting the migrant histories that had shaped their own social and historical environments.

The whitening of urban working-class England was also influenced by newly influential transatlantic discourses of race. What is striking about the language of the rioters in contemporary reports of the riots is how American it was. Ruth Glass records a specific reference by one of the attackers of an African student. 'Just tell your readers that Little Rock learned us a lesson', a reporter is told, a reference to the contemporary struggle for integrated education in Arkansas (Glass 1960: 138). The calls for lynchings to which all contemporary press reports refer also suggest the incorporation of the rhetoric of Southern American sectarianism into new formations of English racism. As imperial reference points were repressed, what might be termed white Atlantic political discourses developed to explain English experience, even though the structure and history of that experience were utterly dissimilar. It was a semantic shift that altered the frame of understanding from an imperial model to an American racial model, a shift that was to shape the urban prophecies of Powell and others in the subsequent decade.

A comparable instability of political discourse was present in the emigrant experience of Notting Hill and its aftermath, for the riots instigated re-alignments of identity amongst Caribbean migrants to London as well as the indigenous English. Pilkington describes the formation of new alliances within the migrant territories of West London and beyond, with Jamaicans from Brixton in particular participating in the defence of other Caribbeans and Africans in Notting Hill (Pilkington 1988: 122). This defence of territory implied a contradictory act of belonging that was quite distinct from the dominant paradigms of the social policy of the time which emphasised gradual assimilation and integration within a 'host' community. It also implied a radical change in self and social definition. One of Pilkington's informants, Baron Baker, states this process of change explicitly: 'Before the riots I was British – I was born under the Union Jack . . . But the race riots made me realise who I am and what I am. They turned me into a staunch Jamaican' (Pilkington 1988: 143). George Lamming, writing in the aftermath of Notting Hill, also argued that migration and the experience of being English in England created Caribbean identities. 'No Barbadian, no Trinidadian, no St. Lucian, no islander from the West Indies', he argues, 'sees himself as a West Indian until he encounters another islander in foreign territory . . . In this sense, most West Indians of my generation were born in England' (Lamming 1984: 214). Whilst the political vision of a West Indian Federation was foundering in the Caribbean, it was being realised in the difficult circumstances of West London.

Regional Race

The Notting Hill riots, then, framed complex re-formations of national identity in metropolitan London. The racialising of Englishness, the repression of imperial memory, the incorporation of contemporary American discourse and the re-alignment of emigrant experiences of Englishness found different expression in the contrasting figures and careers of Enoch Powell and Randolph Turpin. During the 1960s Powell directed the racial turn of Englishness marked by Notting Hill into a politics that fused feudal commitments to the Crown in Parliament with an astute populism that addressed constituencies like that of Notting Dale which had come to manage social and cultural change through new definitions of racial identity. Like those rioters, Powell projected the near future as American even as he erased the imperial history that had brought otherness to England in the first place. The boxer Randolph Turpin was a different version of that other, a black Englishman, born and bred in Leamington Spa, Warwickshire. It was an identity that was at once confirmed and destabilised by his victory over the American Sugar Ray Robinson in 1951. Turpin was celebrated as an English world champion, but he also made the Atlantic journey in reverse and found himself a black Englishman in Harlem. Despite the radical differences in their engagements with race and postcolonial identity, Powell and Turpin also suggest the importance of regionalism in the arguments over postwar English identity. They were West Midlanders and that identity shaped both of their performances within a history of postcolonialism that was resolutely metropolitan in its emphasis.

Enoch Powell remains the most influential English postcolonial theorist, albeit that his was the '*other* postcolonialism', as Bill Schwarz puts it (Schwarz 2000: 22). In the *Daily Telegraph* of 7 November 2007, nearly ten years after his death and nearly forty years after his most notorious speech, Simon Heffer could still write an article entitled 'How Right Does Enoch Have to Be Before the Tories Will Say So?' (Heffer 2007). The use of the Christian name alone suggests the persistent currency of Powell's perceived ideas. However, as Schwarz argues, his influence only makes sense within the context that he most virulently denied, that of imperial history, and through an implicit dialogue with the ideas of those like C. L. R. James in which he would have had no interest. What remains so disconcerting about Powell's theories of Englishness is their resemblance to more recent orthodoxies of academic postcolonial studies. He insisted, for example, that nationhood was an 'imagined community' fifteen years before Benedict Anderson popularised that idea. 'The life of nations, no less than that of men', he told an audience at Trinity College, Dublin, 'is lived largely in the imagination'. Nations, he went on, live by the myths which their citizens – or subjects in Powell's terms – share, and the 'greatest task of the statesman is to offer his people good myths and to save them from harmful myths' (Powell 1969: 245, 246). For Powell, the most harmful English myth was that of empire.

Again anticipating the intellectual concerns, if not the politics, of post-colonial studies, he argued that imperialism worked primarily as discourse. At odds with the imperial nostalgia that gripped sections of his party in the 1950s and 1960s, Powell saw empire as an obsessive illusion that had distracted England from England. 'What is the matter with us', he asked a Waterloo Day meeting in Weybridge in 1968, 'that we, alone of all the nations upon earth, have planted the centre of our world in some other hemisphere – in India, in South-East Asia, in central Africa – anywhere, in short, but where we are, anywhere but where we live?' (Powell 1969: 243). 'Where we are' and 'where we live' were to be the main concerns of Powell's postcolonial Englishness, and their embodiment and expression were at the centre of his idiosyncratic politics. Powell, for all his occasional appeals to the 'earth of England's history' and other such phrases from older discourses of pastoral nationhood, operated in English territories quite distinct from such landscapes, and his political oratory was directed towards their redemption (Powell 1969: 257).

For Powell, the 'good myths' of nationhood were not to be established by logic and persuasion but by acts of witness. Nationhood, as he had affirmed at the time of the British Nationality Act, was not an identity that could be legislated; 'being a nation is, in the last resort, subjective', he argued, 'those who feel they are a nation and behave accordingly are one' (Heffer 1998: 822). This belief explained his distinctive commitment to oratory rather than the written word as the primary means of political action – 'saying is doing', as he told the *Sun* in 1971 (Heffer 1998: 586). In a speech in the House of Commons in 1953 opposing the Royal Titles Bill, Powell made his theory of national performance clear. 'It is because I believe that, in a sense, for a brief moment, I represent and speak for an indispensable element in the British Constitution and in British life that I have spoken', he declared (Powell 1969: 196). This prophetic strain – 'a speaking forth, not a telling in advance' as he put it in a 1970 interview – was to underlie his practice in the series of speeches about immigration he made in the late 1960s (Heffer 1998: 556). Powell not only articulated a calculatedly passionate case against its effects but also embodied and voiced a prophetic Englishness that was to be set against the 'alien' presences that haunted those speeches. In 1969 he spoke in Wolverhampton of having 'an identity of our own, as we have a territory of our own' and it is through that relationship of territory and identity that Powell developed his postcolonial politics (Stacey 1970: 133).

The discrepancy between the prophetic tenor of Powell's utterances and the prosaic, sometimes dismal territories of their performance was frequently acute. The Institute of Office Management, Ealing Young Conservatives and the Wolverhampton Rotary Club all played host to Powell at his most hieratic, and the disjunction of word and place in each case emphasises both Powell's belief in the transformative power of national-political witness and the essentially provincial sources of his national vision. Like Joseph Chamberlain, his imperialist *bête-noire* and the politician who most fascinated him, Powell was a West Midland theorist of Englishness. On the very rare occasions he allowed himself to articulate a vision of the England that he 'represented', the classicist intellectual retreated into a routine ruralist repertoire of village feudalism reminiscent of Stanley Baldwin, a West Midland Conservative politician whom Powell did not admire. But the discrepancy between the myth of an England where 'institutions which elsewhere are recent and artificial creations, appear . . . almost as works of nature, spontaneous and unquestioned' and the actuality of the Road Haulage Association, the Federation of Wholesale Grocers and, most importantly, the streets of postcolonial Wolverhampton was central to his politics (Powell 1969: 257). It allowed him, for a while at least, to pursue a dialectic of national transformation rather than a trajectory of national retreat.

Powell made his most notorious statement of Englishness at the Annual General Meeting of the West Midlands Area Conservative Political Centre in Birmingham on 20 April 1968. What became known as the 'rivers of blood' speech was an intervention in the debate about the second Race Relations Act, a measure introduced by the Labour government of the day to ameliorate the restrictive Commonwealth Immigration Act of the same year. But Powell's speech was interested in performance not political argument. He combined national theory, vernacular expression and a prophecy that drew upon both classical Latin and contemporary American reference points to produce a West Midland modernist meditation on what was presented as a racialised postwar urban wasteland. The performance, the text of which was carefully circulated in time to achieve maximum publicity in the Sunday press, provoked an unprecedented and persistent, if largely disorganised, populist response. It also suggested Powell's skilful exploitation of the contradictions and incoherence of English nationalist discourse.

For the speech is notably and deliberately incoherent, in contrast to Powell's usual ostentatiously crafted classical oratory. The two most virulent passages are not (avowedly at least) in Powell's own words. A reported conversation with a constituent and a letter that relates to his constituency allow him to adopt voices and perspectives that contrast with his own and that in turn allow him to activate discourses of race he avoided in other performances. In contrast to the meditation on the duty of the 'statesman' which begins the speech and the prophetic persona which ends it, they combine to form a visceral commentary on a postcolonial England defined by violence, filth and miscegenation. These passages also predict the ending of the social contracts of a postwar settlement. The 'quite ordinary working man' who initiates the racial discourse of the speech is said to be 'employed in one of our nationalised industries' and to have three children who had been educated at grammar schools. In the speech this habitus, shaped by that consensual wartime trinity of Beveridge, Morrison and Butler, is imperilled not by Powell but by the disillusioned beneficiary of its social planning. 'I shan't be satisfied till I have seen them all settled overseas', the man declares in a reversal of the perceived geography of colonial migrancy, 'in this country in fifteen or twenty years time the black man will have the whip hand over the white man' (Stacey 1970: 84). Blackness and whips, codes of slavery inverted with unacknowledged irony to signify the consequences of 'immigration', intrude rhetorically upon continuities of work and family. Settlement also suffers a semantic shift from social continuity to relocation as the 'ordinary working man', with an irony that this time does seem intentional, is driven abroad by the effects of colonisation in reverse. Powell's England, as in the fantasies of Dilke and early twentieth-century imperial pessimists, is in danger of having to find itself new territories.

A more developed narrative of the collapse of the English settlement is given in Powell's reading of a letter that is 'about something which is happening at this moment in my own constituency' (90). It begins as a contemporary parable: 'Eight years ago in a respectable street in Wolverhampton a house was sold to a Negro'. Eight years later the sole surviving white inhabitant is a war widow who has endured the disintegration of her boarding-house business as respectable English community, profit and personal security had been relentlessly destroyed. 'The immigrants moved in', reports Powell in terms and a tone that he would never ordinarily use. 'With growing fear, she saw one house after another taken over', he continues, 'the quiet street became a place of noise and confusion' (91). Worse than that, it becomes a place of abasement, financial persecution combining with broken windows, excreta through the letterbox and 'charming, wide-grinning piccaninnies' chanting 'Racialist' as she goes to the shops. Imprisoned in a ghetto, the

woman fears actual incarceration if she complains because of the imminent passage of the Race Relations Bill. 'Respectability' and 'ordinariness' again sanction the deployment of inflammatory discourse and a
lurid narrative that the scholarly Powell could never deploy on his own
terms. And it is the scholar's persona that then re-emerges as the
prophetic classicist, looking ahead 'with foreboding', aligns himself
with Virgil in the quotation that was to give the speech its popular title.
'Like the Roman', he claimed in an analogy that few in his audience
must have recognised, 'I seem to see "the River Tiber foaming with
much blood" ' (93). At the end of the speech Powell is England's guide
to the Inferno of a postcolonial Wolverhampton re-imagined as a black
American ghetto.

Powell's speech achieved its effects both from its emphasis upon
witness and its cunning deployment of the full incoherent repertoire of
discourses of English national identity and paranoia. What C. L. R.
James describes as the necessary process of English modernity becomes
a regression, as the respectable street reverts to primitive racialised
anarchy, and a reversal of those currents of migrancy that James and
Garvey identified as the forces of modernity itself. The English working-
man is forced to become a migrant to defend the integrity of his family
and the destructive forces of black America enter England through the
racial disguises of a misguided imperial past. The 'territory of our own'
that Powell appealed to and found so hard to define emerges from the
speech as both embattled and bemused, boarded up like his constituent,
in fear of otherness and anticipating a prophetic nationalism that the
speech itself could not articulate beyond its vision of West Midland disorder. In the mid-1970s, Powell's intellectual eccentricities overcame his
populist instincts and he retreated to an Ulster Unionism wherein, he
argued, the real questions of English history and identity could continue
to be posed (Schwarz 2000: 24). It was, in its way, the political journey
predicted by the 'ordinary working man' of April 1968 who could
remain English only by settling his family elsewhere. But the dour body
of Protestant Loyalism was far from the visceral modernist theatre of
race that Powell had staged in the late 1960s, and his political legacy
largely depended upon memories of that performance of English
nationalism.

Randolph Turpin provides a contrasting narrative of race in the West
Midlands but one that involves oddly similar political and discursive
material. Turpin's Leamington Spa, like Wolverhampton, was part of the
provincial England that shaped distinctive versions of the struggles of race
and English identity in the postwar period that drew upon its own
particular political traditions. Also like Powell, Turpin's main point of

reference for his experience of race in modern England was not empire, though his father was Caribbean, but America. In other ways, though, Turpin represented Powell's worst fears. He was a mixed-race Englishman and so someone who refuted the assertion that England 'underwent no organic change as the mistress of a world empire', Powell's characteristically oblique way of expressing the dread of miscegenation (Powell 1969: 255). As a black Briton before black Britishness, though, Turpin's Englishness was unprotected from the damaging forces of national change.

Turpin was born and died in Leamington Spa, the son of a Guyanese First World War veteran and an English mother. He had no experience of the changing cultural territories of Notting Hill in the 1950s let alone the politics of Garvey and James. However, his success at boxing exposed Turpin to a peculiar and vivid version of the politics of Englishness and the black Atlantic in the postwar period. The sport was unusual in England for having a long tradition of black participation going back to the early nineteenth century. At the same time, though, boxing had policed those encounters fiercely and explicitly. No black fighter was allowed to fight for domestic championships until 1948 when Turpin's brother Dick became the first black boxer to hold a British title (before then they had to compete for Empire belts). Boxing was important, too, in being one of the few sports that allowed a direct performative encounter with America. Turpin's two fights with Sugar Ray Robinson in 1951 offer a way of examining a transatlantic relationship that was outside the political discourses of Garvey and James and outside the white-mediated exchanges of Hollywood and popular music. The meeting with Robinson and his African-American culture was a complex encounter with England's own multiracial future.

Sugar Ray Robinson like all great sportsmen embodied a cultural transition in his articulation of postwar black America. In some ways his visit to Europe in the summer of 1951, complete with large entourage and pink Cadillac, was a revival of the carnivalesque extravagance of the pre-First World War European excursions of Jack Johnson, the first great black heavyweight champion. But Robinson represented a different America from that which had driven Johnson into exile. The casual elegance of his boxing and his fluently expressed racial politics displayed a new sense of postwar possibility. It was a style that found its apogee in that of Muhammad Ali, a fighter who paid direct homage to Robinson and who was also to make a startling visit to London during the next decade. Robinson's stay in England in 1951, though, tested the discursive resources of Englishness to deal with this new America, and, after Turpin's unexpected victory, with its first black English champion.

Sugar Ray's sense of African-American play, opulent extravagance and elegant violence had been easily absorbed into the popular modernist traditions of metropolitan France, where, he claimed, he was treated as an 'artiste' (Robinson 1992: 174). In England, though, Robinson and his party found themselves barred from the Savoy Hotel and forced to find uncomfortable alternative accommodation in the Star and Garter in Windsor, a public house associated with older traditions of English boxing. It was a bizarre residency that was reported in detail in a *Times* editorial on the day after Turpin's victory. Struggling to frame the encounter of black America and a black England, it represented Robinson's party first as characters out of Damon Runyon's tales of (white) New York street-life and then as recollections of the golden age of English boxing which the Star and Garter itself embodied. 'Memory slips from [Robinson] to the old Cockney champion', it mused, 'who drove in an open carriage with his face painted red and white and appeared in the ring smoking an enormous Havana cigar'. A contest between a great African-American champion and a one-time builder's labourer and member of the only black family in Leamington Spa became for *The Times* 'a throw-back to the old Corinthian tradition of prize-fighting' (*The Times* 11 July 1951: 7).

This effacement of the underlying cultural, racial and class politics of the fight by reference to the rituals of Regency prize fighting was characteristic of the unease in other accounts of Turpin's convincing victory over the under-prepared champion. Turpin had long been patronised by the journalistic racial epithets of the day – 'bronze tiger', 'copper-coloured warrior' and the like – but the significance and surprise of the first Robinson fight intensified the need for a discursive means of engaging with his national identity (Birtley 1975: 27, 32). What is striking in the contemporary coverage and later recollections of the bout is how difficult it was for observers to describe Turpin. At times an averred common racial identity of the two boxers overcame personal and cultural differences, quite literally entangling them, though their appearances and physiques were utterly distinct. 'In front of me two dusky gentlemen had their arms entwined around each other', recalled the referee Eugene Henderson of the end of the fight. 'Which was which?' he asked, fearing that he might ultimately award victory to the wrong man (Henderson 1957: 122). The *Daily Express*'s Peter Wilson, after noting the 'strongly colour conscious' politics of Robinson, describes Turpin's most effective punch in the fight, a straight left, as a 'traditional British weapon'. In Wilson's account, this nationalised 'weapon' not only defeated the American but also effected a kind of racial degeneration. It 'turned his slicked-down hair into a golliwog's mop', he reports, 'and ended by leaving him with his swollen, discoloured features blood-bespattered and pain-distorted, looking like the mask of a wounded ape' (Wilson 1959: 124). The entangled, racialised bodies that apparently so confused the referee here become distinct. As Turpin progresses towards victory, he emerges as a traditional 'British' boxer in the mode of *The Times* editorial, just as Robinson regresses from politically artic-ulate and cosmopolitan American artiste to a condition of primitive blackness.

Turpin's Englishness was, then, clarified at the point of victory. He returned to the West Midlands and a lavish reception hosted by the mayors of Leamington Spa and Warwick, and contemporary newsreels record his appearance with his mother on the town hall balcony and a shy, self-deprecating speech. Later he celebrated by taking his mother to the Festival of Britain Ideal Home Exhibition in Coventry (Birtley 1975: 48). But Turpin's public absorption within the discourse of *The Times* and the civic rituals of provincial England was soon complicated by a black Atlantic journey. Contractually obliged to defend his title in America, Turpin travelled to New York for a return bout which was scheduled less than ten weeks after his victory in London. Whilst news-reels again pictured Turpin on his departure as the shy, generous English Corinthian, he arrived in America as a black world champion.

The fight was held in the Polo Grounds in New York and Turpin set up his training base in Harlem, Robinson's home territory and as culturally remote from Leamington Spa as it was possible to be. 'Everybody was waiting for a look at Randy', wrote the American boxing commentator A. J. Liebling, and the gaze of black Harlem was very different from that of the crowds who had celebrated his victory at Earls Court, let alone those who went to welcome him home at Leamington Town Hall (Liebling 1956: 52). Turpin lost the return bout narrowly and the defeat was to be part of an experience of black America that was to be equally determining and ruinous for the fighter. His time in Harlem in 1951 and 1953 when he returned for a non-title fight forms an obscure and disturbing episode of the black Atlantic which brought not only the loss of his world championship but also a relationship that ended in a rape charge filed by an African-American woman, Adele Davies. The case, which was settled out of court, was suggestive of the cultural disturbance of Turpin's black Atlantic journey and the incongruity of his representation in the available discourses of Englishness.

Sugar Ray Robinson had been able to retreat to the cultural and eco-nomic securities of Harlem after his defeat in London, but for Turpin the visit had emphasised the cultural and economic discrepancies of

America and England, as the details of Turpin and Davies' financial transactions which were revealed at the trial the following year made evident (Birtley 1975: 104). He had arrived in Harlem a black boxing champion but he returned to Leamington Spa a black Englishman without a title and with 'things on his mind'. And, as he told reporters at the time, 'any fighter with things on his mind is past his peak before he goes into the ring' (90). Turpin's Leamington Spa, unlike Robinson's Harlem, offered no resources for recovery, as provincial Englishness quickly replaced transatlantic blackness. It was a transition implicitly noted by Kenneth Tynan shortly after his return. 'Randolph Turpin, for a few months, was middle-weight champion, and everyone agreed that the better man had won', he admitted. 'Better, yes; but somehow less sparkling, less magnetic' (Beaton and Tynan 1953: 81). In the compendium of contemporary celebrities that Tynan compiled with the photographer Cecil Beaton, it is Robinson's picture, not Turpin's, that is included.

Randolph Turpin met Sugar Ray Robinson once more in December 1965 when the American invited him to a gala evening at Madison Square Garden to mark his retirement. Robinson had pursued a successful career in the ring well into his forties and had maintained the style that so intrigued *The Times* such that in 1963 the new English magazine *Flamingo* was featuring him as a role model for the aspirant black Briton (Taylor 1963). By then Turpin was working in his wife's transport café in Leamington after a disorderly decade in which his boxing career had rapidly declined and chronic financial problems had driven him to perform in wrestling bouts and work in scrapyards. The journey to America in 1965 was again significant. His biographer notes that the only press-cutting that Turpin kept was a report of the evening at Madison Square Garden and the re-encounter with Robinson provoked the only remotely political remark that Turpin ever seems to have made. It was, he said, 'one of the few times I have been treated like a human being' (Birtley 1975: 84). Five months later, back in the Leamington café, he shot himself.

The history of boxing in both Britain and America has always included many working-class men who were variously incompetent in handling brief periods of celebrity and prosperity. However, Turpin remains an exceptional case in English sport and society, living and working in cultural frames of unusual complexity and in a volatile period of English engagements with race and nationhood. He represents a point of disjunction in both dominant discourses of Englishness and the emergent discourses of postcolonialism and emigration. Neither the paradigm of what Stuart Hall called 'that great unspoken

British value – "whiteness" ' nor that of emergent formations of post-colonialism work in describing Turpin's experience of that nationhood (Hall 1999–2000: 7). His death as a provincial black Englishman in the territory of Powell's West Midlands is in alarming contrast to one of the final photographs of Turpin in the company of Sugar Ray Robinson and Muhammad Ali at the event where he was 'treated like a human being'. The presence of two of the most politically articulate African-Americans counterpoints the sustained inarticulacy of Turpin, a silence that was cultural as well as personal and persisted beyond the balcony of Leamington Town Hall. Developed outside of the main political, cultural and territorial agencies of emergent postcolonial England, Turpin's career exposes the limitations of both England's engagement with issues of race and of a metropolitan model of postcolonialism.

The sense of Englishness as an identity penetrated and destabilised by the consequences of empire had been active since the late nineteenth century. However, it took the dissolution of that empire to demonstrate the range of challenges that imperialism brought. Before the Second World War Marcus Garvey and C. L. R. James first articulated the role of the colonised in the new cultural formations not only of the Caribbean and Africa but also of England itself. It was a philosophy that was to be developed by postcolonial intellectuals such as Stuart Hall and Paul Gilroy and by activists such as Claudia Jones, all of whom engaged with the new circumstances of the nationalisms of former colonies and the consequences of mass emigration from them. Jones's work also confronted directly the shifts in the discourses of indigenous English identity. Her inception of the first Notting Hill Carnival was in response to the violence in the borough in August and September 1958 and recognised the need for new cultural forms to accommodate and develop significant social change (see Sherwood 1999; Schwarz 2003). The racialising of Englishness that the Notting Hill riots expressed was also articulated in the oratory of Powell which, for a short period at the end of the 1960s, threatened to shape a national popular politics. It was Randolph Turpin, though, who despite the disasters of his later life, embodied the Englishness anticipated by Garvey and James. His ambivalent identity and his tentative, troubled negotiation of regional Englishness, postcolonial and transatlantic cultures became not the exceptional experience that it was in 1951 but the beginning of a dominant form of understanding English identity in the last three decades of the century.

Chapter 7

Sport

The fights between Randolph Turpin and Sugar Ray Robinson, as well as suggesting the transatlantic cultural politics of postwar England, illustrated an English problem with sporting style. Robinson, the self-proclaimed 'artiste', confronted what he later termed the 'ruffian style' of the Englishman, a remorseless unrefined battling that led A. J. Liebling, reporting the re-match for the *New Yorker,* to describe it as a throwback to the static pugilistic method of Regency prize-fighters (Robinson 1992: 201; Liebling 1956: 50). It was just this anti-style that was represented by contemporary English journalists as proof of Turpin's essential Englishness – the traditional straight left set against Robinson's transatlantic extravagance. Sporting style has always tended to be treated with caution in English sport and identified with the exotic ways of foreign competitors, a judgement that has a bearing upon the politics of Englishness and its engagement with modernity.

C. L. R. James was perhaps the first theorist of sport to connect the way that a game was played with the social and historical moment of that play. For James, sport was a social and historical theatre, and stylistic innovation was necessarily political innovation. In his writings on cricket the great players – Grace, Constantine, Bradman, Sobers – are presented not as individualists but as embodiments of moments of historical change, whether it is that of industrialising England in the case of Grace or Caribbean independence in that of Constantine and Sobers. In a more recent academic context Eduardo Archetti has made similar claims in his study of the relationship between sport and nationalism in South America. The 'emergence of contrasting styles in sport, particularly in football', he argues, 'is intimately related to a search for national identity (Archetti: 2001: 154). Even in the globalised sporting context of the last twenty-five years, a player like the Argentine Diego Maradona is not beyond the particular social and historical conditions that produced his football. His play and the supporters' interpretation of it represent the particular cultural aspirations and contradictions of his nation.

In these contexts the English problem with sporting style, exemplified in the contrast between Randolph Turpin and Sugar Ray Robinson, is part of wider questions of English national representation. This chapter will explore issues of national style and anti-style in three famous moments in English international sport over a period of sixty years. The 'bodyline' Ashes series of 1932–3, the English football team's defeats by Hungary in 1953 and 1954 and Paul Gascoigne's tears in the 1990 World Cup in Italy all represent broader cultural encounters. Bodyline set the traditions of English cricket in contest with emergent postcolonial identities in Australia, whilst the Hungarian games pitted English professional football against the newly politicised sporting nationalisms of postwar Eastern Europe. Gazza's performance marked England's entry into the globalised sports media, an ambivalent encounter which, like the earlier contests, expressed insular tensions embedded in the social histories of English sport as much as they did the confrontation with emergent foreign traditions. Bodyline exposed the difficult relations between amateurism and professionalism in cricket, for example, whilst the working-class conservatism of English professional football was at issue in the Hungary games.

Douglas Jardine's Cap

'Cricket is a game worth taking trouble over and playing well', wrote Douglas Jardine, the former England cricket captain, in *Cricket: How to Succeed* (1936), 'but like all other games there is a right and a wrong way of playing it' (Jardine 1936: 3). The right way to play and the wrong way to play were much at issue three years earlier when Jardine led the England touring party to Australia. The 1932–3 Test series against Australia was played in the aftermath of England's comprehensive home defeat by the Australians in 1930 and the emergence of the batsman Donald Bradman. His heavy scoring throughout the series (he averaged 139 and made a world record Test score of 334) had ensured Australian victory, so the English priority in 1932 was to develop a way of controlling him. 'Bodyline', or 'fast leg-theory' as Jardine always called the method that he devised, worked on the principle of containing a batsman by limiting his range of strokes and encouraging error. This was done by bowling short, fast deliveries on the line of the body. Such deliveries provoked uncontrolled or risky shots that could result in a catch to one of the six or more fielders stationed on the leg side. It also made batsmen vulnerable to orthodox deliveries aimed at the stumps as they anticipated a short-pitched ball. As Jardine always pointed out, this kind of tactic had been used before in cricket, but it had never been developed as a consistent strategy over a long and high-profile Test series. It was to prove the most politically contentious innovation in the history of international cricket.

The English bowlers' tactic of targeting the body led to the Australian Board of Control making an unprecedented formal protest about 'unsportsmanlike' behaviour and to moments of threatened disorder at the grounds which brought wider questions of colonial relationships into play. It also tested the complex social dynamics of English cricket, bringing together two men who exemplified the social and cultural differences embedded in the game: Douglas Jardine (Winchester and Oxford University) and Harold Larwood (Kirkby Woodhouse Board School and Annesley Colliery). Together captain Jardine and fast bowler Larwood created a vivid theatre of ambivalent English class and colonial relationships when, like Randolph Turpin, they set out to contain a brilliant innovator from an emergent sporting and political culture.

For bodyline was richly performative. Even though the series became known for the English sanction of fast bowling at the body, its deep cultural meanings were developed through a range of symbolic exchanges and disjunctions that drew upon a whole repertoire of national, imperial and social discourses. Throughout the series the laconic English captain was willing to expose and explore systems of meaning in the game that had previously been left implicit, forcing his own team, the Australians and the Australian crowds into difficult interpretations of what the codes of cricket meant or could mean. The difference between the right way and the wrong way to play became technical, moral and cultural, as Jardine set his version of Englishness against the emergent Australianness of Donald Bradman. A notorious incident that took place on the second day of the third Test in Adelaide provides an illustration of the semiotic richness of the encounter.

Late in the afternoon Bill Woodfull, the Australian captain, had been struck above the heart by the final ball of an over by Larwood who was then bowling to an orthodox field. Whilst Woodfull was recovering, Jardine went over to the bowler and said, 'Well bowled, Harold'. During his run-up at the beginning of his next over to Woodfull, Larwood was halted by his captain. Jardine then moved the field to the leg side, initiating a series of short-pitched balls from the bowler to the injured batsman, an action that provoked great hostility from the huge crowd and fears of a pitch invasion. It also provoked an unprecedented questioning of the values of English sport. What Laurence Le Quesne describes as the 'moral turning-point' of the series depended upon a sequence of calculated ambiguities and exploitations of the codes of cricket (Le Quesne 1983: 30). Jardine's remark to Larwood was in one sense a conventional display of support from a gentleman captain to his professional bowler, a social distinction marked by the use of the first name. But it was also an oblique statement of intent outside of the amateur spirit of the game, expressing support for bowling that had led to the temporary disabling of an opponent. As such, some witnesses argued, it was meant to be overheard by Bradman, the other batsman at the time. The unusual decision to halt Larwood's run-up at the beginning of his next over was also ambiguous. Such an action would normally suggest a change of mind on the captain's part, an admission that the field placing that had been decided before the over began had been mistaken. Here, though, it was a premeditated act. Batsmen and crowd were being made to witness the movement of fielders to the leg side and all that it represented for the colonial politics of bodyline.

At the Adelaide Oval on 14 January 1933 Jardine isolated certain performative acts in the generously coded sport of cricket and demanded new interpretations of them. Meanings were duly made, and it was this passage of play that led to the most intense abuse from the crowd and Woodfull's contrastingly eloquent re-statement of sporting values delivered to the MCC tour manager Sir Pelham ('Plum') Warner when he enquired after the Australian captain's condition. 'I don't want to speak to you, Mr Warner', Woodfull reportedly replied. 'Of two teams out there, one is playing cricket, the other is making no effort to play the game of cricket. It is too great a game for spoiling by the tactics your team are adopting' (Le Quesne 1983: 32). Leaked to the press, it represented the day's most drastic political act. A Dominion player had lectured a representative of the MCC – the guardian of cricket's laws and values – on the right way and the wrong way to play the game.

The 1932–3 series was seen at the time as initiating a radical change in cricket, separating it from the 'traditions' of the so-called Golden Age of the decade or so before the First World War. The Australian journalist and cricketer Arthur Mailey gestured towards 'something modern' that was happening to cricket; to the *Argus* newspaper bodyline was a demonstration of a new set of values established by 'Philistines of a ruthless modern age' (Mailey 1933: 12; Stoddart 1979: 136). C. L. R. James also read the series in these terms, though he saw Jardine's strategy as an escalation of cricketing tendencies already established by Bradman himself. 'It was the violence and ferocity of our age expressing itself in cricket', he writes in *Beyond a Boundary* (James 1963: 186). The parallel with the arms races of the 1930s was emphasised in the metaphors routinely used in contemporary reports – Mailey termed Jardine's response to Woodfull's being hit a 'war measure', for example (14). Warner also used this metaphor when he confided his feelings about the crisis and his captain to his wife. 'D. R. J. has almost made me hate cricket', he wrote. 'He makes it war' (Howat 1987: 128). Even *Wisden*, normally a measured arbiter of the English game, deplored the tendency for Test matches to become 'battles rather than pleasurable struggles' (Southerton 1934: 332).

The modern warfare perpetrated on the cricket grounds of Australia in 1932–3 was a contradictory one, however. Jardine, its theorist and instigator, was no obvious revolutionary – even Warner described him as someone 'versed in cricket lore and history' (Warner 1951: 136). Jardine's 'war' was seen as a personal pathology by Warner. 'When he sees a cricket ground with an Australian on it he goes mad!' he wrote to the Governor of South Australia (Douglas 1984: 175). But it was Jardine's historical sense rather than personal prejudice that lay behind his modern methods of combating the emergent postcolonial style of Bradman's batting. For Jardine's cricketing and political identity was colonial more than national. He came from a family of administrators and lawyers in India, a country with which he identified to the extent of calling it 'the land of my birth' on his arrival there as MCC captain in 1933 (163). In the context of imperial India, cricket was an expression of cultural unity rather than competition and that imperial tradition was the primary imaginative resource for the expression of Jardine's sporting politics. When Warner protested at his forcing the English professional Eddie Paynter out of his hospital bed to bat during the fourth Test, for example, Jardine responded, 'What about those fellows who marched to Kandahar with fever on them?' a reference to the Second Afghan War of 1873–4 (Warner 1951: 141). Such anachronistic codes of imperial conduct were directly challenged by Bradman's cricket and by the Australian crowds.

Bradman's fast, relentless accumulation of runs, his technique, his walk to the wicket, his *look* were perceived by Australians as embodying an emergent national style. As one commentator on the Ashes series of 1928–9 wrote, 'if I were ever confused about whether I was English or Australian, my doubts evaporated in those precious seconds before Bradman received a ball' (Perry 1995: 127). Bradman's ruthless batting, his youth (he was only 24 at the time of bodyline) and his acute sense of the economics of a developing mass sporting culture combined to make him a new kind of cricketer. He was professionally adventurous, embarking on a promotional tour of America before the 1932–3 series and engaging in prolonged disputes with the Australian Board of Control about his right to make money from journalism whilst playing cricket. In a still notionally amateur sport, he demanded financial rewards for his skills, an exchange that presented a century every 2.88 innings throughout his career to the huge crowds who paid to see him bat. And despite taking place at a time of severe economic depression in Australia – and perhaps because of those conditions – the bodyline Tests attracted record attendances: 50,962 witnessed the Adelaide incidents and the crowd contributed wholeheartedly to the challenges to cricketing codes and interpretation that Jardine set there. And Jardine, in his turn, was obsessed with the political meanings of Australian cricket spectators.

Australian crowds first appear in the second paragraph of *In Quest of the Ashes* (1933), Jardine's account of the series, and they are never far from his thoughts thereafter. The penultimate chapter of the book is devoted to them. 'To take the most charitable view of the position', he writes with characteristic disdain, 'the behaviour of Australian crowds at its best, when judged by the standards accepted by the rest of the world, is not naturally good' (Jardine 1984: 198). Setting cricket against baseball and football, and equating it with lawn tennis and golf, Jardine insists upon the etiquette implied in the formal transaction between spectator and player. By behaving at a Test match like a working-class English crowd behaved at a football match, he suggests, Australians were reneging upon what he termed 'the Imperial responsibilities of cricket' (212). They also posed a more direct political challenge. After describing a crowd's barracking of a visiting dignitary, Jardine's conclusion is explicit:

> Here was Democracy arrogating to itself the right to demand its full pound of flesh, for which it had paid the magnificent sum of a shilling or two at the gate, and refusing to concede three minutes of a whole day's cricket to a visit which should mean as much to the crowd as it does to the officials of the ground and the players concerned. (209)

The economics and style of Australian popular sport, he suggests, contributed to a populist threat to cricket as the game that best expressed traditional English and imperial values. It was a view of the political theatre of Australian cricket confirmed by Australians themselves. Even the conservative politician Robert Menzies made the connection between crowd behaviour and local Australian freedoms. At a reception for the English team in Melbourne, he responded to Warner's plea for better behaviour by commenting, 'whether Englishmen hit out or sit on the splice, we will have the satisfaction of barracking them. It is our prerogative' (Derriman 1984: 54). This prerogative of the colonial Demos found its equivalent in the devastating cricket of the ruthless, mercenary, bumptious, up-country Donald Bradman.

Jardine's response to the emergent postcolonial dialectic of Bradman and the Australian crowds was to initiate a dialectic of his own. He made extravagant play of his status as an English gentleman amateur. Larwood records Jardine's reaction to the crowds in Adelaide. ' "Listen to the bastards yelling", he said. "I think I'll go in myself and give the bastards something to yell at" '. Choosing the 'most outlandish . . . long-peaked creation' of a cap he opened the second innings and took four hours and fifteen minutes to score 56 (Larwood 1965: 12). As with his interruption of Larwood's approach to the wicket, this was calculated theatre and an ostentatious display of colonial hierarchy. Jardine's Harlequin cap signified that he was an Oxford cricket Blue, but more than that, it confirmed his adherence to the values of a sporting tradition and a politics rooted in English public schools and the universities. Such performances made him 'a barracking gift from the gods', as Jack Fingleton put it, but that was the point (Derriman 1984: 12). The display of the most gaudy symbol of amateurism before one the biggest popular crowds in cricket history was his rebuttal of suggestions of a lack of sportsmanship and an aggressive provocation of what he took to be their worst qualities. His batting, defined by a 'policy to hasten slowly', as he put it, prolonged the display and again emphasised his difference from the famously fast-scoring Bradman (Jardine 1984: 140).

The performance was a colonial theatre that disguised English cricket's own internal contradictions, however, for the campaign against Bradman was both dependent upon and challenged by the captain's relationship with Harold Larwood. To succeed Jardine needed sufficiently fast, accurate and strong-minded bowlers to carry 'fast leg-theory' through on the sometimes slow Australian pitches and in the face of popular and official disapproval. His main bowlers were Larwood, Bill Voce and George 'Gubby' Allen, the first two professional players at Nottinghamshire, the latter a Middlesex amateur. Of the three, it was Larwood and Allen who shared the most overs and wickets, but the pair disagreed about Jardine's tactics. Allen refused to bowl 'fast leg-theory'. 'I just hate it and will not do it', he wrote to his family during the tour (Swanton 1985: 127). Larwood did do it and his thinking about the tactic and its wider meanings is developed in two books separated by over thirty years. In *Body-Line?* (1933), published in the immediate aftermath of the tour, Larwood pursues the arguments put forward by Jardine who contributed an aggressive foreword. Defending this 'new application of the ball', he attributes any controversy to unsporting Australian crowds and their 'ingrained inability to take a licking'

(Larwood 1933: 163, 152). He distinguishes between '*English* cricket, the real cricket' and that traduced by the 'effeminate outcry' of the Australian critics (48, 33).

Larwood's later recollections of bodyline complicate the earlier narrative. Admitting that the strategy was one of intimidating Bradman, something consistently denied by Jardine, Larwood also stresses the class dynamic that underlay its planning and execution. '[Jardine] asked me to bowl leg theory and I did', he writes. 'I wouldn't say I was told to bowl leg theory. I was asked to do it and I complied. In any case, I was convinced that I wouldn't get many wickets any other way' (Larwood 1965: 97–8). The passage is eloquently opaque. Refusing to accept Jardine's absolute control of his bowling, he is also clear about whose theory it was (in Jardine's account, the key decision after the Woodfull incident is – incredibly – assigned to Larwood) (Jardine 1984: 136). The 'compliance', as studiedly neutral a term as Larwood can muster, is linked to a professional cricketer's pragmatic assessment of Australian pitches and, implicitly, to Bradman's abilities on such pitches – Larwood had been dismissively handled by the batsman in two previous series. All the professionals in the team, with the exception of Wally Hammond, were either supportive of or indifferent to the bodyline approach. Allen, the fast bowler who demurred, was an amateur, the implications of which Larwood merely trails when he remarks, 'I know what would have happened had I raised a similar objection' (Larwood 1965: 105). Even had Larwood worried about bowling at the body – and he didn't seem to – the economic and social relations within cricket would have presented him with none of the room for moral manoeuvre that Allen made for himself.

The events of the bodyline tour, then, exposed contradictions in English cricket as it looked outward to the innovations in the game being developed in the style of 'colonial' players like Bradman and inward to its own resources to compete with them. Radically conservative, Jardine acknowledged the need for technical innovation and ruthlessness but found the resources for new approaches in old prerogatives of class and empire, the very ascendancies that Bradman, the superstar from Bowral, so cockily opposed. Jardine politicised his relationship with Australian crowds and he exploited Larwood's professional status as well as his professional skills in the colonial theatre that he created. For him the tour was indeed a 'quest', a latterday march on Kandahar that sought to re-establish correct behaviour in a colony that was displaying perilous tendencies towards independent democratic politics both on and off the field. It was, in Plum Warner's words, 'stern policy', but, as that phrase implies, it is also the kind of thing England might be expected to do when its back was up against a colonial wall (Warner 1951: 141).

There is 'a right and a wrong way of playing' as Jardine was to say, and the ambiguity between moral and technical semantics in the sentence was to define the aftermath of the victories in Australia. The catastrophically effective pairing of Jardine and Larwood and the cricket that they created defined a modernity that English cricket could not countenance in the long term even though bodyline had been successful in its immediate objectives. It was an anti-style set against colonial innovation and expressive of no emergent English identity, depending instead upon old hierarchies of empire and class. The subsequent careers of bodyline's main players suggest the cultural outcome of the series. Larwood never again played for England, Jardine resigned the captaincy for the Ashes series of 1934 and Don Bradman retired from Test cricket in 1948 with a batting average of 99.94.

Hungarians, Class and Tears

Issues of style, nationhood and class were also evident in English football in the second half of the century. Football was never an imperial sport, but in the postwar period it dramatised an encounter between English and emergent European national styles. Two international games against Hungary in 1953 and 1954 exposed an English sporting culture that was introverted and focused upon domestic competition – league, cup and 'home internationals'. Unlike cricket, football was a wholly professional game but its professionalism was defined by conservative traditions of class and labour. It was played by what James Walvin calls 'perpetually and lowly paid indentured workers' who worked for 'Victorian and Edwardian institutions, often fiercely resistant to change, determined to maintain their methods and traditions' (Walvin 1975: 166; Walvin 1986: 17). Walter Winterbottom, the England national team's first manager (though one unable to pick his side), reflected on the early 1950s as the climax of this period of isolation: 'We felt that if we played our own brand of football we were the kings of the game', he commented, 'and this carried on for many years and of course it meant us getting more and more lost in the wilderness' (Bowler 1998: 102).

The games with Hungary in 1953 and 1954, which England lost 6-3 and 7-1 respectively, both exposed English sport to emergent national styles and emphasised the social and cultural contradictions in its national game. 'I sometimes think I have a little insight how Paul felt on the road to Damascus', wrote Ron Greenwood, a future England manager, about his experience of watching the Hungarians (Greenwood 1984: 140). 'Their players were free agents', he recalled. 'They used *moving* triangles . . . they used space wherever it was' (142, 143). The close skills, fast movement, new geometries of passing and effective finishing baffled an English team which, as Jeno Buzanszky remarked, was always predictable because a player's shirt number would indicate just where on the pitch he would play (Puskas 1997: 94). Nándar Hidekúti, wearing the Hungarian number 9, by contrast, rarely went anywhere near the traditional centre forward's position. 'It was like playing people from outer space', recalled one English player (Taylor and Ward 1995: 112). More accurately, it was like playing a team from an East European state interested in using football as an expression of the modernity of its political system.

'The Hungarian philosophy of sport', writes Andrew Handler, 'envisioned every competitive, especially international, event as a make-or-break test of self-image, national pride, and ideological conviction' (Handler 1994: 49). But there was an important ambivalence in this aspiration. Whilst demonstrating the virtues of Soviet-style central planning, the team's success was also interpreted as a reassertion of nationalism against foreign dominance. 'Ironically, our victories made it possible for ten million Hungarians to regain and celebrate their "Hungarian-ness" in a way the state could hardly disapprove of', commented the goalkeeper Gyula Grosics (Puskas 1997: 105). In sharp contrast to the indentured labour experienced by English professionals, the Hungarian coach Gusztáv Sebes established an innovative, expansive sporting culture for his 'amateurs' that introduced calisthenics, art and theatre, as well as training sessions that anticipated the specific conditions of foreign fixtures. His vision of 'imaginative and effortless interaction between the midfielders and the strikers' was developed at a time when the English team was still being decided, position by position, on a show of hands by an FA selection committee (Handler 1994: 19; Matthews 2000: 311). 'We knew each others' dreams, every movement', recalled Hidekúti, a sentence that in its idiom as much as in its meaning suggests the distinction between the two national teams (Taylor and Ward 1995: 107). Gil Merrick, the English goalkeeper, ingenuously reflected the social and cultural limitations of the English game in his account of entering the dressing rooms at the Budapest stadium. 'When we first walked in', he recalled, 'we had to make sure that we were not in the directors' room' (Merrick 1954: 96).

Reporting the Wembley game for *The Times*, Geoffrey Green registered its implications immediately. 'Within ten minutes of the interval', he wrote, 'the past was dead and buried forever'. The English team not only lost an undefeated home record, but had become 'strangers in a strange world' (Green 1992: 67, 65). What the Hungarians exposed was a national style that had been preserved by the dual forces of the economic and administrative conservatism of the game's national structures and the social conservatism of the players and managers themselves. English football 'mirrored working-class male solidarities', John Williams and Rogan Taylor suggest of the period that shaped Merrick's deferential wonderment. 'There was no room here for "fancy dans" or indeed, for the deviousness and dishonesty associated . . . with the "feminised" foreign traditions of playing the game' (Williams and Taylor 1994: 219). Even after their exposure to that 'strange world' of European modernity in 1953 the forces of English anti-style persisted. Ferenc Puskas recalled the return match in Budapest in May 1954: 'Within minutes we realized that the English hadn't even changed their tactics since our last encounter . . . They just played the same; it was the only way they knew how to play and they stuck to it' (Puskas 1997: 114). England lost again, this time 7-1, and the past was ready to be buried again. Willy Meisl, the emigrant Austrian journalist, commented, 'suddenly nobody mentioned the unfailing prescription any more which has been our supposed cure-all before any match with foreigners: "Tackle 'em hard!" and "Get stuck in!" ' (Meisl 1955: 155–6). Meisl's was to prove an optimistic interpretation of that silence.

The English anti-style that Meisl referred to can be better understood by reference to England's own fancy dan of the period, Stanley Matthews. Matthews was undoubtedly a player of singular style, but his role in the team and his own self-representation merely confirmed the dominant conservatism and mistrust of his skills. He was, in Tony Mason's words, a 'special case' who in a 'professional sport . . . appeared to represent skill as against force' (Mason 1990: 160). That opposition led to Matthews being perceived – by himself and by others – as an unassimilable individual playing in a limited area of the field rather than as a model for the team as was the case with Puskas or Hidekúti. It was a gifted isolation that was social as much as technical. Alf Ramsey recalled him as often being 'in a quiet corner of the field by himself' and later in his career he frequently trained separately from his team (Ramsey 1952: 86). This physical separation defined a peculiarly persistent trait of English football culture that could cherish exponents of skilful play like Matthews but remained sceptical of the application of those skills to the broader game, instead remaining wedded to traditional values of force, labour and getting stuck in.

Six years after the Budapest defeat, change was still being anticipated. Bob Ferrier, like Meisl before him, was predicting a new English football that encouraged 'much more exchanging of roles . . . a constant and fluid switching and swopping throughout the team, of positions, functions, responsibilities' (Ferrier 1960: 184). Its implicit reference to the Hungarian model of the early 1950s and the emergent Brazilian teams of the late 1950s where individual creativity was put at the service of collective endeavour proved hard to develop in a football culture still largely determined by working-class masculine values of effort and brawn. These survived both the disappearance of the industries and communities that shaped such traditions and what Chas Critcher has called the 'self-conscious . . . embourgeoisement' of English footballers after the abolition of the maximum wage in 1963 (Critcher 1979: 165). Thirty years after Ferrier's vision, and nearly fifty years after the Hungarian defeats, the England forward John Barnes was telling Pete Davies, 'in England, they place too much importance on position – if you're midfield you're midfield, if you're a winger you're a winger' (Davies 1990: 325). Chris Waddle, an Englishman playing in Marseilles, summed up the strategy of the England coach Bobby Robson in dismissively national terms. 'He's used to thinking English English English', he despaired (392). 'English' in 1990 meant roughly the same, in terms of footballing conservatism, as 'English' in 1953. It was a meaning that was about to be tested in new ways by an apparently new kind of English stylist who also heralded wider changes in the game's marketing and national perception.

Paul Gascoigne, in the words of the demanding sports journalist Brian Glanville, displayed 'a flair, a superlative technique, a tactical sophistication, seldom matched by an English player since the war' (Glanville 1997: 307). That he also displayed a large pair of plastic breasts on an open-top bus parade to 'celebrate' England's semi-final defeat to Germany in 1990 suggested that Gascoigne was no Sir Stanley Matthews, however. The meanings that Gascoigne's performances generated in both popular and academic contexts demonstrated changes and continuities in the vexed question of English sporting style. 'Gascoigne does not look like an English footballer', the Czech manager Jozef Venglos commented after watching the performance that assured the player a place in the England squad in the 1990 World Cup (Hamilton 1998: 28). That un-Englishness, the unusual skill, beauty and adventure that his football could display, was famously offset by another kind of un-English display when he wept openly towards the end of the semi-final. Fortuitously, Gazza's tears flowed directly into a new style of television coverage of football in a tournament that had

Luciano Pavarotti's performance of 'Nessun Dorma' rather than the chirpy populist bounce of the *Match of the Day* theme as the soundtrack to what was now presented as 'the beautiful game'. Gazza (briefly) became part of an operatic melodrama that left him and his football open to unprecedented cultural interpretation. No previous English footballer had at once been lionised by tabloid journalists and made the subject of an essay by the pre-eminent sociologist of the day and of a book by a metropolitan literary editor and poet. Anthony Giddens's 'Gazza's Goal Slump' (1990) and Ian Hamilton's *Gazza Agonistes* (1994) were part of a new national discourse that found in Gascoigne an apt metaphor for a transformation of national sporting style.

The change in English football that occurred in the years around 1990 appeared to be a revocation of the working-class heritage that had defined Gil Merrick's view of the Budapest dressing-room and the exclusivity of Stanley Matthews' football, and which, by the 1970s and 1980s, had decayed into a physically and ideologically violent occupation of the barren and dangerous environments of many English football grounds. In 1985, the year of the Bradford City fire in which fifty-six died and the Heysel Stadium riot in Belgium in which thirty-nine were killed, football attendance had fallen below 18 million for the first time and Gazza's tears came only a year after ninety-six Liverpool supporters had died at an FA Cup semi-final at Hillsborough (Russell 1997: 208). The game's response to decline and disaster was both financial and discursive. Hillsborough led to the modernisation of English football stadia; commercial investment and media coverage of football allowed the English Premier League to break away from the conservative traditions of the Football League in 1992; and new styles of football coverage were introduced – hence 'Nessun Dorma' – to attract new audiences for games. Football attracted new kinds of cultural commentary, too, something exemplified by Giddens's and Hamilton's writings on Gascoigne. Brian Glanville's long-standing complaint about the lack of a serious English sporting literature and journalism equivalent to that of many other European countries and of America was partially answered by a growth of fanzines (unofficial supporters' magazines), literate and opinionated football periodicals such as *When Saturday Comes*, and Nick Hornby's football-based memoir *Fever Pitch* (1992) and its many successors (Glanville 1999: 12–24, 245–52). This popular writing on the game was also complemented by what was to become a substantial literature produced by new academic centres for the study of sport.

The discursive turn that these various innovations represented had two main tendencies. First was an attempt, encouraged by sports authorities, media and clubs alike, to broaden the appeal of football by dissociating it from the restrictive cultural codes that had marked its earlier history in England. The World Cup of 1990 and later the European Championships of 1996 held in England suggested that television viewers could be persuaded to see the game as a kind of popular theatre rather than a masculine class ritual. For this strategy to be successful, and for advertising revenues to be maintained, the more visceral local hatreds, racism and violence that had been features of English football since the 1970s had to be seen to be curbed. The popular theme-song of the 1996 championships, Frank Skinner and David Baddiel's 'Three Lions', articulated this process in its calculated reference to a national homecoming, rhetorically achieved by bypassing the 1970s and 1980s and a return to the footballing successes and the perceived social stabilities of the 1960s.

A second and related tendency was a questioning of the perceived link between football and an unproblematised *lumpen* masculinity. Football, for fans and marketing departments alike, came to be represented through discourses of emotion and passion, feelings expressed in proliferating radio phone-in shows and later on internet message boards. This new emphasis on the subjectivity of fans displaced the largely inarticulate social rituals of football's past, a process that was apparent in the new literature of the sport. Richard Haynes, for example, argues that the football fanzine contributed to a culture that 'enabled male producers and readers to redefine their ideas of masculinity when watching football' (Haynes 1995: 129). Hornby's *Fever Pitch*, which became the definitive piece of new football writing, presented the game as a kind of male therapy rather than as an uncomplicated assertion of masculinity. The autobiographical narrative shows how the game shaped his personal life, allowing him as a boy to rebuild his relationship with his father, for example. Paul Gascoigne also contributed to this discursive turn but in ways that suggested its contradictions as well as its strengths.

Gascoigne's emergence as a skilful, beautiful player in an England team that included John Barnes, Chris Waddle and Gary Lineker raised the possibility of a truly cultured national football that wasn't reductively 'English, English, English'. His 1990 tears also seemed to confirm what Richard Giulianotti and Michael Gerrard termed an 'epistemic shift' in English football. If Matthews was a classic local working-class player and George Best had been representative of the individualistic social mobility that came with money and celebrity in the 1960s, Gascoigne, they argue, achieved a 'postmodern stardom' that signified 'the end of "class identity", the entropy of the social, the victory of the mass' (Giulianotti and Gerrard 2001: 135). The capacity of this postmodernity to be endlessly reproduced and reinterpreted was there for all to see on the t-shirts that featured the weeping Gazza. No other English footballer had so publicly shed tears (in other times, like so much else, the lachrymose player, if he had existed at all, tended to be kept firmly in the dressing-room). But that image was just one part of Gascoigne's unusually rich iconography which complicated established codes of professionalism and masculinity. A much-reproduced photograph of the Wimbledon defender Vinnie Jones squeezing Gascoigne's genitals after the player had displayed his skills too ostentatiously summed up his role in a changing game. The villainous Jones represented an older tradition of uncompromising physicality, violence and getting stuck in; Gascoigne, neither adult nor child, athlete nor victim, professional nor amateur, suggested a different, more playful future for the national game which emphasised pleasure over function and skill over efficiency.

As with all revivals of Englishness, however, this new era of the national game proved a contradictory affair. Like Jardine's bodyline, the new style of English football was defined by conservatism as much as by modernity, and proved more socially evasive than nationally inclusive. The emotional resources of the new writing and broadcasting about football, as 'Three Lions' suggested, were to be found in historical references to the late 1960s rather than in any new formation of the game. This was a transitional period of English football after the end of clubs' feudal control of their players but before the onset of 'postmodern stardom'. It was also the period of England's success in the World Cup of 1966 and Manchester United's victory in the European Cup of 1968. As Anthony King notes, 'the period of the best English club and national team performances was conveniently coupled with an era of social democratic consensus', not only before Bradford, Heysel and Hillsborough but also before Ulster's civil war, the winter of discontent and the Miners' Strike (King 1998: 182). The decline of English football culture into violent sectionalism in the 1970s was variously linked to the effects of the breakdown of that consensus by the new sociology of sport which was part of its 1990s 'revival'. Football violence and racism was read by academics as the bitter end of working-class collectivism or as the product of new competing social formations resulting from that breakdown. The football terrace in the period and its attendant problems could be seen as 'the last place where you can be a white, Anglo-Saxon man and not have to worry what anybody else thinks about it', as one England fan expressed it, or as representing the emergent culture of 'the upwardly mobile, individualistic fraction of the (male) British working class which has done relatively well out of the restructuring of

British industry' (Back et al. 2001: 241; Taylor 1991: 19). Whatever the cause, though, the 'transformation' of football in the 1990s was marked by attempts to erase those politics and histories through discourses that emphasised personal rather than political pasts.

Although the work of Hornby and his contemporaries makes actually quite ambitious claims to national cultural meaning, these are distanced by their emphasis on the personal and the individual over the collective. In earlier forms of English sports writing – those of C. L. R. James and Brian Glanville, for example – sport is explicitly presented as a game that is shaped by historical, social and political forces. The individual who plays and watches it is able to experience and analyse those forces. It is definedly a public political theatre. A book like *Fever Pitch*, by contrast, presents English football as primarily a discourse for understanding and expressing an individual sensibility only tentatively linked to any coherent public history. Hornby presents his relationship to the game as obsessive, abnormal and self-consciously 'male', a knowing and ironic counterpoint to the difficulties and failures of family and heterosexual relationships. In James's writing watching cricket and thinking about it is part of a broader cultural landscape that includes literature, theatre and political oratory. The new football writing, on the other hand, tends to present sport as evidence either of a humorous individual pathology ('*For alarmingly large chunks of an average day I am a moron*', Hornby declares at the beginning of *Fever Pitch*) or as proof of a personal investment in older traditions of family or community (Hornby 1992: 10). Even Anthony Giddens begins his piece on Gascoigne by assuring the reader of his long-sustained allegiance to Tottenham Hotspur (Giddens 1990: 11).

These are essentially conservative positions. The game becomes a means of restoring both personal and national breaches of sensibility not, as in James's model, representing new social and political possibilities. The essays in an early collection of 'new football writing', *Saturday's Boys: The Football Experience* (1990), a book dedicated to 'our Dads', are notably about discontinuity, distance and absence (Lansdown and Spillius 1990). Their main theme is the loss of familial, social and civic landscapes, their nostalgia laying claim to personal but also to imagined social resources of coherent Englishness that lie not in the village or the meadow but in the football grounds of the period 1966–70. This imagined community of the past both elides and redeems the period that follows, as well as offering means of addressing contemporary challenges of class and gender. Hornby, often a shrewd analyst of the rhetoric he deploys, acknowledges that 'the temptation to apologise (for Cambridge, and for not having left school at sixteen and gone on the dole, or down the pits, or into a detention centre) is over-whelming' (Hornby 1992: 96). Instead, he negotiates a discourse where such irony can both define and validate his 'middle-class' relationship with football, one that is more articulate but no less 'passionate' than the working-class fan's. It is a strategy that is also used to shape a res-olutely masculine discourse that is at once attentive to feminist critiques of sporting obsession and persistent in maintaining the gendered values of that obsession. 'How was I supposed to get excited about the oppres-sion of females if they couldn't be trusted to stay upright during the final minutes of a desperately close promotion campaign', is a typically coy example of Hornby's strategy in *Fever Pitch* (105).

New football writing, then, coalesced with the aim of clubs and media in the 1990s to project a game that was classless yet traditional, masculine yet sensitive and beautiful and passionate not remorseless and violent. However, the politics of that revision remained locked into a nostalgic version of Englishness and an individualised rather than a transformative social politics. Paul Gascoigne, as if validating James's theory of the relationship between style and history, performed just this contradiction. For Gascoigne may have been un-English, feminised, innocent and beautiful in a game that had long stressed an earnest devo-tion to muscle, manliness and the professional approach, but he also represented an Englishness that was stubbornly local, class-bound and untranslatable into the terms established by a writer like Hornby. In 1969, in one of the utopian moments that punctuated postwar English sports writing, the *Sunday Times* journalist Arthur Hopcraft antici-pated new social developments in the game, citing Sheffield Wednesday's Sam Ellis as a 'representative of the new breed of professional player' with his ten 'O' levels and 'A' levels in economics, history and geogra-phy (Hopcraft 1968: 49). Gascoigne, born a year before Hopcraft's book was published, was proof positive of the English game's resistance to such transformations just as it had largely resisted the lessons of Hungarian football. His first biographer begins his narrative with images of working-class life that would not be out of place in Gracie Fields' autobiography, and Gascoigne himself confesses to his therapist the old markers of social restriction, 'we had an outside toilet and a tin bath, you know', he tells him (McGibbon 1990: 17; Gascoigne 2006: 138). The cultural project anticipated by Hopcraft never materialised, despite economic changes in the game. Though Gazza could be idealised as a Rimbaud by his poet-biographer, he remained absorbed in a con-servative version of English culture and masculinity, unable to articulate the complex relationship between his social reality and the football that he played.

Gascoigne's sad memoir of footballing unemployment, *Being Gazza* (2006), demonstrates relentlessly the paucity of English cultural resources in sport. Unlike Diego Maradona, a footballer with whom Gascoigne shared midfield skills, charisma and tendencies to self-destruction, he had no possibility of falling back on equivalents of the two 'Big Beards' that the Argentine credits with his survival – God and Fidel Castro. As Eduardo Archetti argues, the discourse of South American football has always been integrated within that of a wider national-cultural identity and Maradona was routinely and popularly linked with both the revolutionary hero José de San Martin and the tango singer Carlos Gardel (Archetti 2001: 151). There has been no such resource in English football. In his autobiography Gascoigne moves restlessly between a discourse of laddish camaraderie and the formalist drone of therapy, evoking only the cultural bipolar disorder of Dunston's Excelsior Working Men's Club and Cottonwood de Tucson private residential treatment centre in California. During his playing career Gascoigne had notoriously flirted with the political symbolism of two of the most factional clubs in Europe, Lazio and Glasgow Rangers, with the same *brio* with which he had donned plastic breasts on the open-topped bus. This political frivolity bespoke not only personal ignorance but also the absence of any English national cultural style that could acknowledge and frame the wider meanings of the sport. If Gascoigne as a player represented for a period the possibility of a new 'un-English' English game, he also came to represent the schismatic, culturally inarticulate Englishness that underlay and belied the style and promise of 1990.

Sport in twentieth-century England, then, engaged frustratingly with its own two Big Beards – empire and class. The bodyline series, the Hungarian games and the career of Paul Gascoigne all suggest more general limitations in national expression. If, as James and Archetti argue, sporting style is shaped within and is expressive of political and social change, an inability to make a style, indeed the active suspicion of the very idea of style, is indicative of the fault-lines in Englishness itself. Its sporting confrontation with emergent postcolonial styles was marked by instincts of consolidation rather than innovation. The modernity of bodyline foundered upon its own anti-style (it was not sporting expression but sporting denial), the reactionary politics of Jardine's imperialism and the uneasy class alliances upon which the tactics' success depended. Far from heralding a new national style, as Bradman's batting did for Australia, it attempted to re-affirm the social and political structures against which Bradman batted. Larwood's subsequent retirement to Australia suggested a symbolic acknowledgement of where history was heading. Postwar English football also suggests a national game struggling with expressive body cultures. The ideological separation of style from work that Stanley Matthews' career illustrated and the persistence of tactics determined by stability rather than innovation emphasised the restrictive social contexts of the sport. Even as Gascoigne's performances seemed to suggest a new kind of English style that could express domestic and global changes, the cultural politics of its most stylish player also confirmed an English game that is at best still incompletely transformed from the social deference and introspection that the Hungarians exposed in 1953.

Chapter 8

Voices

In Edgar Bateman's song 'I'm Using Sunday Language All the Week' (1910) an East End Londoner explains to the audience his problems coping with his wife who has found a job in the West End and now insists upon proper speech at home. 'I'll just give you an instance how I have to pick and choose / The words that your poor humble has to speak', he sings, 'When I'm "stoney broke" I say that I'm "financially embarrass'd" / 'Cos I'm using Sunday language all the week' (Scott and Bateman 1910). Bateman's song dramatises a contemporary struggle between an emergent concept of a spoken Standard English and a diversity of accent and idiom that was to be central to debates about English national identity and social change throughout the century. It was written in a period of elocutionary polemics which centred upon the virtues of a deterritorialised English voice and its role as a 'cure for dialects', as one educationalist termed it (Barber 1934: 25). The speech training of the private Athenaeums and elocution classes which were particularly popular in the Midlands and northern England was one expression of this aspiration to 'the ideal of a pure English speaking nation' (11). Its objectives and techniques also entered the curricula of state elementary education as well as the policy of the newly formed BBC in the first quarter of the century (11).

Dialect and local idiom, though, remained stubbornly resistant to elocutionary cures, as the coster in 'Sunday Language' suggests. Their role in articulating dissenting social and political positions can be seen in the work of D. H. Lawrence and Tony Harrison. Both writers dramatise the contradictory social meanings of dialect as cultural relic and as cultural weapon, as well as exploring the implications of strategies of mimicry that were characteristic of the modern history of English elocution. Lawrence's sense of dialect as a component of social contest is demonstrated in accounts of his own early encounters with metropolitan modernist culture in Edwardian London and in his late return to the theme of English identity in the three versions of *Lady Chatterley's Lover* written in the 1920s. Harrison's sonnet sequence *The School of Eloquence* (1971) revisits the question of voice and regional and national identity in the context of post-Second World War education and social change, providing an ambivalent sense of the continuing cultural power of Standard English and the local expressiveness of dialect.

English popular song provides different inflections of voice, power and mimicry. Cecil Sharp's project to revive English folk-song, as with his work with the morris dance, was part of a nationalist strategy which, like that of the elocutionists, intended to purify the traditional English voice from the corruptions of modernity. However, the commercial culture of the music-hall song, which Sharp held responsible for the disappearance of traditional song, produced over a period of twenty years an innovative expression of modern Englishness, one that was attractive to urban and rural singers alike. The figure of the serio-comic Londoner, such as the protagonist of 'Sunday Language', performed on new national popular theatre circuits by Marie Lloyd, Gus Elen and Vesta Victoria embodied and expressed conflicting versions of that nationhood. In their performances, the cockney inheritor of pre-industrial freedoms and communal customs was confronted with the social consequences of relentless urbanisation and attempted to make comic sense of that conjunction. It was a song tradition most perfectly realised by Bateman, staff writer for Francis, Day and Hunter, the leading commercial music publishers of the period, and lyricist of some of the most acute popular cultural analyses of turn-of-the century urban England. But Bateman's career also marked the end of this brief emergence of a realised popular expression of English modernity. The rapid incursions of transatlantic musical forms in the 1920s effectively displaced the indigenous, stylised English popular voice, replacing the codes of the Cockney with those of America. Such mimicry did not end distinctively English expression, however. As the song styles of Gracie Fields and Noël Coward in the 1930s were the first to suggest, English song negotiated an English identity within an unprecedented transatlantic dominance by means of that mimicry.

Speaking Properly

In 1930 Kate Emil-Behnke, a prolific polemicist for a family tradition of vocal training, identified physical corruption at the heart of English elocution. Hers was a bleak analysis of the national speaking body with its tendency to flat foot, feet widely turned out, knock knees, bent knees, weakness of the abdominal muscles with consequent protrusion below the belt, flat chests, round backs, stretched, weak muscles at the base of the back of the neck, resulting in an ugly bulge, with, towards middle age, frequently a considerable deposit of fat there, and as a result of the weak muscles a badly-carried head and outstretched chin.

(Emil-Behnke 1930: 70)

It is a description that recalls the images of decline in *Scouting for Boys* and, like Baden-Powell, the elocutionist prepared for a conflict that was at once physical, moral and national. 'Clear and accurate pronunciation is evidence of firm, decisive action and character', declared Emil-Behnke, and she was herself firm and decisive in initiating quasi-military physical reforms in the private schools of speech training (np). 'Muscles of respiration' were to be 'trained, developed, and brought under control', 'lung drill' was to be introduced and the jaw was to be 'mobilized' (Emil-Behnke 1937: 63, 29, 88).

The crisis in English speech identified by elocutionists like Emil-Behnke was given less lurid but more influential expression by academic linguists and educational theorists in the first third of the twentieth century. In 1909 Daniel Jones, then lecturer in phonetics at University College, London, published *The Pronunciation of English*, a textbook 'for the use of English students and teachers, and more especially for students in training-colleges' (Jones 1914: vii). It was an innovative venture, the second edition of 1914 using accompanying gramophone records of Jones himself reading from sample texts, and emphasising a 'scientific' approach to the study of speech. Nevertheless, its descriptive phonetics was directed at prescriptive elocutionary ends. Jones addresses the textbook to teachers 'whose aim is to correct cockneyisms or other undesirable pronunciation in their scholars', and commits himself wholeheartedly to an oral standard defined as that 'most usually employed by Southern English persons who have been educated at the great public boarding-schools' (vii; 1). This combination of scholarly objectivity and the promulgation of socially and culturally specific ideals of speech training came to be integrated into reforms of the general English curriculum after the First World War.

In 1920 the Board of Education established a committee chaired by the poet Sir Henry Newbolt to report on the teaching of English in schools. Its conclusions, published as *The Teaching of English in England* (1921), formed an influential document that offset a relatively liberal educational outlook ('the first thought of education must be the fulness of life, not professional success') with a prescriptive elocutionary mission to conquer 'habitual lip laziness' through training in Standard English (Board of Education 1921: 60, 61). One of the committee's members, the London headmaster George Sampson, developed these ideas of compulsory elocution in his essay *English for the English* (1921). 'This country is torn with dialects', he declared, adding a political urgency to the issue by defining 'difference of speech [as] a symbol of class antagonism' (Sampson 1921: 40, 44). Only by overcoming linguistic divisions was national integration possible, he argued, for 'if there is a unity called England there should be a unity called English' (44).

Unlike Daniel Jones, however, Sampson was evasive about what constituted that 'unity', appealing to English common sense with an off-handedness that anticipates George Orwell. 'There is no need to define standard English speech', he writes.

> We know what it is, and there's an end on't. We know standard English when we hear it just as we know a dog when we see it, without the aid of definitions. Or, to put it another way, we know what is *not* standard English, and that is a sufficiently practical guide . . . it is the kind of English spoken by a simple unaffected young Englishman like the Prince of Wales, or by Mr Balfour (born in Scotland). (41)

The apparent lack of irony in the inclusion of the Prince of Wales and a former Prime Minister educated at Eton and Trinity College, Cambridge, amongst his 'unaffected' Englishmen suggests the hidden politics of establishing a standard in the democratic environment of universal education. For even if the cultural and technological contexts for transmitting it were changing – and the BBC was founded the year after Sampson's essay was published – such speech was never going to be socially neutral. The urge for children to be 'trained to talk naturally', as a later report has it, inevitably entailed conflicts of class and social values (Board of Education 1925: 12).

Evidence for the issues provoked by Standard English in this period can be found in the performances and the writing of England's only major modernist writer who did not speak it, D. H. Lawrence. In 1910 Lawrence, then twenty-five, attended a literary evening at the Hampstead home of the editor Ernest Rhys. W. B. Yeats and Ezra Pound dominated the occasion, accompanied by Winifred Emery, dressed in robes, who intoned mystical verse to the accompaniment of a psaltery. Rhys described Lawrence's contribution:

> He rose nervously but very deliberately, walked across to a writing-desk whose lid was closed, opened it, produced a mysterious book out of his pocket, and sat down, his back to the company, and began to read in an expressive, not very audible voice. One could not hear every word or every line clearly, but what was heard left an impression of a set of love-poems . . . interspersed with others written in dialect not easy to follow:

> Whativer brings thee out so far
>   In a' this depth o' snow?
> – I'm takin' 'ome a weddin'-dress,
>   If yer mun know.

His reading went on too long and he had to be persuaded off stage to allow Pound back (Rhys 1931: 253–4).

This grim soirée staged very English conflicts of language, region and metropolis within its apparently cosmopolitan context. Rhys's account presents Lawrence as a gauche provincial, 'shy and countrified' as he puts it, his performance suggesting the need for elocutionary intervention to improve posture, clarify diction and replace dialect with the kind of good literature that Sampson advocated for the education of the working-class voice and mind (251). However, Lawrence continued to resist metropolitan training. His stepson recalled that sixteen years after the Hampstead débâcle Lawrence had 'retained a markedly Midlands accent, e.g.: "Sargent, sooch a bad pēynter" ' (Nehls 1959: 70). It is also possible that the performance in Hampstead was not as naïve as his host made out. 'Whether or Not', the poem that Rhys cites, is a very long dialect piece with an explicitly sexual theme, a choice that suggests studied confrontation as much as it does inexperience. Lawrence's insistence upon East Midlands dialect in this environment also counterpointed the extravagant but culturally unrooted heteroglossia of Pound, Yeats and the other performers. And as his later accounts of the evening at Rhys's house and his treatment of orality in *Lady Chatterley's Lover* confirm, he retained a sharp sense of the political and cultural meanings encoded in that dialect.

Lawrence, the life-long East Midlands speaker, was also a life-long mimic, and his imitation of the performance of Winifred Emery at Rhys's soirée was a favourite routine. 'Lawrence rose languidly, arranging imaginary robes that flowed and trailed around him', recalled Achsah Barlow Brewster of an evening in Capri in 1921, 'seating himself gracefully and played with languishing movements long arpeggios upon the psaltery, chanting in an ecstatic voice' (Nehls 1958: 77). Such comedy was characteristic. David Garnett recalled Lawrence as 'the only great mimic I have ever known', and again it was the evening in Hampstead that was the reference point: 'he told you that he had once seen Yeats or Ezra Pound for half an hour in a drawing-room, and straightaway Yeats or Pound appeared before you' (Nehls 1957: 176). Mimicry, like elocution, can be the reproduction of an admired original, but, as recent postcolonial theory has emphasised, it can also represent a strategy of cultural defence and attack. A mimic operating within unequal relationships of social power can display competence in structures and styles of speech and movement in order to assume some of the privileges of his or her superiors. At the same time, though, acts of mimicry can establish an ironic distance between imitator and imitated, a gap in which a politics of resistance can be developed. Lawrence's performances as Pound, Yeats and Emery suggest both a critique of the pretensions of the night and a sense of the cultural significance of that long poem which he had spoken there in the voice of his father.

Fifteen years after Rhys's soirée Lawrence returned to the politics of elocution, dialect and mimicry, and provided a kind of fictional intervention in the contemporary debates around Standard English. All three versions of his final novel contain a playful de-elocutionising scene in which the gamekeeper attempts and fails to teach Connie Chatterley Derbyshire dialect. 'She would never be able to imitate his speech. You couldn't even spell it', Connie admits in *The First Lady Chatterley*, significantly translating Parkin's speech into the terms of writing. 'He didn't say "these" but "thaese", like the Italian *paesano*. And not "nowt" but "neôwt", a sound impossible to write' (Lawrence 1973: 82). Connie is fluent in Italian but inarticulate in her lover's Derbyshire. 'Tha canna do't . . . dunna thee try', Parkin tells her in the first version, a sharp delimiting of his social superior's access to a local power implicit in the exclusive world of dialect (part of the frequently unnoticed comedy of the novels is Connie's inability to master the shared North-East Midlands vowel of their once notorious sexual words) (Lawrence 1973: 131).

Lawrence also explored the social function of mimicry. The bilingual 'gentleman-worker' Mellors replaces the monoglot Parkin in the third version of the novel and his competence in Standard English is crucial to the politics of the story. His is a knowing and mocking skill in language which is both demonstrated and withdrawn at will, allowing Mellors to operate as a socially mobile figure. He can speak dialect, but unlike Parkin he is not a dialect-speaker. His position between languages represents his refusal to accept the limitations of any class identity, and it is this instability that enables the lovers' relationship to develop in the final version, a dynamic that is explored further in the next chapter. For whilst it did not matter to the redemptive project of the novel that in the end Lady Chatterley could not learn Derbyshire, it certainly did matter that her lover was able to speak properly.

As the case of Mellors suggests, the elocutionist perspective on the 'intractable tongue' of region and class proved remarkably durable (Emil-Behnke 1937: 99). Lawrence, who knew the cultural value of dialect, also came to recognise that it was those same values that stalled his narrative of national revival in the first two versions of *Lady Chatterley*. But Mellors' bilingualism also signalled a change in the social meanings assigned to dialect and Standard English. In the second third of the century elocution textbooks began to abandon the more virulent forms of 'lung drill', emphasising instead the social and career benefits of 'good English'. Some variations in accent also began to accrue cultural value. During his 'English journey' in 1934, J. B. Priestley noted that 'as a rule I like local accents and have kept one myself', that sense of choice in the matter enacting a striking inversion of the usual imperatives of elocution (Priestley 1968: 290). Priestley's maintenance of his mild Bradford inflections was to contribute to his extraordinary popularity as a broadcaster in the early months of the Second World War where it demonstrated an Orwellian ordinariness in contrast to the class-defined norms of BBC voices. It was a sign of the growing importance of radio in debates about English voice and of the contradictory effects of the medium on English speech.

In some ways the BBC reinforced the oral and cultural values stated by Daniel Jones and George Sampson, and did so in an even more influential context than universal education. Its first Director-General, John Reith, though Scots, was of the lung drill school of English elocution. 'One hears the most appalling travesties of vowel pronunciation', he noted two years after the BBC was incorporated. 'This is a matter in which broadcasting may be of immense assistance' (Reith 1924: 161). A. Lloyd James indicated in the first *B.B.C. Handbook* what that assistance might be. Radio enabled 'a certain type of language to be heard simultaneously over the whole extent of these islands', he argued, with children hearing speech 'quite unlike the language that their parents use' (Lloyd James 1928: 357). The Corporation, in other words, could supply a free private education for the nation's children in the values of Standard English.

Yet language proved harder to control within the changing cultures of public broadcasting than John Reith and his staff anticipated. The BBC had always used non-standard voices. It was no surprise, perhaps, that these included the first radio comedian, the Yorkshireman John Henry, but beyond such stereotypical assignments, radio did not just reinforce elocutionary norms (Briggs 1961: 286). Hilda Matheson, head of the Talks Section from 1927, noted in 1933 that broadcasting had also heightened a sense of linguistic difference and initiated debates about English as a plural rather than a standardised expression. It 'has made several million people conscious, if not of their own speech, at least of the speech of others', she argued, 'the violence of emotion produced in quite mild people by unfamiliar pronunciation, vowels, accent, is an astonishing proof of this heightened consciousness' (Matheson 1933: 61). Matheson's cultural position was inevitably a conservative one. 'One would not . . . choose a reader with Cockney vowels or a Northumbrian burr to read English lyrics', she commented, whilst acknowledging that such voices would be appropriate for 'a talk of new careers in engineering, or on fifty years of memories in shipbuilding' (68). Nevertheless, although she saw the medium as an 'education of the ear', she was also alert to the difficulties of imposing language and the dangers of creating 'a single type of degraded pseudo-cultivated English which is full of hybrid sounds and ugly shams' (62, 70). Radio, she argued, was not only an educational tool but had to engage with a range of English voices. It was a view that found its test case in the career of Wilfred Pickles.

The notably uxorious Pickles was no Oliver Mellors. However, this graduate of the Halifax Athenaeum School of Elocution articulated in the most influential public medium of the century a version of the linguistic conflicts and accommodations that Lawrence had explored in the *Chatterley* novels. His employment in the BBC's North Region was initially possible because of the mastery of Standard English that he had achieved at the Halifax Athenaeum, but he became the first radio announcer to use a version of 'Northern English'. 'I was thinking only of the long or short "a" ', he recalled of the broadcast when he reverted to something approximating Halifax speech (Pickles 1949: 95). A short time later he became the first announcer to articulate that 'short "a" ' nationally. During the Second World War, Pickles was drafted into the London BBC, apparently on the instructions of the Minister of Information, Brendan Bracken, who felt 'listeners [were] getting a little tired of the so-called Oxford accent; and as a security measure because [his] accent might not be so easily copied by the Germans' (133). Pickles' homely manner negotiated the transition and heralded the more linguistically egalitarian postwar broadcasting in which certain regional voices became acceptable, and even desirable. The Shakespearean scholar and Fellow of Jesus College, Cambridge, A. P. Rossiter, for example, gave talks on language in which he defined dialect as 'the mark of our history upon our tongues' and boasted that he 'grew up to talk broad Glo'ster' (Rossiter 1953: 52, 35).

Social changes impelled by the Second World War also altered the terms of the elocution/dialect debate in education – or, at any rate, appeared to alter them. Butler's Education Act of 1944 initiated competitive entry to grammar schools and the strategies of competence and mimicry that interested Lawrence in the 1920s came to have a much broader relevance. In the 1950s, Brian Jackson and Dennis Marsden discovered that Mellors' bilingualism was a grammar school way of life in Huddersfield:

> Parents with middle-class ambitions were as conscious [of accent] as their children, and a small number (especially girls) were soon taking elocution lessons. Others spoke of themselves as good 'mimics' who quickly learned to speak as others and the teachers spoke. This group, 'the mimics,' were perhaps the largest body, and they certainly knew what they were about.
>
> (Jackson and Marsden 1966: 114)

Such strategic mimicry was not interested in the re-definition of Englishness that Lawrence projected but in assimilation within existing social structures of class, 'working-class children turning into middle-class citizens', as Jackson and Marsden describe it (15). The mimics, they found, 'spoke the idiom better than the native born' (150).

The processes of language and class observed by Jackson and Marsden and other postwar sociologists became the focus of more critical analyses in the 1960s and 1970s both by a new generation of sociolinguists and by writers who were themselves the products of the postwar grammar schools. Tony Harrison's *The School of Eloquence*, a sequence of sonnets begun in 1971, is a meditation on the relationship of class, language and culture which takes its bearings from the academic revision of working-class history in the 1950s and 1960s and from his own early life in Leeds. The title of the sequence is taken from E. P. Thompson's *The Making of the English Working Class* (1963) and refers not to the aspirational Athenaeums that produced Wilfred Pickles but to the revolutionary reading clubs of the early nineteenth century. The voices and politics that Thompson unearthed, rooted in local – and particularly northern – industrial cultures, are evoked to make sense of Harrison's own experience of English culture and class in 1950s Yorkshire. Like Lawrence in Hampstead and Mellors in Derbyshire, Harrison appears in his sequence as a sceptical bilingual English speaker.

'Them & [uz]' is perhaps Harrison's most famous poem and offers a concise statement of the cultural politics of the sequence as a whole, as well as of the sociolinguistic trends of the time. The two sonnets that make up the poem perform a witty analysis of the class implications of English speech and English literary culture. The first describes the young Harrison's humiliation in an English literature class at Leeds Grammar School. The teacher's elocutionary dictum, 'We say [ʌs] not [uz]', establishes the institutional authority of Standard English vowels in the North, an authority that extends to prohibiting those on the wrong side of the phonetic divide access to Keats and the leading parts in Shakespeare (Harrison 1987: 122). The second sonnet responds to the teacher's final emphatic demand – '*E-nun-ci-ate*!' – by doing just that, but in a voice that claims to reclaim the sounds and functions of northern vernacular speech for English poetry. 'So right, yer buggers, then! We'll occupy / your lousy leasehold Poetry', the poet declares, noting that 'Wordsworth's *matter/water* are full rhymes' and making poetic tradition a source of oral variety not of social differentiation (123).

Such strategies were also evident in contemporary educational theory in which the prescriptive elocution at work in the Leeds classroom was replaced by a sense of the history and value of ordinary speech. In *Accent, Dialect and the School* (1975), for example, Peter Trudgill argued against the idea of 'correct speech' in English teaching. 'All normal adult native speakers know and therefore use their own dialect of English perfectly', he writes. 'No grammatical form which occurs in any English dialect is an error' (Trudgill 1975: 45). Whilst a 'bi-dialectal approach' could be used to introduce certain kinds of written norms, Trudgill argued that education should commit itself to developing oral diversity rather than restrictive usage. He concludes:

> Above all . . . by not criticising their 'bad grammar' or 'slovenly speech', we can encourage children from all areas and classes to become confident speakers and writers who can express themselves clearly and without embarrassment, and who are articulate users of English which is, in the true sense of the word, good. (103)

It was a version of Lawrence's vision of an England in which disabling markers of social difference are broken down.

The anti-elocutionary argument won the ground to the extent that 'Them & [uz]' itself became a set text on 'A' level syllabuses, occupying the leasehold of the educational canon, as it were, or at least of its examination boards. However, such success also poses a problem expressed in the poem itself. Its attack on the class appropriation of poetry is mounted through a self-advertising deployment of West Yorkshire vernacular, but the status of that voice, of the 'we' to which the poem appeals, remains in doubt. Its idealised heteroglossia is offset by a cultural ambivalence and tonal insecurity that are characteristic of Harrison's most interesting work. 'My first mention in the *Times* / automatically made Tony Anthony!' the poem ends, the point apparently being one about the stubborn propriety of the (then) establishment English newspaper which insists upon the poet's full name (Harrison 1987: 123). But the lines also boast an achievement that fits neatly with the cultural trajectory of the Leeds Grammar School of the 1950s. As was the case with Oliver Mellors in *Lady Chatterley's Lover*, the most vital question becomes that of establishing where the mimicry begins and ends. The poet both recalls his working-class voice ('*mi 'art aches*') and

celebrates the success of the very classical education that is implicitly crit-
icised – the sonnet, after all, begins with a Greek quotation. Like Mellors
and Wilfred Pickles, the Harrison of 'Them and [uz]' is positioned
between those oppositions, arguing the value of dialect only through his
capacity to transcend it through mastery of the standard.

Harrison's *School of Eloquence* and his later long poem *v.* (1987),
like the work of Trudgill and other sociolinguistics, insist upon the diversity rather than the hierarchy of English speech. Yet as that poetry also
suggests, the hierarchies of English voice remained stubbornly in place,
shaping the articulation of that diversity rather than dissolving to create
a true relativism of voice and accent. The end of the century consequently saw the resurgence of a popular sociolinguistics more associated
with the reformist elocution of the 1920s than that of Peter Trudgill.
John Honey argued in *Does Accent Matter?* (1989) that the 'genuine
"openness" of any child's future' was inevitably compromised by the
'closed system' of a non-standard accent (Honey 1989: 175–6). In a
country 'torn by dialects', as George Sampson had it sixty years before,
'speakers of certain localized forms of English . . . have a right to be
pointed in the direction of the standard accent . . . and to be given every
facility in acquiring it' (177). Such elocutionary prescription at the end
of the century was reflected in a continuing popular perception of the
social divisiveness of English speech patterns. Research commissioned
by the Department of Trade and Industry in 2006 found 'accent or the
way I speak' to be surpassed only by age and long-term illness as the
main perceived focus for workplace discrimination (Grainger and
Fitzner 2006: 3). The vexed question of English speech, like other forms
of English popular expression, continues to resolve on familiar conflicts
involving tradition and modernity, region and metropolis and on the
absence of an inclusive national identity. Speaking is still an inevitably
oppositional act, and mimicry, in its various ambivalent forms, an
inevitable means of negotiating hierarchies of voice that have remained
remarkably stable over a century.

Singing in English

The contested relationship of English voice and English culture is also
evident in the history of modern song, though here the singing voice confronted outside oppositions as well as domestic discriminations. A
founding myth of twentieth-century Englishness locates the re-discovery
of its authentic voice in the encounter between Cecil Sharp and John
England, gardener at the rectory of Hambridge, Somerset, on 22 August

1903. While he worked, England sang the traditional song 'The Seeds of Love'. 'I tackled him then and there', wrote Sharp in one of several versions of the story, '[and] made him sing his song whilst I noted down the tune and my friend the words. I at once saw I had captured a prize' (Schofield 2004: 492). He harmonised the song for piano accompaniment and his friend Mattie Kay, a trained contralto, sang it that evening at a choir supper. The day's work was entirely characteristic of Sharp. Despite his later celebration of the 'communal effort' that refined folk music over time, 'just as the pebble on the sea shore is rounded and polished by the action of the waves', Sharp's cultural practice was always marked by untraditional speed (Sharp 1907: 16). Three months after England's performance, he was lecturing on folk-song in Hampstead and his theoretical work *English Folk-Song: Some Conclusions* (1907) was published only four years later. As with his work with morris dance, Sharp intended the music to recover, shape and disseminate a pure English culture endangered by urbanisation and mass production. But just like that later project, folk-song expressed the contradictions and conflicts within Englishness rather more than it resolved them.

Sharp's 'capture' and rapid transformation of 'The Seeds of Love' suggest the social and cultural strategies that were to inform his movement. The gardener was at the supper and, Sharp's biographers suggest, was 'proud, but doubtful about the "evening-dress"; there had been no piano to *his* song' (Fox Strangways and Karpeles 1955: 33). This hint at the gardener's ambivalence is removed from Karpeles' more eulogistic revision of the biography, perhaps because it raised the question as to why Sharp did not invite England to sing it himself. But the 'prize' that was won at Hambridge was not the 'undiscovered jewel' of the song itself – the journal of the Folk-Song Society had printed versions two years before, describing it as 'one of the best-known traditional songs' (*Journal of the Folk-Song Society*, 1. 3, 1901: 86–7). It was the sense of the possibilities of mediating traditional performance. The day's work at Hambridge was reproduced on a much wider scale three years later when Sharp's *English Folk Songs for Schools* (1906) was published, for Sharp, like George Sampson, was always alert to the possibilities of using mass education to inculcate a version of the authentic English voice.

A different perspective upon the meeting of tradition and modernity at Hambridge is provided by John England himself. Whilst no one could have had a more appropriate name or job for the role that he was assigned in the folk-song movement, it was Sharp that fashioned England's traditional Englishness for him. He was a thoroughly modern Englishman, only thirty-eight when Sharp met him and with a contemporary taste in music. 'Though he had scores of Music Hall songs', Sharp noted, 'he had no more Folk Songs – we had robbed him of his only jewel' (Schofield 2004: 493). For Sharp, England exemplified a corrupted peasantry almost lost to the forces of modernity and mass culture, his 'one jewel' representing the last threatened hope for a revival that he was himself unable to achieve. It required Sharp to identify and transform the truly valuable elements of a national culture almost unknown to its possessors. For John England, though, silent at the supper as his song was sung, his other repertoire unrecorded, it was a denial of his identity as a modern English traditional singer.

Some sense of what might have made up England's repertoire can be projected from recordings made nearly fifty years later. The Dorset shepherd Charlie Wills would have been twenty-six when Sharp collected 'The Seeds of Love', but it was not until 1950 that his singing was recorded by Peter Kennedy. Wills's stock of songs was quite small, and though it included versions of classic ballads such as 'Lord Thomas' and 'Barbara Allen', he favoured boisterous comic songs, particularly ones with sexual themes. Kennedy recorded all Wills's repertoire, including songs from 'composed' sources such as 'It's A Wonder I'm Alive to Tell the Tale', a husband's account of a parsimonious wife's perilous 'household remedies'. 'It's a Wonder' is a significant item because it is not one of the early nineteenth-century music-hall songs which had always had a half-life in oral and broadside traditions but a song that had been composed in 1898 by the London comedian Harry Randall with lyrics by Edgar Bateman, the writer of 'Sunday Language'. Where a shepherd, who, by his own account, learned most of his songs in the 'traditional' way from his mother and grandfather, heard it is unclear. However, Wills sings this metropolitan song in a Dorset accent and with obvious relish:

> And when I had a face which swelled as big as Primrose Hill,
> I had the earache awful, and my gum-boil took a chill;
> She thought she'd try her grandad's cure, a thing she knew by heart,
> And some sweet oil and a feather seemed to play the leading part.
> > She tried to stop the earache with some sweetened paraffin,
> > > You'd have thought I was a bedstead from a sale;
> > But that beastly low-flash oil blew off my lovely boil –
> > > It's a wonder I'm alive to tell the tale!
> > > > (Randall and Bateman 1898)

Like John England, Charlie Wills was not a peasant, and, the sophisticated hexameters and metropolitan reference points of Bateman's lyric posed him no problems. Whilst the performance indicates the social penetration of the new mass industries of song publishing and music-hall performance that so troubled Sharp, it also suggests that a singer like Wills – and, by implication, England – made no aesthetic or generic discrimination between such a song and the 'traditional' elements of his repertoire. Unworried by threats to English cultural integrity, he learned pieces that appealed to him and that were suitable for performance in the rural public houses of Somerset and Dorset. Wills's singing of 'It's a Wonder' provides evidence of the way urban music halls were shaping modern English popular culture by the end of the nineteenth century, and also suggests the particular qualities and voices of that new national culture that made it so appealing to the young shepherd.

Francis, Day and Hunter was publishing up to ninety popular songs a month with print-runs of never less than 25,000 at the time it released 'It's a Wonder' (Abbott 1959: 21, 42). However, within this industrial process a writer like Bateman was able to develop a distinctive form of English song that explored the changes that such mass culture brought about. His development of the coster character song – a stylised idiom based on the voice and experience of the working-class Londoner – allowed him to express the condition of English men and women who dwelt in modernity but were not themselves wholly modern. In his best songs Bateman and his performers present liminal figures who provide a baffled, sometimes violently comic commentary on metropolitan modernity – its endless expansion, the proliferation of its commodities, new disciplines of labour and new pressures on marriage and family.

'Making Room for Mighty London Town' (1902), a fantasy of the ultimate triumph of the English metropolis written for Arthur Reece, suggests Bateman's methods. 'Now the word has come at last', the singer reports, 'ev'ry other town must go, / All the lot are coming down to give old London room to grow'. The song is full of Bateman's characteristic extravagance and wit ('Engineers are hard at work running up a tidy bill, / Blew up Snowdon yesterday – they're making room for Primrose Hill'), but it also suggests the qualities of self-conscious localness and shrewd irony that characterise Bateman's vision of changing nationhood (Murray and Bateman 1902). England might be becoming London, but that expansion only deepens a metropolitan self-absorption that Bateman recorded in loving detail. In 'The Cockney's Travels' (1896), for example, the 'traveller' deplores the parochialism of fellow Londoners but he himself never gets beyond the capital's mainline stations, and in ''Ackney with the 'Ouses Took Away' (1900) Vesta Victoria's visit to the countryside is relentlessly translated into the terms of the East End (Le Brunn and Bateman 1896; Le Brunn and Bateman 1900).

Bateman was capable of articulating in popular comic forms the depth of modernity's incursions into the ordinary experience of the city.

In 'A Nice Quiet Day' (1901), for example, written for Gus Elen, the most thoughtful of the coster comedians, he depicts a postman's bleak Bank Holiday excursion with his family around London's outer postal districts ('West Ham, Wanstead, Woolwich, Walthamstow') (Scott, Baynes and Bateman 1901). Far from representing the formalised division between labour and leisure which the 1871 Bank Holiday Act envisaged, the postman is trapped within the patterns of his urban labour, unable and unwilling to shake them off. The great metropolis has to be trudged, mapped and endured even on holiday, any residual attraction to feast and festival subordinated to the impulses of his work. And the private family man must impose upon that family the imperatives of his labour.

In other contemporary songs, though, Bateman does suggest ways in which the disciplines of modernity that so dominated the postman could be combated. The costers' resources in 'Folkestone for the Day' (1901) and 'The Girls from Bryants and May' (1901), the former sung by Marie Lloyd and the latter by her sister, Bella, lie in the residual disorder offered by pre-modern festive custom. Folkestone, 'a place where costers seldom go, / Look on us as low, / Stuck-up lot, *you know* . . .', is invaded by twenty 'ladies' with their 'blokes in tow', 'all intent on having a spree'. This consists of arguing with 'would-be-if-they-could-be toffs', brawling with publicans, occupying the beach, assaulting dowagers and swells, and throwing a policeman in the sea (Le Brunn and Bateman 1901a). The insistence on the right to a 'spree' is repeated in the second song where 'two 'undred jolly girls' from the Bryants and May match factory and their men storm the upper-class territory of the Henley Regatta. The violence of this 'beano' is even more marked than in the Folkestone excursion, with men and women pitched into the river, a concertina rammed down a toff's throat, heads pelted, and suits and their contents stolen. 'Arriett, Sall, and Ann Maria', the song concludes

> Setting the blooming Thames afire!
> And ev'ry time they strike a match the folks up 'Enley way,
> They always think of brimstone and the girls from Bryants and May.

The release from work – the spree, the beano – allows Sall and Ann Maria and the rest to make a point about modern industry and the meaning of its commodities. The upper classes of Henley are made to remember the human labour behind the matches that they light by the 'brimstone' those workers brought to its territory during their leisure time (Le Brunn and Bateman 1901b).

Bateman reached his sophisticated heights as an interpreter of metropolitan England in the period before the First World War. After the war he published just two songs. The genre that in Cecil Sharp's view had corrupted true English song and, from another perspective, had provided a new national voice that attracted Dorset shepherds and Somerset gardeners as well as the Londoners on whose speech rhythms it was based had lost its dominance. In 1919, the year of Bateman's penultimate song, the Original Dixieland Jazz Band played a three-month season at the Hammersmith Palais de Dance. The first visit of an American jazz band to England (albeit made up of white musicians) confirmed the end of the coster. The songs and the voices which would dominate English popular culture for the rest of the century were to be American.

American Dreams

This was no sudden event. Francis, Day and Hunter had established an office in New York as early as 1905, and American songwriters were already publishing in large quantities through British-based subsidiaries by the turn of the century. Edgar Bateman himself, sharp observer of developing mass culture that he always was, had noted the intrusions of American popular culture into English life. His ''Liza Johnson; or, The Rag-Time Coster' (1901), sung by Kate Carney, is a cockney woman's complaint about her man who has 'got mashed upon a Yankee and her ragtime melody'. She provides a scathing analysis of his obsession with things American: 'When he takes yer out a-walking it's enough to make yer smile, / 'Cos he tries to do the cake walk, people think he's off his tile' (Le Brunn and Bateman 1901c). Nevertheless, within twenty years, her bloke's taste was the norm and the English performer had to deal with the wholesale incorporation of the English style that Carney represented by the rhythms and vowels of America.

Neither the idiom of music hall that Bateman had helped bring to maturity nor Cecil Sharp's revival of 'traditional' folk-song was flexible enough to challenge the sexuality, romance and perceived modernity of American dance and song styles. In 1934 *The Times* complained that the default voice of British entertainment had become American. Each week the BBC Variety Department 'listens to a dozen crooners offering a fairly accomplished imitation of Bing Crosby, and a dozen impersonators who follow Florence Desmond and Beryl Orde in impersonations of Mae West and Zasu Pitts' (Briggs 1965: 110). Four years later Tom Harrisson noted in his study of Bolton dance-halls that jazz 'has become or is becoming the religious ritual of post-War youth, and these songs of hope and happiness in a dream-world every moon-night are the hymns of young England' (Harrisson 1938: 66). For the first time, in popular music at least, Englishness was being shaped by a foreign language.

The 'disappearance' of the English voice, like all such moments of English decline, fall or absence, is more equivocal than it first seems, however. As with the conflicts over Standard English, mimicry was important to the post-Bateman history of English popular song. Those singers who responded most successfully to the coming of America constructed a popular voice that gave them an English room for manoeuvre. Simon Frith has argued that the best popular songs are 'those that can be heard as a struggle between verbal and musical rhetoric, between the singer and the song' (Frith 1996: 182). The relevance of this to English song can be heard in the work of the two singers of what might be termed the first post-English generation of popular music in the 1920s and 1930s. Gracie Fields and Noël Coward developed contrasting performance styles that incorporated a knowing interaction of irony and burlesque with sentiment and American popular idioms to create a new kind of English singing.

As was suggested in Chapter 5, Fields became a star because she established a nationalisable version of Northernness. But her success also depended upon her integration of American styles in a display of apparently unsophisticated Englishness. The best evidence of this is a recording of her performance at the Holborn Empire, London in October 1933. The nine-song set begins with a parody of the American rural lament 'There's a Cabin in the Pines' (1933), which she sings in a pastiche of Al Jolson's style disrupted by her usual whistles, groans and Lancashire exclamations. This is followed by three Northern music-hall style comic songs, including 'The Rochdale Hounds' (1931), one of Fields' most characteristic exercises in this genre. A parody of a late nineteenth-century parlour ballad is then set beside Irving Berlin's recent song 'I Can't Remember' (1933). Two encores emphasise the cultural poles of her act. 'Sally' (1931), Fields' signature tune, is a sentimental English song sung straight, whilst the finale is 'Stormy Weather' (1933), a current hit for Ethel Waters and the Duke Ellington Orchestra. Fields again sings it straight and in American this time with virtuoistic jazz stylings. At the height of her success, then, her act moved easily across available popular forms without ever resting upon a single voice or a single culture. Although she asks her (London) audience to imagine themselves in her Rochdale home after a 'nice tea', she is also, implicitly at least, asking them to imagine themselves in the Cotton Club in Harlem (*Gracie Fields – Stage and Screen* nd).

Noël Coward counterpointed Fields' apparently ingenuous stardom with an equally adept construction of class and engagement with dominant American styles which relied on quite another repertoire of English voice. Coward's work emerged from English musical theatre and revue genres which were facing increasing competition from imported American musicals and films after the First World War – a process acknowledged in the knowing anachronism of his *Cavalcade* (1932). His response was simultaneously to celebrate and mock English identity in camp performances that made room for conflicting responses of amusement – a favoured Coward term – and disdain. If Fields guyed and used stereotypes of Northernness, Coward exaggerated the mannerisms of Received Pronunciation – rolled r's, clipped delivery, elongated vowels – as he both performed and satirised the aristocrat, the imperialist and the metropolitan socialite. At the same time, though, the exaggeration and posture also created space for an expressive, if ironic and understated, romanticism and patriotism unusual in English popular song in the period. That his voice was emphatically artificial to the point of self-parody was one of the means by which this was achieved; another was an accompaniment that had thoroughly absorbed the styles and harmonies of jazz.

Coward's Englishness was defined through the play between these styles. The songs that advertise the absurdities of fading aristocracy and failing empire also allow the expressive resources of a more reserved nationalism to be taken seriously. Thus the mockery of 'The Stately Homes of England' (1938) allows the patriotism of 'London Pride' (1941), and against the banal chatter of 'I Wonder What Happened to Him' (1944) is set the stoic, reticent romanticism of 'I Travel Alone' (1934) and 'I Follow My Secret Heart' (1934). Not attempting naturalness, and locating his voice firmly in a class register that advertised its imminent obsolescence, Coward maintained an English popular voice that understood but did not imitate the expressive language and culture of jazz. Like Fields, Coward combined performances of English class and culture with American musical style to create songs that both acknowledged and denied its dominance.

In many ways Fields and Coward were one-offs who, despite their popularity in mid-century, established no sustainable tradition of English performance. Fields retired early after an unsuccessful wartime excursion to Hollywood, and in later life Coward was appearing in cabaret in Las Vegas and adorning self-conscious English film capers like *The Italian Job* (1969). But whilst their repertoires and personae were idiosyncratic, their strategies for maintaining a distinctive English popular voice in the context of transatlantic hegemony of language and style proved to be remarkably resilient. It was Fields' and Coward's ironic performance of Englishness, their hybrid repertoire and their insistent dialogue with the popular music of America, that set a pattern for the voice of English popular music throughout its later phases through skiffle, to rock and roll and beyond.

English voices, in speech and song, have been involved in familiar struggles. The idea of a standard English speaking voice, like that of a pure English singing voice, was always undermined by the implication of such projects in the exertion of forms of cultural and social authority. Dialect was to be eradicated and John England sat silently while his song was sung by someone else. At the same time, regional speech and song were always in lively dialogue with those dominant forms, whether through Charlie Wills' fascination with Bateman's music-hall song or the more strategic deployment of dialect by D. H. Lawrence. Despite the cultural and technological power of the BBC in its early days, the Corporation could not educate the English voice in the way its Director-General might have wanted, in the end absorbing regional difference in its own expression. And English popular music, facing an unprecedented formal and performative challenge from America, developed strategies of mimicry, irony and accommodation to maintain its own cultural distinctiveness in hybridity rather in an imagined purity.

Chapter 9

Romance

The exploitation of reticence, parody and pastiche that characterised Noël Coward's songwriting in the 1930s and 1940s is also evident in his script for the classic film of English romance, *Brief Encounter* (1945). The film presents what became a much-parodied vision of provincial middle-class England in which the two married lovers sacrifice their passion for family and social propriety. As often in English popular culture, though, *Brief Encounter* engages obliquely with wider questions of national identity and the social and cultural conflicts that frustrate and complicate its expression. Here it concerns the role of gender in the making of nationhood and the peculiar uncertainties of its role in Englishness. As was noted in the Introduction, England never 'adopted [an] ideal of manliness and built its national stereotypes around it' in the way that George Mosse argued was characteristic of nineteenth- and twentieth-century European nationalisms (Mosse 1985: 10). Instead, a far less secure projection of both masculine and feminine roles was evident in the national organisations of the early twentieth century – the Scouts and Guides, the folk-dance movement and the Women's Institutes, for example. George Orwell argued something similar in 'The Lion and the Unicorn' when he defined popular mistrust of militarism as a particular feature of Englishness (Orwell 1968: 79). Patriarchy may have shaped and dominated English institutions, as Virginia Woolf argued in *Three Guineas*, but overt displays of masculinity as defining of nationhood were rare.

Romance isn't much associated with the English, let alone the making of English identity, but its narrative means of negotiating between representations of masculinity and femininity make it unexpectedly important in thinking about the popular expression of gender in English culture. Whilst *Brief Encounter* and the other case studies of the chapter, *Lady Chatterley's Lover* and the popular presentations of the life of Lady Diana Spencer, are all shaped by male agency in one way or another, their sexual narratives are ones of gendered contest rather than gendered conviction. These contests are structured by other social and cultural forces. Lawrence's novel, for example, as the previous chapter suggested, is also concerned with issues of language and voice, and its complex regional geography shapes its sexual narrative and its project of national revival. *Brief Encounter* is a meditation on English cinema and its relationship with that more potent factory of desire Hollywood in the 1940s, whilst Diana's lifelong exploitation of romance conventions produced an unlikely political critique of monarchy in the late twentieth century.

The Democracy of Touch

'When a "serious" young man said to me the other day: "I can't believe in the regeneration of England by sex, you know", I could only say, "I'm sure you can't" ', D. H. Lawrence writes in the essay 'A Propos of *Lady Chatterley's Lover*' (1930). 'He had no sex anyhow: poor, self-conscious, uneasy, narcissus-monk as he was' (Lawrence 1968: 496). Lawrence himself had come to believe in the necessity of just such regeneration and devoted his last novel and its earlier variants to describing it. *Lady Chatterley's Lover* remains a singular English modernist text as much because of its extra-textual life as its literary significance. Its initial suppression brought it notoriety; in 1960 it was the centre of a legal case that contributed to the liberalisation of English obscenity laws; and in the 1970s it became the object of a second-wave feminist critique of its phallocentric sexual politics. Several exploitative film adaptations also contributed to *Lady Chatterley*, alone of its modernist contemporaries, having a common, if frequently debased, currency in national popular culture.

This after-life of the novel both maintained and distorted Lawrence's insistence that Englishness and sexuality should be addressed as common problems. If, as Linda Ruth Williams has argued, his primary concerns in the late fiction are 'to render the unspeakable spoken, to bring into the public realm the private, secret, the taboo: "the secret entrances" ', those entrances have as much to do with place as they do with sex (Williams 1993: 104). For *Lady Chatterley* is not only concerned with the relationship between Englishness and sexuality, but with that of Englishness, regionalism and sexuality. The 'democracy of touch' that it projects is not an abstract vision of national-sexual revival, but one fought out in the cultural and geographical landscapes of the English North-East Midlands, at first sight an unlikely place for such a resurrection (Lawrence 1960: 79).

Lawrence's return to the question of English identity was prompted by a final visit to his home region in the summer of 1926 and the three versions of *Lady Chatterley* represent his ambivalent re-engagement with the territory of the Nottinghamshire-Derbyshire border. After a long walk around Eastwood with an old friend, Lawrence was apparently dismissive of his hometown and its culture. 'I asked him when he was coming over again', recalled Willie Hopkin. 'His reply was "Never! I hate the damned place"' (Nehls 1959: 93). It is a judgement reflected in Connie Chatterley's evocation of the 'awful ugly Midlands' and 'its disfigured countryside' (Lawrence 1973: 61, 63). However, other texts suggest different approaches to what Lawrence called, in a letter to Rolf Gardiner in December 1926, the 'country of my heart' (Lawrence 1997: 329). His essays of the period combine what he calls in 'Return to Bestwood' (1926) 'a devouring nostalgia and an infinite repulsion' (Lawrence 1968: 257). In one visionary text, for example, he presents his hometown transformed into a William Morris-like utopia, a 'golden city' with 'Sherwood Forest grown dense again' and in 'Nottingham and the Mining Countryside' (1930) he imagines an alternative historical geography for the industrial East Midlands (Lawrence 1936: 829, 831). 'What opportunities, what opportunities!' he laments. 'These mining villages *might* have been like the lovely hill-towns of Italy, shapely and fascinating. And what happened?' (134). What happened was the 'utter negation of natural beauty, the utter negation of the gladness of life . . . the utter death of the human intuitive faculty' which he describes in the final version of *Lady Chatterley* (Lawrence 1960: 158). But those possibilities of other histories and other geographies remain tangible in the novel and are connected to its more evident project of national-sexual redemption.

Connie Chatterley felt that she 'seemed to have left England altogether' when she arrives in the East Midlands from Sussex in *John Thomas and Lady Jane*. It was 'some weird and unnatural country where everything came from underground. It was no country. It was another no-man's-land' (Lawrence 1972: 150). But that 'no country' is revealed as a place of historical and cultural struggle and transformation which has as its absent centre the gamekeeper's enclosure within the Wragby woodlands. The latter form the 'remnant of the great forest where Robin Hood hunted and [the] riding was an old, old thoroughfare coming across country. But now, of course, it was only a riding through the private wood' (Lawrence 1960: 44). That two-sentence history of English land enclosure and the transition from what E. P. Thompson calls 'customs in common' to the discipline of private ownership provides the political context for the novels' study of England (Thompson 1991).

Clifford Chatterley projects onto his enclosed woods a comparably limiting national vision. 'I consider this is really the heart of England', he tells his wife, making the ancient forest and its embodiment of nationhood a personal possession to be protected and preserved by aristocratic power and sensibility. 'We who have this kind of property, and the feeling for it, *must* preserve it', he continues (45, 46). This embattled Tory nationalism is set within a familiar paradox of English tradition and modernity as the old England is economically sustained only by the forces that will eventually destroy it, represented in the novels by Chatterley's collieries and by the pit villages and miners that encroach upon the estate. His journey into the wood (into 'the heart of England') finds him literally bogged down as his wheelchair is unable to traverse the ground that he claims as his own. Connie's relationship with the land of the East Midlands is more volatile, however, and it is her exploration of its historical geography that first allows her to find a new way of being English.

The proprietal rights that Clifford claims are challenged in the woodlands both by the incursions of the miners as poachers and by the adultery of his wife, trespasses that share a common politics. Chatterley's preoccupation with poaching, the subject of his dialogues with the gamekeeper whose job it is to beat the bounds of private property, is part of a wider history of what Bob Bushaway has called 'the transition from custom to crime' (Bushaway 1981: 209). The enclosure of the forest to create a private estate entailed the restriction of common rights of access and use, and the redefinition of such rights as trespass and theft. Mellors, trapped in a social contradiction of his own, finds his 'only and last freedom in life' in the spaces in the wood where he can negotiate a temporary release from both the economic power of his employer and the actual violence of the miners/poachers (Lawrence 1960: 91). It is a freedom that is grounded in a 'secret little clearing, and . . . secret little hut' reached by 'a track that seemed to lead nowhere' (90). Connie's entry into that place is experienced by him as 'a trespass on his privacy', a transference of the term associated with the property of Connie's husband to the keeper's determined maintenance of a free social space (91). Their subsequent struggle over access to this secret place – she insists upon a key to his hut – becomes a political struggle over private ownership and common rights. Her demand for access is extended through the property rights of her husband; Mellors' resistance is a defence of a place maintained outside of those laws.

The sexual relationship that develops between Connie and Mellors, and which has for various reasons preoccupied discussions of the novel, is actually determined by this politics of place. Both lady and keeper have to abandon class and role and learn to become trespassers in the clearing. The abdication of power that this implies on both sides allows the possibility of a 'democracy of touch', and, in the visionary national politics of the novels, for the private land of the wood to be redeemed as ancient forest. However, Lawrence is also attentive to the ways in which the couple's sexual and political relationship is hedged and threatened by forces embedded in the physical geography of the East Midlands. 'The seclusion of the wood was illusory', Mellors acknowledges, and the novels set themselves the problem of devolving the politics of the clearing to the contested ground of modern England (124).

In the first two versions of the story the democracy of touch cannot survive its passage into industrial England. *The First Lady Chatterley* presents desire foundering embarrassingly on the realities of a working-class tea when Connie visits Parkin in Sheffield. In *John Thomas and Lady Jane* the Parkin of the wood becomes a 'pinched, rather insignificant little working-man of Blagby Street' (367). Only in the final version of the novel is there the possibility of developing the transformation of history and society achieved in the clearing to a wider England. The shift from Parkin to Mellors (Connie exclaims in *The First Lady Chatterley*, 'Parkin – the very name seemed ridiculous to her') represents a transition in social identity (Lawrence 1973: 81). Mellors, embodying the 'no-man's-land' of the wood, does not resolve into a fixed class identity when he leaves it. As noted in Chapter 8, he can move between voices and varied social environments, and draw upon wartime experience as an officer. But the 'regeneration of England by sex' still remains a problematic enterprise in the novel. As soon as the lovers move from the clearing to Mellors' cottage and beyond, law, class and custom encroach upon sex. The comedy of the novels, particularly the account of the scandalous return of the gamekeeper's wife which Lawrence retained in all three versions acts as a reminder of the incongruity of a sexual revival of Englishness taking place in what Connie calls 'that dismal mess of the East Midlands' (273–4).

Banality and bathos are integral to the national vision of *Lady Chatterley*, although it has always been the more grandiloquent passages that have attracted critical – and popular – attention. Beyond the simplistic cultural binaries of Englishness – North/South, rural/urban, traditional/modern – the territory of the Derbyshire–Nottinghamshire border offer the necessarily unstable and complicated ground for imagining a new England. Whilst part of its purpose was to provide the cultural resources for seeing 'Sherwood Forest grown dense again', Lawrence also shows the couple's lovemaking being interrupted by an aubade of the hooters from Tevershall pit. The banalities and absurdities of English romance are more significant in the novels than critics of their phallocentric excesses tend to acknowledge. And whilst they do insist upon sexuality as the means of national regeneration and class dissolution they also acknowledge, through their comedy as much as anything, the uncertainties of gender identities in England.

Between Delirium and Baluchistan

Lady Chatterley's Lover and David Lean's film *Brief Encounter* (1945) are at first sight an odd pairing. Lawrence's deliberately provocative novel of sexual politics ended a career of modernist literary experiment, whereas *Brief Encounter* was a modest adaptation of a Noël Coward play aimed at a popular cinema audience. However, both are texts that pose questions of English identity as questions of sexual identity in the aftermath of war and *Brief Encounter*, like *Lady Chatterley's Lover*, has provoked conflicting accounts of that questioning. Viewed as either a classic representation of middle-class sexual reticence or as an ironic study of that reticence, as a women's picture or as a coded gay narrative, Lean's film became central to academic revisions of mid-century British cinema and culture in the 1990s (see Medhurst 1991; Light 1991; Dyer 1993; Gledhill and Swanson 1996). Like *Lady Chatterley*, too, *Brief Encounter* is definitively English, but, like Coward's songwriting, it is also alert to its relationship with the commanding genres of contemporary transatlantic cultures.

Its story is that of a doomed, quasi-adulterous romance between Laura Jesson, played by Celia Johnson, a married, middle-aged, middle-class housewife, and Alec Harvey, played by Trevor Howard, a married, middle-aged doctor in a northern market town just before the Second World War. Over seven Thursdays they meet, are attracted to each other, fall in love, attempt sex, fail and agree to part. The film's subdued atmosphere and lack of dramatic action led its producers to laud an innovative realism on its release. 'This is a story in which the happenings are like life and not the conventional film script', they claimed; 'nothing happens in the Hollywood sense', its director added (BFI *Brief Encounter* File; Lean 1947: 32). Such characterisations were generally accepted by contemporary reviewers. 'No Hollywood glamour', the *Standard* noted, 'but warm and sympathetic insight into real emotion, powerfully felt' (*Standard* 23 November 1945: np). The trade press, more shrewdly, emphasised its likely appeal to a female audience. *Kinematograph Weekly*, for example, noted that 'its appeal to the woman fan's heart and mind is unbounded' (*Kinematograph Weekly* 15 November 1945: 24). The 'woman fan's heart and mind' is also the film's central interest, for Laura's 'brief encounter' is a junction for competing representations of English sexuality and desire. Like Connie Chatterley, she is both wife and lover, but the challenge to her sexual identity comes not from the domestic exoticism of a cross-class relationship but from her engagement with popular entertainment.

The end of the Second World War marked a high point of English cinema attendance, divorce and illegitimate births (Lant 1991: 24; Smart 1996: 93; Webster 1998: 12). The coincidence reflects the social and sexual dislocations of the war, and the cinema of 1945 reflected these changes. Laura is one of the 'women fans' referred to by *Kinematograph Weekly*, albeit located in a pre-war context. Her Thursday afternoons are spent in one of Milford's two cinemas and she knows their weekly programmes by heart. The illicit relationship with Alec develops when they go to the pictures, the Palladium balcony allowing a safely darkened environment for it to prosper. More significantly, though, the cinema provides her with a language and syntax for her own English love story. Going to the pictures in the afternoon seals her fate – as she might say – and as the audience sees Laura feeling guiltily happy and happily guilty in the three-and-ninepennies, it witnesses English cinema at work reflecting on the relationship of cinema-going, desire and nationhood.

This self-referentiality was to make *Brief Encounter* popular in film criticism forty years later but it also acknowledged a cultural truth. As the surveys of J. P. Mayer and Mass-Observation in the 1930s and 1940s confirm, the enthusiastic routine of English film-goers, the majority of whom were women, inculcated a remarkable grammar of cinematic narrative and a critical knowledge of its genres, conventions and history (Mayer 1948; Richards and Sheridan 1987). When *Brief Encounter* was released in the winter of 1945–6, Laura was telling her story to audiences able to cross-reference its discourses and narrative with a range of contemporary romances. An average film-goer, for example, might well have seen Leslie Arliss's racy historical romance *The Wicked Lady* (1945) a few weeks before *Brief Encounter* played. This provides a gaudy parallel to Laura's story, with Margaret Lockwood's anti-heroine relieving problems of marital boredom through adultery with a highwayman, robbery and murder. *The Seventh Veil* (1945), which, like *The Wicked Lady*, had James Mason as its sadistically sultry male lead, also focused on a woman's sexual dilemmas, and *Waterloo Road* (1944), a film about the temptations of adultery during a husband's wartime absence, was still showing in provincial cinemas in spring 1946. Powell and Pressburger's *I Know Where I'm Going!* (1945) was also an independent British production which featured a headstrong heroine and celebrated romantic passion and tradition winning out over money and modernity, whilst the re-release of Laurence Olivier's *Pride and Prejudice* (1940) reminded audiences of Hollywood's more routine approach to the English romance genre. Two other American films circulating in the months of *Brief Encounter*'s release suggest contrasting transatlantic approaches to romance. Otto Preminger's *Fallen Angel* (1945) and Billy Wilder's *Double Indemnity* (1944) developed the moral ambiguities of what was to be known as *film noir*, the murderous Barbara Stanwyck in the latter acting as an amoral agent of revenge for the disappointments of marriage. Laura the film-goer constructs her provincial romance both through and against these competing genres of cinematic fantasy.

Like *Double Indemnity*, *Brief Encounter* is structured as a confession, but it is a silent one. Laura tells the story of her encounter to her husband Fred, but only in an internal monologue. The film's audience is thus privy to a subjective and retrospective commentary on the seven Thursdays, the Englishness of which is immediately foregrounded. Laura's confession begins with three assertions of 'ordinariness', a claim supported by Celia Johnson's lack of make-up or stylish costume. She is conspicuously not Barbara Stanwyck, not even a star pretending not to be a star. But that ordinariness is gradually destabilised by the cultural resources available for transforming the mundane and imagining an alternative reality. For whilst Laura defines herself by her everyday qualities, the film does not allow us to see her every day; we see her only on Thursdays, her 'Milford days'. These are times marked by her consumption of varieties of modern fantasy – romance fiction from the Boots library, lunch in the orientalist Kardomah restaurant and, most importantly, film. The relationship with her 'lover' – the term can't survive this English context without quotation marks – is shaped by these places of leisure just as surely as Connie Chatterley's is by the woods of Wragby.

The leisure and fantasy experienced alike by Laura and the audiences of *Brief Encounter* provide an escape from the realities of English domestic order, a family economy that we glimpse only in the relatively few scenes when Laura is at home in Ketchworth, a train-ride away. Initially, Milford days are routine avoidances of routine, ritualised escapes into reading, lunching and film-watching controlled by the omnipresent timetables of railway and family. But as her relationship with Alec intensifies and 'real' romance enters her leisure hours, Laura starts to lose track of time, the film fan's greatest thrill and the commuter's greatest fear. Thursdays then become not sanctioned periods of release but, like the cinema that she attends, a space in which Laura can create a different life for herself beyond the restrictions of provincial routine and beyond its securities of role and timetable. Fleeing from a half-hearted attempt to consummate her relationship with Alec, Laura wanders through Milford for three hours, 'but it didn't seem to be any time at all' she remarks (Coward 1999: 65). The film audience is thus reminded of its own guilty implication in Laura's romantic escape, for her experience of the slippage of time is its own, and the dangerous, adulterous pleasures and agonies that she endures are those to be found in the cinema that they both attend.

Laura Jesson, in Laura Mulvey's terms, is a scopophile, a looker whose reflections and refractions of herself are a means of entering other, more interesting worlds of desire (Mulvey 1975). Whether at the dark window of railway carriages, her bedroom mirror or the cinema screen, Laura is always looking and re-making herself. Her English ordinariness is disordered by the fantasies that she creates, from Venetian gondolas to the rendering of Milford after dark as a threatening urban landscape. But *Brief Encounter*, unlike *The Wicked Lady*, never allows such moments the full expression of a cinematic narrative. Provincial England is never allowed to transform itself into the totality of Leslie Arliss's Restoration setting. Instead, *Brief Encounter* is punctuated by alarms, whistles and interruptions which emphasise the process of imagination and spectatorship, as the viewer, like Laura, is removed from its pleasures and returned to everyday reality. Laura's capacity for losing herself, is set in opposition to the codes of English bourgeois womanhood that she also articulates, with their various prescriptions against smoking in public, staying out late and having extramarital sex. In a particularly heightened moment she can conjure an image of a life with Alec that recalls the Parisian flashbacks of *Casablanca* (1942) and any number of other Thursday afternoon romances in the Palladium. But the film must end and the last train must leave for Ketchworth: 'the palm trees changed into those pollarded willows by the canal just before the level crossing', Laura's commentary notes flatly (51).

Such moments suggest Coward and Lean's wry critique of the banality of English spectatorship, the inability of English film to sustain with conviction Hollywood's definitive cinematic narratives of desire. The inadequacy of English performances of the codes of Hollywood melodrama lies at the centre of the film. Lean recalled a mortifying preview in Rochester in which the audience openly mocked its love scenes, laughing at the couple's failure to perform the passion that they talk about so much (Brownlow 1996: 203). It is true that Laura isn't very good at it and Alec, inevitably the initiator, isn't any better. They move together too quickly; they grab and heave, and demonstrate no erotic style. But, then, neither is schooled in touch, democratic or otherwise. Theirs is a performance of physical passion staged in the context of Hollywood films and romantic novels and it necessarily falls short of the mark. The disjunction is uncomfortable and embarrassing, something that seems to have been registered in the Rochester response. Yet the sexual and cultural politics of the film lies precisely in that gap between the passionate intensity of Laura's commentary and the ineptitude and disappointment of the actions that it interprets. At the end of the film Laura and Alec try to re-enact the concluding sacrifices of *Casablanca* but instead have to be polite to Laura's friend Dolly Messiter, and after Alec leaves, Laura tries (and fails) to be Greta Garbo in *Anna Karenina* (1935). Whilst Robert Krasker's cinematography sporadically reproduces the atmosphere of Preminger's *Fallen Angel*, these moments are always in tension with irreducibly English landscapes, voices and bodies that have to return to Ketchworth and Churley. A few years later such discrepancies were to be at the heart of Ealing Studios' national comic style.

For all its knowing pastiche and irony, however, *Brief Encounter* is not an Ealing comedy and the film engages seriously with the process of female spectatorship, the 'desire to desire', as Mary Ann Doane terms it (Doane 1987). The enduring power of the film lies not in its irony but in its irresolution, its indecision about where it stands on contemporary issues of sexuality, femininity and family. The narrative is uneasily located between melodramatic subjectivity (the confessions of Laura in love) and the everyday realism its producers celebrated (Milford, Fred and the children). The discrepancies are comic, or at least embarrassing, but they also point up the social codes of class and gender from which Laura's melodrama is struggling to escape. The least clumsy moment of Alec and Laura's physical relationship is actually their first encounter. Laura is momentarily blinded by a piece of grit, and Alec steps in, removes it and she sees him for the first time. Their touch here is more intimate than at any point in the film because it is legitimised by male professionalism. 'I happen to be a doctor', says Alec self-deprecatingly as he moves towards her and that status enables him to establish an immediate physical contact (Coward 1999: 26). By contrast, his parting touch, seen twice at the beginning and end of the film, is a bizarre, alienated action that marks the restrictions, rather than the opportunities, of middle-class professionalism. Interrupted in their farewell, Alec can only signify his emotion by squeezing Laura's right shoulder with his left hand. Ornately formal, the action encodes an encouragement to emotional resilience and an absolute refusal to risk public disgrace.

Laura's difficult experience of modern English romance is also explored in the film's close attention to gendered social environments. As noted earlier, the 'realism' of the film is disordered by an exclusive concentration on the exceptional day, Thursday. Whilst Laura's commentary attempts to assert the orderliness and stability of her bourgeois lifestyle, the perspective of the Thursdays distorts this, and the audience sees unexpected challenges to the routines of family encouraged in the popular guides to housekeeping of the postwar period (for a particularly gruelling example of these, see Buckner 1951). The implicit gendered order of male professionalism and female domesticity, alluded to in the first meeting with Alec, is reversed in the representation of Laura's home. Fred is always 'in' and Laura is frequently 'out'. His hat, fore-grounded in shots of the hallway, marks his hapless occupation of the domestic space rather than his entry from a male public world – Laura's hats, by contrast, are emphatically on throughout the film. And whilst Fred is dressed for professional male duty – tie and jacket for an evening crossword that significantly locates 'desire' alongside 'delirium' and 'Baluchistan'– he is always housebound because of his wife's persistent Thursdays. Signs of male authority are denied to him. Although Alec declares his profession in his first sentence, Fred's remains unknown. 'Have it your own way', he tells Laura, a good-natured relinquishing of patriarchal role that, like much else in the film, is more radical than it might first appear.

Whilst Fred tries to keep order at home, Laura, like the English wartime women whom she anachronistically resembles, gets about. Set against the 'solid, comfortable-looking house' in Ketchworth is Milford Junction, a liminal area of social crossing that leads to the heaven and hell of her romance (Coward 1999: 12). Set between that opposition is the second private space in the film, the 'service flat' which belongs to the consultant Stephen Lynn. Alec has a set of keys and after an intense struggle with self-doubt Laura goes there on the sixth Thursday, implic-itly to have sex. Stephen's unexpected return leads to Laura's hurried exit down a 'tradesmen's staircase', her distraught wandering through Milford's rain-drenched streets and the ending of the relationship one Thursday later (61). In terms of an otherwise tightly wrought and highly motivated plot, the scene in the flat makes little sense. The building itself, with its lobby and palms and service restaurant, is an anomaly in the otherwise resolutely provincial Milford, and Alec has no reason to have a key when he is seen to return to his family on the other Thursday evenings. But the flat is crucial to the film, not just as the location of a still excruciating scene of sexual failure but also as a site for arguments about postwar English gender, sexuality and power. Like Wragby and Tevershall in *Lady Chatterley's Lover*, Stephen's flat and Laura's house define the social limits from within which new kinds of desire struggle to emerge.

The flat is an ambivalently gendered space. Coward describes it in his script as 'rather a bleak little room' and Lean spoke of it as 'really a hostile place, uncosy, unwelcoming' (Coward 1999: 60; Brownlow 1996: 200). It is also awkwardly set between the privacy of Laura's home and the public space of the railway tearoom. Stephen's ownership, at first understated but embarrassingly evident when he returns, releases a conflicting set of gendered values and judgements. For the first time in the film Alec's social authority is removed – Stephen is both visible property-owner and professional superior – and the fleeing Laura becomes instantly lower-class, forced to use the tradesman's entrance, and immoral, the secret mistress. Stephen, like the flat he lives in, is an oddity in a film apparently committed to provincial ordinariness. Coward describes him as 'a thin rather ascetic-looking man', and Lean notes his 'Puritan countenance' (Coward 1999: 61; Brownlow 1996: 200). Although his judgement – a damningly English expression of 'disappointment' in his friend – effectively ends the affair, the incongruity of the person passing judgement and the space in which it is passed complicate rather than clarify *Brief Encounter*'s treatment of English sexuality.

The scene in the flat, like so much else in the film, is shaped by fantasy. Stephen ironically imagines Alec and Laura's brief encounter by his fireplace as an interview with an 'hysterical' patient. Laura, absent from the action for the only time in the film, later imagines Alec and Stephen's conversation as a knowing meeting of men of the world. Both have their truths – Stephen is the only character in the film to point out the gendered inequality of the affair, Laura's hysteria was later to become a point of Freudian interest in academic discussions of the film, and the scene is the only homosocial encounter in a remarkably heterosexual film. But the flat also embodies the problems of the 'modern age' that Stephen defines and to which Laura's fantasies incline. It is a putatively metropolitan place within provincial England, one that, as its owner sarcastically remarks, 'caters for all tastes' (Coward 1999: 61). But such apparent sophistication disguises older forms of power and judgement. Laura's approach to it finds Robert Krasker relishing his most noirish camerawork as her image is trapped in the ever-deepening grids and bars of the stairway and lift. Film fan that she is, Laura is imagining her journey to sexual fulfilment as *Double Indemnity* not *Casablanca*. This is no enclosure in the Wragby woods that can bring sexual renewal but instead a 'hostile place' that confronts the lovers' desires with English realities.

Brief Encounter is a knowing treatment of the questions of English sexuality and gender at the end of the Second World War developed through transatlantic film genres and styles. If it is never as serious as its protagonist and narrator in its presentation of women's sexual dilemma, it is also not as parodic as some of its ironic strategies might suggest. Laura's construction of her own melodrama, as contemporary reviews and the film's modest commercial success suggest, did speak to the imaginative world of at least a section of the English popular film market. It also offered a more complex gender politics than its more lurid and finally more conservative Gainsborough competitors. For if Stephen suggests the persistent puritanism concealed at the centre of wartime modernity, Laura's journey through the melodrama of romance provides counter-discourses that suggest a rather less stable ideological function. The film's later importance as a gay English text, exploring the tensions and idealisms of covert sexual expression, acknowledges one aspect of this. Another is embedded in its treatment of the English bourgeois family itself.

At the end of the film Laura, traumatised by the break with her 'lover', returns to the family home, its order contrasting with the emotional chaos that she has just narrated. Yet rather than this being a return to a patriarchal frame, peacetime conformity replacing wartime release as it were, Ketchworth is shown to present unlikely possibilities of change in English gender relations. Unlike Stephen, that self-styled representative of the modern age, Fred passes no judgement on her, and his response reminds the audience of the tolerance that he has extended throughout the film. Whereas Laura's fantasy has been projected through a romance with a Mills and Boon doctor who always tells her what to do and think, Fred has maintained a domesticity that abjures all such forms of control. And it is with Fred that the last word lies in this strange, oddly radical view of Englishness. Laura's dream, he suggests, was not a happy one, a critique of the inherently conservative gender politics of the cinema that he never attends and the romances he never reads. Beyond the beguiling but finally normative discourses of heterosexual desire, he is entirely willing to readjust the patriarchal structures of the English nuclear family as he has demonstrated throughout the film. Against the odds of a Rachmaninov soundtrack, the possibilities of postwar relationships are shown to lie not in the modernity of American cinema or between delirium and Baluchistan but within the inexpressive structures of provincial England – which is just where Lawrence located them, of course.

The Romance of Royalty

A photograph of a young Lady Diana Spencer provides another image of English romance. She is shown reading a novel by her step-grand-mother, Barbara Cartland, but there is not just one book in the picture; at least five more are strewn around, all Barbara Cartlands. It is as though Diana is involved in dreamy but intensive research into the genre to which Cartland contributed so amply. Only a few years later Diana was, indeed, involved in a national romance of unprecedented scale, albeit one that ultimately devolved into the cognate genre of gothic horror. Like the image of Laura reading her Boots library book only seconds before the beginning of her brief encounter, the photograph suggests the processes of English romance in action. Diana, like Laura, mastered its codes and styles and applied them to her life and times. But hers was a more ambitious project than Laura's escape from Ketchworth. For whilst it did not countenance the regeneration of England by sex in the style of Connie Chatterley, it did attempt to re-imagine England's political centre, the Crown.

'Monarchy', wrote the Labour politician Richard Crossman, 'is a deeply rooted national myth which canalizes and purges the emotions of a mass democracy exposed to mass media in an irreligious age' (Crossman 1972: 41). Crossman was reflecting on the work of Walter Bagehot, the most celebrated theorist of English monarchy, who a century earlier and with elegant cynicism had laid the ground-rules for English political modernity and the role of monarchy within it. Bagehot argued in *The English Constitution* (1867) that if oligarchic caste rule was to be maintained in England during a period of democratic agitation, a powerful symbolic mediation of that undemocratic political power was needed. This was the role of a monarchy replete with the signs of tradition and continuity but also endlessly adaptable to the changing circumstances of the modernity it apparently denied. 'It is needful to keep the ancient show while we secretly interpolate the new reality', Bagehot noted (Bagehot 1963: 262). This was no Powellesque obeisance to the sanctity of Crown in Parliament, but a shrewd assessment of the need to make English tradition relevantly traditional in order to prevent truly radical political change. 'I found no point of *The English Constitution* more completely truthful to real life today than the chapter on the monarchy', writes Crossman, a former and future Cabinet Minister

(Crossman 1972: 38–9). But, by 1972, what Bagehot termed the 'secret prerogative' of monarchy was in difficulties (Bagehot 1963: 100).

Bagehot's strategy depended upon what he called the 'mystery' of monarchy. 'Above all things', he wrote in a famous passage, 'our royalty is to be reverenced, and if you begin to poke about it you cannot reverence it . . . Its mystery is its life. We must not let in daylight upon magic' (100). This strategic mystification was in tension with changing political conditions, however. Royal Englishness had encountered modernity not by taking the gradually retiring path of its relatives in other European monarchies. Instead, it had projected a boldly contradictory position located within what Judith Williamson has termed 'the structure of a feudal aristocracy and the culture of the capitalist bourgeois and petit-bourgeois' (Williamson 1986: 86). The extravagant panoply of an unreformed monarchical constitution was set over what purported to be a recognisably ordinary domestic unit, the Royal Family. By the late 1960s the demands of petit-bourgeois culture had become unusually evident and royalty came to be represented and to represent itself more as Laura's family in Ketchworth than any aristocratic English imaginary. The BBC's documentary *The Royal Family* (1969) was one response to the demands of secular egalitarianism and a newly influential national media. Bagehot's 'mystery' was risked against performances of ordinariness. It was a gamble that was to reach its reckless extreme nearly twenty years later in *It's a Royal Knockout* (1987). This demeaning game show, produced by the Queen's youngest son, allowed members of the Royal Family to perform an unreflecting parody of aristocratic tradition and privilege in the garish populist context of a 'McDonald's Restaurants Knock a Knight' tournament. As Barbara Windsor remarked, it was 'like filming *Carry on Camping* in *Carry on Henry* costumes' and it consequently defined a moment at which any possibility of mystery seemed to be at an end (Edward 1987: 121).

Such performances, oddly like Bagehot's own ironic patrician stance, underestimated the visceral power of royalty in the popular constitution of English identity. As Tom Nairn argues, the 'glamour of backwardness' that it represented was no kitsch relic but a political force at the heart of the English problem of 'permanent [national] immaturity' (Nairn 1988: 137). Against the political odds and beyond the sophistication of Bagehot's theory, monarchy still worked as a significant, irrational social agency. Mass-Observation's anthropological project developed from just this perception when its founders witnessed popular responses to Edward VIII's abdication in 1936. Charles Madge and Tom Harrisson surmised that people 'marvelled at the open emergence of forces so powerful, and realised as never before the sway of superstition in the midst of science' (Madge and Harrisson 1937: 10). The same could have been written nearly seventy years later in the aftermath of the death of Diana, Princess of Wales. That 'potent mixture of popular culture and undogmatic religiosity' as Anthony O'Hear called it, was proof that Diana of all her generation of royals had understood how Bagehot's 'secret power' could be maintained at the end of the twentieth century (O'Hear 1998: 190). Her strategy was one of romance.

Diana's revision of *The English Constitution* applied the lessons of her early study of Barbara Cartland's fiction and her later mastery of the semiotics of *Vogue, Tatler, Hello!* and a newly virulent English tabloid press. Like Laura Jesson, though, she both constructed herself and was constructed by the narratives and discourses of this popular culture. Her courtship by the heir to the throne was cast as a fairy-tale romance – 'the first Queen-to-be to go to an ordinary school', as one contemporary account had it, stretching the concept of ordinariness to its limits (Craven 1982: 39). The 'crowded' marriage that followed became in multiple retellings a royal *Rebecca*, with its ingénue heroine intimidated by the presence of erotic ghosts and crippled by social naivety. Courtiers 'hung on my every word . . . only I had none', Diana recalled of an early visit to Balmoral, telling her biographer in true Daphne du Maurier style that on her honeymoon she 'dreamt of Camilla the whole time' (Skinner and Hussein 1998: 87; Morton 1997: 43). Her post-divorce emotional career resorted to other narratives drawn from Cartland and Mills and Boon. Army officers, sports stars, charismatic surgeons and playboys constituted the full range of the masculine stereotypes of English romance and their narratives were eagerly consumed by readers of the popular press. Such feminised narratives, whatever their accuracy or implication, established Diana as a royal at odds with the stodgy compromises of royal pageantry and bourgeois family life visible elsewhere. But it was in her mastery of image within these narratives that her real political power lay. Diana came to realise that in an age of digital technology, mass circulation press, populist television and an expanding culture of the celebrity, Bagehot's secret power was to be maintained not through absence or populist compromise, but by relentless, managed presence and style. Excess of Diana did not make her more knowable. Quite the reverse. It made her more mysterious, as cultural theorists found to their profit after her death.

Diana entered the world of English signification when she was nineteen and at the beginning of her ill-fated royal relationship. Famously, she was photographed posing with children outside the 'Young England' kindergarten where she was then employed. 'She was not to foresee the mistake of not wearing a slip under her skirt that day', comments

Debrett's Illustrated Fashion Guide archly, 'quite unaware that her long shapely legs were clearly visible through the flimsy, and by now transparent, skirt' (Fincher and Fincher 1989: 6). It was a very English gaffe which established a paradox that a mature Diana would come to exploit. The performance was designed, if it was designed at all, to suggest innocence, caring and an interest in future royal child-bearing. This in turn was offset by heart-shaped patterns on her dress, symbols of virginal romance and an early indication of her desire to play the 'queen of hearts' as she was to put it later. The absence of the slip, though, inserted a sexuality that was otherwise absent in the moment and, indeed, in the whole public performance of her royal relationship. Such a confused representation of romance was quite quickly to become an assured and innovative command of royal iconography.

The subsequent history of Diana, Jude Davies argues, presented a 'narrative of . . . liberation from containment in symbolic forms (model wife, national mother, princess)' (Davies 2001: 25). It was a recasting of royalty away from state function and bourgeois family, the two strategic roles of twentieth-century monarchy. The most memorable photographs of Diana were those that were uncertainly poised between formality and informality; evidently performing a public function, her body was shown to be transgressing conventions of royal behaviour. The 'Young England' mistake became strategy as Diana brought the sexuality of contemporary fashion to previously conservative dress codes and made calculated introductions of informality and personal confession into formerly rigid protocols. Ben Pimlott notes her restoration of touch as a royal prerogative, particularly in her work with AIDS patients, and such contrasting images as those of the lovelorn wife in front of the Taj Mahal and the stylish marital escapee at the Serpentine Gallery were unprecedented combinations of state function and personal narrative (Pimlott 1996: 644).

Diana's revision of Bagehot's theory of monarchy made her, in Jude Davies's term, a 'multivalent sign' (Davies 2001: 36). Instead of representing a continuity of English tradition that disguised political change, Diana was perceived as embodying that change. After her death Julie Burchill characterised her as a 'true Utopian', Beatrix Campbell argued that she undermined 'the patriarchal foundations of the monarchy' and Mica Nava imagined a Queen Diana inaugurating a postcolonial nation 'where sexual desire and intermarriage produce a new generation of racially indeterminate Britons' (Burchill 1998: 142; Campbell 1998: 7; Nava 1999: 116). An academic study was subtitled 'The Making of a Media Saint' (Richards et al. 1999). Ten years later the extravagance of these assessments has itself become a point of historical and cultural interest, suggesting that her shoe designer, Manolo Blahnik, made the shrewdest assessment of her political and cultural legacy when he remarked, 'I do miss her image continually' (Coward 2004: 266).

Diana's strategy of political obfuscation was in the end entirely consistent with that laid out by Bagehot in the 1860s and in retrospect it was the rest of the family that had failed to respond appropriately to the demands of the times. Her various romance narratives were always defined by social mores that offered no possibility of political change – no Connie Chatterley she – but only lessons in adaptation. That cultural commentators of Englishness could think otherwise and, in the aftermath of her death, argue that Diana's life was a fable of oppression, resistance and innovation was proof not of the fallibility of second-wave feminism but of the persistent power and adaptability of the Crown in England. Her struggle for the maintenance of the title HRH after her divorce suggests that Diana was also aware of this. She recognised that however close her strategy appeared to be to that of contemporary celebrity culture, her charisma was absolutely defined by her implication in what Nairn calls 'Royalty-fetishism' (Nairn 1988: 157). Politically she was, at most, interested in an adjustment of the charitable focus and casual racism of an English social elite – in itself no mean ambition, of course. However, her radicalism lay only in the understanding of the means by which royal iconography could be modernised in the 1990s. Her refusal to wear gloves, her hugging and touching, her couture, but especially her understanding of cameras made Diana's career the only significant twentieth-century appendix to *The English Constitution*'s treatment of monarchy.

Diana's political insight has been confirmed rather than contradicted by the remarkable fading of her national significance in the decade since her death. The removal of her body to a sepulchre on an island in the grounds of her family's seat in Althorp, Northamptonshire was represented at the time as the final stage of a romance narrative. She became a Tennysonian princess returning to ancestral English ground in the 'Rose of the Shires' and away from the betrayals of an un-English court, as Earl Spencer implied in his funeral address. Such a narrative was inevitably bounded. As Diana knew well, postmodern royalty depended upon the reproduction of imagery and the development of narrative. Monumental stability, as Althorp's current website with its dry account of the male line of aristocratic history confirms, revealed only the reactionary politics behind the mysteries of the 'ancient show' and modern romance alike, and that was something that Diana – and Bagehot – would not have advised.

Connie, Laura and Diana suggest the ways in which Englishness has never completely represented that 'distinctly homosocial form of male bonding' argued by Andrew Parker and his fellow editors of *Nationalisms and Sexualities* (1992) to be favoured by classical nationalist histories (Parker et al. 1992: 6). Whilst all three were variously shaped by masculine discourses of nationhood, each demonstrated the ways in which Englishness is both defined and challenged by gender. The national crisis depicted in *Lady Chatterley's Lover* is expressed and potentially solved by a relationship that is itself shaped by the geography and culture of conflicting tradition and modernity. The changes brought about in women's roles in the Second World War are central to *Brief Encounter* and other films of the later period of the war. Whilst again they are represented through the conventions of heterosexual romance, the film also examines the terms of that romance and its implication in contemporary popular culture. Laura's identity as an English consumer allows an ambivalent critique of the gendered relationships of family and film, as well as a distinctive contrast to Hollywood conventions of the period. Diana's revision of late twentieth-century royal iconography was similarly ambivalent. Whilst she remained trapped in romance narrative conventions, her construction of new versions of royal performance suggested a sense of the peculiar force of monarchy in English life and the need for a changing means of representation to maintain its conservative political reality.

Conclusion

That a book about English popular culture ends by the tomb of a princess on an artificial island in the grounds of a South Midlands stately home might seem to confirm that, at the end of the twentieth century, Englishness still occupied traditional ground defined by archaic hierarchies of social station and myths of rural settlement. The case of England ten years later is no less contradictory, with plenty of evidence for a persistent popular interest in the question of nationhood, but a banal range of resources to satisfy that interest. Studying Englishness can still be quite embarrassing. This is, in part at least, a result of the way in which the English question continues to be framed. Ever since the time of Cecil Sharp, the 'revival' of England has been couched in terms of nationalism, reconstruction and recovery, all cultural and political processes that England had previously and notably avoided. Instead of inventing its own nation, as the rules of nationalism demand, England had invented entirely different national and colonial structures to stand in for it. One of the reasons that the St George flag will always be tainted with its association with the Far Right is that it never had any previous existence as a popular collective symbol. The English were quite content to be British and allow the national question to slide between those two slippery near-synonyms.

The half-heartedness of English nationalism, a result of a political centre putting its nationalising energies elsewhere, is evident in the struggles of the revivalist movements of the Edwardian period. Quirky, individualistic and improvised organisations took the place of state-sponsored initiatives, and the notable struggles with gender and class that characterised their development suggest the divergence of English traditions from populist nation-formation on the one hand and masculinist militarism on the other. The organisations of Sharp, Neal and Baden-Powell struggled to articulate a coherent national identity in the face of the social and cultural divisions that their initiatives highlighted rather than resolved. The absent centre that Tom Nairn and Perry Anderson define was not just an intellectual and political one; it represented itself in the cultural practices of Englishness. The failure to be revolutionary in 1968 was linked to the eloquently ambivalent politics of George Orwell, to the contradictory land politics of H. J. Massingham and even to Douglas Jardine's stern policy with Australian crowds. The fascination with the rural, the hidden and the revelatory moment discussed in Chapter 4 was an expression of that entrapment, and the most challenging exponents of the genre – Edward Thomas, C. E. Montague, Powell and Pressburger – recognised that.

Where popular Englishness did take on an ostentatiously modern aspect – in late nineteenth-century Blackpool, for example, or in the mass culture of turn-of-the-century music hall – that modernity was combined with a re-statement of traditional forms of experience. The glamour of Blackpool Tower and the innovative civic amenities of leisure were dependent upon the traditional disciplines of the wakes week, a connection that the town's greatest comedian, Frank Randle, emphasised in his idiosyncratic performances of local resilience. Likewise, the great achievement of the relatively brief period of the classic music hall was its development of a discursive critique of the modernity that it embodied. Bateman's costers, lost in the new city but still attentive to the demands of community and custom, performed comic negotiations between the urban past and present. These contradictions were to have wider and more directly political manifestations. In an irony that Perry Anderson could not have anticipated in 1968, the most significant challenge to the English state in the second half of the century came not from a mature Marxism on the continental model but from the localised struggles of the 1984–5 Miners' Strike which had heritage as their central imperative.

The inward turn, marked officially by the South Bank Exhibition of 1951, was also a turning away from structures of identity that were potentially far more radical in their implications than the half-hearted nationalism that replaced them. Even when Stanley Baldwin made his secret confession of Englishness in the security of the Royal Society of St George, he did so with implicit recognition of the necessary strategic performances of other identities elsewhere. English imperialism had developed a transnational network of cultures that ultimately displaced dominant metaphors of centre and periphery. The idea of an English imperial hub, as C. L. R. James quickly realised on his arrival in England in the 1930s, was illusory. He developed theoretically what Marcus Garvey already knew from experience: that English expansion had created diasporic systems of connection that could be used not just to maintain the iniquities of the imperial project, but to transform them. That transformation necessarily included England as one point on the circuits of Europe, the Caribbean, North America and Africa that Garvey, James and later postcolonialists travelled – literally and figuratively.

The rapid and bloody abandonment of imperial and colonial possessions after 1947 led to a deliberated forgetting of their legacy that became central to the effectiveness of Enoch Powell's populist nationalism in the 1960s. A logical social and economic consequence of imperialism came to be classified pejoratively as 'immigration'; questions of postcolonial identity were translated into questions of race; and the particular historical formations of migration were simplified by largely irrelevant comparisons to North American political ethnography. These were displacements that denied the fact that the ideology as well as the economy of empire were ramified throughout the experience of Englishness no matter how stringently it came to be denied – and the brutal depth of the denial was clearly evident from Notting Hill in 1958 onwards. The forgetting of empire was also a forgetting of the structures, if not the politics, that offered the means of transforming Englishness from unachievable nationalism to an identity that could engage with different problems and possibilities raised by its transnational past.

The possibility of experiencing Englishness as a meeting point of the global histories that its strategies of expansion had initiated came to be expressed in various postcolonial politics. C. L. R. James's insistence on the necessary and transformative political and cultural dialogue of colonised and coloniser was one such, while Stuart Hall and Paul Gilroy's projection of a convivial cultural diversity against the pernicious amnesia – and anaemia – of the dominant English experience of postcolonialism was another. Englishness could be redeemed from insularity by a transformation of historical instincts of expansion and global interest from economic exploitation to cultural recognition.

The problem with such models, however, was the exclusiveness of their application to contemporary English experience. By developing a theory of conviviality that centres upon London, postcolonialism reinforced old metropolitan hierarchies that might have different meanings in, say, Darlington, Burnley or Leamington Spa from those in Walthamstow, Hammersmith or Hackney. The case of Randolph Turpin suggested the ways in which the black Atlantic circuits foundered on a provincial Englishness that proved difficult to include in the emergent politics of London, the Caribbean and Harlem. Turpin's liberation and destruction were entailed by his journey to America as a black world champion boxer and his return to Warwickshire as a provincial Englishman. The intractability of local English experience was not just a condition of Turpin's exceptional experience but part of a wider question of national cultural geography.

Turpin's history is one early argument for the model of English conviviality to be extended to include regional England as well as the metropolis. The construction of Englishness over a century has remained dependent upon a model of metropolitan hegemony albeit one extended to the rural South and West wherein reciprocal relationships and codes of identity were established. But the England beyond that reciprocity fared unequally. The characterisation of 'the North' as an English other, a trope that defined both George Orwell's and Mass-Observation's domestic anthropology, disguised its real place in English modernity. As Frank Randle's decrepit hiker declared in resolutely vulgar fashion, the northern industrial body *was* English modernity, just as his Blackpool was a unique social formation of English mass culture. Gracie Fields represented another version of this modernity. The most significant negotiator of mid-century transatlantic challenges to English popular song and performance, she depended upon specifically northern discourses of community and labour to mount that defence. Her career and Randle's less accommodating cultural practice suggest that there was need for the displacement of the exceptional South East as a normative model for English identity just as England itself displaced from being an imperial hub to being a component of postcolonial transatlantic circuits. Such domestic reconfiguration of cultural geography has proved just as hard to achieve, however.

The revision of Englishness, as D. H. Lawrence's late work suggests, does depend upon a radical examination of the histories of region and its relationship with the cultural, economic and political capital. The struggles of land, class, voice and sexuality that the *Lady Chatterley* novels explore are sketches of this process and affirmations of the need to recognise that the potential for change is not exclusively metropolitan – or even metropolitan at all. Lawrence's return to the East Midlands renders it a meeting place for unresolved historical forces and the source for a re-articulation of nationhood drawn from the encounter of modernity and tradition that the 'secret place' in the East Midlands allows. The twentieth-century history of regionalism, by contrast, has been one of political attenuation and distortion. The change from the civic radicalism and internationalism of the late nineteenth-century West Midlands into the barren racialised political landscape of Enoch Powell and Peter Griffiths in the 1960s is one striking example of this. The recognition of the particular social and cultural energies of a federal England remains a necessary accompaniment to the transnational re-imaginings of the old imperial centre even if the means for achieving it are currently difficult to conceive.

England, then, remains in search of itself as a nation and that search has been an integral part of its culture and politics for over a century. The secret truth that there was nothing to be found remains a secret despite the Millennium Experience's extravagant attempts to reveal it. But the stories that have been told in the preceding chapters suggest some of the ways in which England makes meanings outside of established patterns of nationalism and through its engagements with the most difficult and most productive consequences of its imperial history and expressions of its regional tradition and modernity. It is in those networks of difference and diversity that England and its Englishness can best be understood and developed.

Bibliography

Abbott, John (1952), *The Story of Francis, Day & Hunter*, London: Francis, Day & Hunter.

Adeney, Martin and John Lloyd (1986), *The Miners' Strike 1984–5: Loss Without Limit*, London: Routledge & Kegan Paul.

Allen, Vic (1981), *The Militancy of British Miners*, Shipley: The Moor Press.

Anderson, Benedict (1983), *Imagined Communities: Reflections on the Origin and Spread of Nationalism*, London: Verso.

Anderson, M. D. (1940), *Design for a Journey*, Cambridge: Cambridge University Press.

Anderson, Perry (1968), 'Components of the National Culture', *New Left Review* 50, 3–57.

Appleyard, Bryan (1989), *The Pleasures of Peace: Art and Imagination in Post-War Britain*, London and Boston: Faber.

Archetti, Eduardo P. (2001), 'The Spectacle of a Heroic Life: The Case of Diego Maradona', in David L. Andrews and Steven J. Jackson (eds), *Sport Stars: The Cultural Politics of Sporting Celebrity*, London and New York: Routledge, 151–63.

Ashley, Peter (2006), *Unmitigated England: A Country Lost and Found*, London: Adelphi.

Back, Les, Tim Crabbe and John Solomos (2001), *The Changing Face of Football: Racism, Identity and Multiculture in the English Game*, Oxford and New York: Berg.

Baden-Powell, Agnes (1911), *The Handbook for Girl Guides or How Girls Can Help Build up the Empire*, London: Thomas Nelson.

Baden-Powell, Robert (2004), *Scouting for Boys: A Handbook for Instruction in Good Citizenship*, ed. Elleke Boehmer, Oxford: Oxford University Press.

— [Lord Baden-Powell of Gilwell] (1933), *Lessons from the Varsity of Life*, London: C. Arthur Pearson.

— (1908), *Scouting for Boys: A Handbook for Instruction in Good Citizenship*, London: Horace Cox.

Bagehot, Walter [1867] (1963), *The English Constitution*, London: Fontana.

Baldwin, Stanley (1926), *On England and Other Addresses*, London: Philip Allan.

Banton, Michael (1955), *The Coloured Quarter: Negro Immigrants in an English City*, London: Jonathan Cape.

Barber, Ethel C. (1934), *The 'Guide' Handbook of Elocution*, Birmingham: Davis & Moughton.

Batsford, Harry (1940), *How to See the Country*, London: B. T. Batsford.

The Battle of Orgreave (2006), dir. Mike Figgis, Artangel Media and Channel 4.

Baucom, Ian (1999), *Out of Place: Englishness, Empire, and the Locations of Identity*, Princeton, NJ: Princeton University Press.

B.B.C. Handbook 1928, London: BBC.

Beaton, Cecil and Kenneth Tynan (1953), *Persona Grata*, London: Allan Wingate.

Belloc, Hilaire [1903] (1910), *The Old Road*, new edn, London: Constable.

Bennett, Tony (1986), 'Hegemony, Ideology, Pleasure: Blackpool', in Tony Bennett, Colin Mercer and Janet Woollacott (eds), *Popular Culture and Social Relations*, Milton Keynes and Philadelphia: Open University Press, 135–54.

Benyon, Huw (ed.) (1985), *Digging Deeper: Issues in the Miners' Strike*, London: Verso.

Birtley, Jack (1975), *The Tragedy of Randolph Turpin*, London: New English Library.

Blair, Tony (2004), *Tony Blair in His Own Words*, ed. Paul Richards, London: Politico's.

Blatchford, Robert [Nunquam] [1893] (1976), *Merrie England*, London: Journeyman Press.

Blyton, W. J. (1937), *English Cavalcade*, London: John Murray.

Board of Education (1925), *General Report on the Teaching of English in London Elementary Schools*, London: HMSO.

— (1921), *The Teaching of English in England*, London: HMSO.

Bowler, Dave (1998), *'Winning Isn't Everything . . .': A Biography of Sir Alf Ramsey*, London: Victor Gollancz.

Boyes, Georgina (1993), *The Imagined Village: Culture, Ideology and the English Folk Revival*, Manchester and New York: Manchester University Press.

Bragg, Billy (2006), *The Progressive Patriot: A Search for Belonging*, London: Bantam Press.

Breen, Max (1934), 'Gracie Fields Wants to Do Nowt', *Film Pictorial*, 3 February, 8, 25.

Briggs, Asa (1965), *The History of Broadcasting in the United Kingdom, Vol. 2: The Golden Age of Wireless*, London: Oxford University Press.

— (1961), *The History of Broadcasting in the United Kingdom, Vol. 1: The Birth of Broadcasting*, London: Oxford University Press.

Brown, Gordon (2006), 'The Future of Britishness', http://fabians.org.uk/speeches/the-future-of-britishness.

Brownlow, Kevin (1996), *David Lean*, London: Richard Cohen Books.

Bryan, H. S. (1936), *Troublesome Boy*, London: C. A. Pearson.

Bryson, Bill (1995), *Notes from a Small Island*, London: Doubleday.

Buckner, Rose (1951), *Rose Buckner's Book of Homemaking*, London: Odhams Press.

Burchill, Julie (1998), *Diana*, London: Weidenfeld & Nicolson.

Bushaway, Bob (1981), *By Rite: Custom, Ceremony and Community in England 1700–1880*, London: Junction Books.

Calder, Angus (1991), *The Myth of the Blitz*, London: Jonathan Cape.

Calder, Angus and Dorothy Sheridan (eds) (1984), *Speak for Yourself: A Mass-Observation Anthology, 1937–49*, London: Jonathan Cape.

Campbell, Beatrix (1998), *Diana Princess of Wales: How Sexual Politics Shook the Monarchy*, London: Women's Press.

— (1984), *Wigan Pier Revisited: Politics and Poverty in the Eighties*, London: Virago.

Chidell, E. F. [Viator] (1903), *Africa and National Regeneration*, London: Simpkin, Marshall.

Clarke, John Henrik (ed.) (1974), *Marcus Garvey and the Vision of Africa*, New York: Vintage Books.

Clifford, Sue (2006), *England in Particular: A Celebration of the Commonplace, the Local, the Vernacular, and the Distinctive*, London: Hodder & Stoughton.

Colley, Linda (1992), *Britons: Forging the Nation, 1707–1837*, New Haven, CT: Yale University Press.

Collis, Henry, Fred Hurrill and Rex Hazlewood (1961), *B-P's Scouts: An Official History of The Boy Scouts Association*, London: Collins.

Colls, Robert (2002), *Identity of England*, Oxford: Oxford University Press.

Colls, Robert and Philip Dodd (eds) (1986), *Englishness: Politics and Culture 1880–1920*, Beckenham: Croom Helm.

Colls, Robert and Bill Lancaster (eds) (1994), *Geordies: Roots of Regionalism*, Edinburgh: Edinburgh University Press.

Conekin, Becky E. (2003), *'The Autobiography of a Nation': The 1951 Festival of Britain*, Manchester and New York: Manchester University Press.

Correia, Alice (2006), 'Interpreting Jeremy Deller's *The Battle of Orgreave*', *Visual Culture in Britain* 7.2, 93–112.

Coward, Noël (1999), *Brief Encounter*, London: Faber.

Coward, Rosalind (2004), *Diana: The Portrait*, London: HarperCollins.

Cox, Ian (1951), *The South Bank Exhibition: A Guide to the Story It Tells*, London: HMSO.

Craven, John (1982), *Charles and Diana*, London: Sparrow Books.

Crick, Michael (1985a), *Scargill and the Miners*, 2nd edn, Harmondsworth: Penguin Books.

— (1985b), 'Reporting the Strike', *Granta* 15, 243–50.

Critcher, Chas (1979), 'Football Since the War', in John Clarke, Chas Critcher and Richard Johnson (eds), *Working-Class Culture: Studies in History and Theory*, London: Hutchinson, 161–84.

Croft, Andy (1990), *Red Letter Days: British Fiction in the 1930s*, London: Lawrence & Wishart.

Croft, W. D. (1927), 'Fifteen Years' Progress', *English Folk-Dance Society's Journal* 2nd series 1, 3–16.

Crossman, Richard (1972), *Inside View: Three Lectures on Prime Ministerial Government*, London: Jonathan Cape.

Davies, Jude (2001), *Diana, A Cultural History: Gender, Race, Nation and the People's Princess*, London: Palgrave Macmillan.

Davies, Pete (1990), *All Played Out: The Full Story of Italia '90*, London: Heinemann.

Deller, Jeremy (2002), *The English Civil War Part II: Personal Accounts of the 1984–85 Miners' Strike*, np: Artangel.

Derriman, Philip (1984), *Bodyline*, Sydney: Collins/Sydney Morning Herald.

Dilke, Sir Charles (1890), *Problems of Greater Britain*, vol. 2, London and New York: Macmillan.

Doane, Mary Ann (1987), *The Desire to Desire: The Woman's Film of the 1940s*, Basingstoke: Macmillan.

Donoughue, Bernard and G. W. Jones [1973] (2001), *Herbert Morrison: Portrait of a Politician*, London: Phoenix Press.

Douglas, Christopher (1984), *Douglas Jardine: Spartan Cricketer*, London: George Allen & Unwin.

Douglass, Dave (2002), 'Scargillism and the Miners', *Weekly Worker* 456, 4–6, http://www.cpgb.org.uk/worker/454/scargillism.

Doyle, Brian (1989), *England and Englishness*, London: Routledge.

Dyer, Richard (1993), *Brief Encounter*, London: BFI Publishing.

— (1979), *Stars*, London: BFI Publishing.

Easthope, Anthony (1999), *Englishness and National Culture*, London: Routledge.

Edward, HRH The Prince (ed.) (1987), *Knockout: The Grand Charity Tournament: A Behind-the-Scenes Look at the Event of the Year*, London: Collins.

Elton, Oliver (1929), *C. E. Montague: A Memoir*, London: Chatto & Windus.

Emil-Behnke, Kate (1937), *The Technique of Good Speech*, London: J. Curwen.

— (1930), *Speech and Movement on the Stage*, London: Oxford University Press.

The Emperor of Lancashire, BBC Radio 4, broadcast 24 September 1989.

Epstein, Brian (1965), *A Cellarful of Noise*, London: Four Square.

Fea, Allan (1913), *Quiet Roads and Sleepy Villages*, London: Eveleigh Nash.

Ferrier, Bob (1960), *Soccer Partnership: Billy Wright and Walter Winterbottom*, London: Heinemann.

The Festival of Britain 1951 (1951), London: HMSO.

Fields, Gracie (nd), *Gracie Fields – Stage and Screen*, The World Record Club, SH 170.

Fincher, Jayne and Terry Fincher (1989), *Debrett's Illustrated Fashion Guide: The Princess of Wales*, London: Webb & Bower/Michael Joseph.

Foot, Paul (1969), *The Rise of Enoch Powell: An Examination of Enoch Powell's Attitude to Immigration and Race*, London: Cornmarket Press.

Fox, Kate (2004), *Watching the English: The Hidden Rules of English Behaviour*, London: Hodder & Stoughton.

Fox Strangways, A. H. and Maud Karpeles (1955), *Cecil Sharp*, 2nd edn, London: Geoffrey Cumberlege and Oxford University Press.

Frayn, Michael (1963), 'Festival', in Michael Sissons and Philip French (eds), *Age of Austerity*, London: Hodder & Stoughton, 319–38.

Frith, Simon (1996), *Performing Rites: On the Value of Popular Music*, Oxford: Oxford University Press.

Frost, Frank (1951), 'At the Pleasure Gardens', *Britain Today* 184, 12–15.

Fussell, Paul (1976), *The Great War and Modern Memory*, London, Oxford and New York: Oxford University Press.

Gascoigne, Paul (2006), *Being Gazza: My Journey to Hell and Back*, with John McKeown and Hunter Davies, London: Headline.

Gate, E. M. (ed.) (1933), *Roland Phipps: Boy Scout*, 2nd edn, London: Roland House.

Geller, Deborah (2000), *The Brian Epstein Story*, ed. Anthony Wall, London and Boston: Faber.

Gibbs-Smith, C. H. (1950), *The Great Exhibition of 1851: A Commemorative Album*, London: HMSO.

Giddens, Anthony (1990), 'Gazza's Goal Slump', *Times Higher Educational Supplement* 21 December, 11.

Gill, A. A. (2005), *The Angry Island: Hunting the English*, London: Weidenfeld & Nicolson.

Gilroy, Paul (2006), 'Multiculture in Times of War: An Inaugural Lecture Given at the London School of Economics', *Critical Quarterly* 48.4, 27–45.

— (2004), *After Empire: Melancholia or Convivial Culture?* Abingdon: Routledge.

— (1987), *'There Ain't No Black in the Union Jack': The Cultural Politics of Race and Nation*, London: Hutchinson.

Glanville, Brian (1999), *Footballers Don't Cry: Selected Writings*, London: Virgin.

— (1997), *The Story of the World Cup*, revised edn, London: Faber.

Glass, Ruth (1960), *Newcomers: The West Indians in London*, London: Centre for Urban Studies and George Allen & Unwin.

Gledhill, Christine and Gillian Swanson (eds) (1996), *Nationalising Femininity: Culture, Sexuality and British Cinema in the Second World War*, Manchester and New York: Manchester University Press.

Golding, Florence (1914), 'What Shall We Wear?', *English Folk-Dance Society's Journal* 1.1, 14–15.

Grainger, Heidi and Grant Fitzner (2006), *Fair Treatment at Work Survey 2005: Executive Summary*, Employment Relations Research Series No. 63, London: Department of Trade and Industry.

Grant, Bob (1999), 'When Punch Met Merry', *Folk Music Journal* 7.5, 644–55.

Green, Geoffrey (1992), 'Match of the Century I', in Ian Hamilton (ed.), *The Faber Book of Soccer*, London and Boston: Faber, 65–8.

Greenwood, Ron (1984), *Yours Sincerely*, with Bryon Butler, London: Willow Books.

Griffin, Nick (2007), 'Building Nationalist Strongholds', *Identity* 81, 4–7.

— (2002a), 'Can You Afford to Wait Any Longer?', *Identity* 22, 4–7.

— (2002b), 'Moving Forward for Good', *Identity* 21, 4–7.

Guilianotti, Richard and Michael Gerrard (2001), 'Evil Genie or Pure Genius? The (Im)Moral Football and Public Career of Paul "Gazza" Gascoigne', in David L. Andrews and Steven J. Jackson (eds), *Sport Stars: The Cultural Politics of Sporting Celebrity*, London and New York: Routledge, 124–37.

Hall, Stuart (1999–2000), 'Whose Heritage? Un-Settling "The Heritage", Re-Imagining the Post-nation', *Third Text* 49, 3–13.

— (1978), 'Racism and Reaction', in *Five Views of Multi-Racial Britain*, London: Commission for Racial Equality, 23–35.

Hamilton, Ian (1998), *Gazza Agonistes*, London: Bloomsbury.

Handler, Andrew (1994), *From Goals to Guns: The Golden Age of Soccer in Hungary 1950–56*, Boulder, CO and New York: East European Monographs and Columbia University Press.

Harrison, Tony (1987), *Selected Poems*, 2nd edn, London: Penguin Books.

Harrisson, Tom (1938), 'Whistle While You Work', *New Writing* new series, 1, 47–67.

Hartley, Dorothy (1935), *The Countryman's England*, London: B. T. Batsford.

Haynes, Richard (1995), *The Football Imagination: The Rise of Football Fanzine Culture*, Aldershot: Arena.

Heffer, Simon (2007), 'How Right Does Enoch Have to Be Before the Tories Will Say So?', *Daily Telegraph* 7 November, 24.

— (1999), *Nor Shall My Sword: The Reinvention of England*, London: Weidenfeld & Nicolson.

— (1998), *Like the Roman: The Life of Enoch Powell*, London: Weidenfeld & Nicolson.

Heimann, Judith M. (1997), *The Most Offending Soul Alive: Tom Harrisson and His Remarkable Life*, Honolulu: University of Hawai'i Press.

Henderson, Eugene (1957), *Box On*, London: Stanley Paul.

Henderson, Hamish (1992), *Alias MacAlias: Writings on Songs, Folk and Literature*, Edinburgh: Polygon.

Heseltine, Michael (2000), *Life in the Jungle: My Autobiography*, London: Hodder & Stoughton.

Hewison, Robert (1987), *The Heritage Industry: Britain in a Climate of Decline*, London: Methuen.

— (2001), 'Cultural Policy', in Anthony Seldon (ed.), *The Blair Effect: The Blair Government 1997–2001*, London: Little, Brown, 535–53.

Higson, Andrew (1995), *Waving the Flag: Constructing a National Cinema in Britain*, Oxford: Clarendon Press.

Hill, Robert A. (ed.) (1983), *The Marcus Garvey and Universal Negro Improvement Association Papers: Volume 1 1826–August 1919*, Berkeley, CA: University of California Press.

Hilton, Jack (1940), *English Ways: A Walk from the Pennines to Epsom Downs in 1939*, London: Jonathan Cape.

Hissey, James John (1917), *The Road and the Inn*, London: Macmillan.

Hitchens, Christopher (2002), *Orwell's Victory*, London: Allen Lane/The Penguin Press.

Hobsbawm, Eric and Terence Ranger (eds) (1983), *The Invention of Tradition*, Cambridge: Cambridge University Press.

Hoggart, Richard [1965] (1974), 'Introduction to *The Road to Wigan Pier*', in Raymond Williams (ed.), *George Orwell: A Collection of Critical Essays*, Englewood Cliffs, NJ: Prentice-Hall, 34–51.

Holt, Richard (1989), *Sport and the British: A Modern History*, Oxford: Clarendon Press.

Honey, John (1989), *Does Accent Matter? The Pygmalion Factor*, London: Faber.

Hopcraft, Arthur (1968), *The Football Man: People and Passions in Soccer*, London: Collins.

Hopkins, Harry (1963), *The New Look: A Social History of the Forties and Fifties in Britain*, London: Secker & Warburg.

Hornby, Nick (1992), *Fever Pitch*, London: Victor Gollancz.

Howard, James (1996), *Michael Powell*, London: B. T. Batsford.

Howat, Gerald (1987), *Plum Warner*, London: Unwin Hyman.

Hughes, M. V. (1927), *About England*, London and Toronto: J. M. Dent.

Irwin, Colin (2005), *In Search of Albion*, London: André Deutsch.

Jackson, Brian and Dennis Marsden [1962] (1966), *Education and the Working Class*, Harmondsworth: Penguin.

James, C. L. R. (2003), *Letters from London*, ed. Nicholas Laughlin, Oxford and Port of Spain: Signal Books and Prospect Press.

— (1984), *C. L. R. James's 80th Birthday Lectures*, ed. Margaret Busby and Darcus Howe, London: Race Today.

— (1963), *Beyond a Boundary*, London: Stanley Paul.

— (1938), *Black Jacobins: Toussaint Louverture and the San Domingo Revolution*, London: Secker & Warburg.

Jardine, Douglas [1933] (1984), *In Quest of the Ashes*, London: Orbis.

— (1936), *Cricket: How to Succeed*, London: Evans Bros.

Joad, C. E. M. (1934), *A Charter for Ramblers or The Future of the Countryside*, London: Hutchinson.

Jones, Daniel (1914), *The Pronunciation of English*, 2nd edn, Cambridge: Cambridge University Press.

Joyce, Patrick (1991), *Visions of the People: Industrial England and the Question of Class, 1848–1914*, Cambridge: Cambridge University Press.

Judge, Roy (1989), 'Mary Neal and the Espérance Morris', *Folk Music Journal* 5.5, 545–91.

Karpeles, Maud (1967), *Cecil Sharp: His Life and Work*, London: Routledge & Kegan Paul.

Kerr, Rose (1932), *The Story of the Girl Guides*, London: Girl Guides Association.

Kidson, Frank and Mary Neal [1915] (1972), *English Folk-Song and Dance*, Wakefield: E P Publishing.

King, Anthony (1998), *The End of the Terraces: The Transformation of English Football in the 1990s*, London and New York: Leicester University Press.

Kirby, John (1993), *The Festival of Britain: A List of Information Sources*, Sheffield: PAVIC Publications.

Kumar, Krishan (2003), *The Making of English National Identity*, Cambridge: Cambridge University Press.

Lamming, George [1960] (1984), *The Pleasures of Exile*, London: Allison & Busby.

Lansdown, Harry and Alex Spillius (eds) (1990), *Saturday's Boys: The Football Experience*, London: Willow Books/HarperCollins.

Lant, Antonia (1991), *Blackout: Reinventing Women for Wartime British Cinema*, Princeton, NJ: Princeton University Press.

Larwood, Harold (1965), *The Larwood Story*, with Kevin Perkins, London: W. H. Allen.

— (1933), *Body-Line?*, London: Elkin Mathews & Marrot.

Lawrence, D. H. (1997), *The Selected Letters of D. H. Lawrence*, ed. James T. Boulton, Cambridge: Cambridge University Press.

— (1973), *The First Lady Chatterley*, Harmondsworth: Penguin Books.

— (1972), *John Thomas and Lady Jane*, Harmondsworth: Penguin Books.

— (1968), *Phoenix II: Uncollected, Unpublished and Other Prose Works*, ed. Warren Roberts and Harry T. Moore, London: Heinemann.

— (1960), *Lady Chatterley's Lover*, London: Heinemann.

Lawrence, D. H. (1936), *Phoenix: The Posthumous Papers of D. H. Lawrence*, ed. Edward D. McDonald, London: Heinemann.

Le Brunn, George and Edgar Bateman (1901a), *Folkestone for the Day*, London: Francis, Day & Hunter.

— (1901b), *The Girls from Bryants and May*, London: Francis, Day & Hunter.

— (1901c), *'Liza Johnson; or, The Rag-Time Coster*, London: Francis, Day & Hunter.

— (1900), *'Ackney with the 'Ouses Took Away*, London: Francis, Day & Hunter.

— (1896), *The Cockney's Travels*, London: Francis, Day & Hunter.

Lean, David (1947), 'Brief Encounter', *Penguin Film Review* 4, 27–35.

LeJeune, C. A. (1947), *Chestnuts in Her Lap 1936–1946*, London: Phoenix House.

Le Quesne, Laurence (1983), *The Bodyline Controversy*, London: Secker & Warburg.

Liebling, A. J. (1956), *The Sweet Science*, London: Gollancz.

Light, Alison (1991), *Forever England: Femininity, Literature and Conservatism Between the Wars*, London and New York: Routledge.

Linsell, Tony (2001), *An English Nationalism*, King's Lynn: Athelney.

Lloyd James, A. (1928), 'Announcers' English', *B.B.C. Handbook*, London: BBC, 357–9.

Lovejoy, John (2000), 'A Paradox', in Tony Linsell (ed.), *Our Englishness*, Hockwold-cum-Wilton: Anglo-Saxon Books, 75–94.

McCall, Cicely (1943), *Women's Institutes*, London: William Colins.

McCullin, Don (1987), *Perspectives*, London: Harrap.

— (1979), *Homecoming*, London and Basingstoke: Macmillan.

MacDonald, Kevin (1994), *Emeric Pressburger: The Life and Death of a Screenwriter*, London and Boston, MA: Faber.

MacDonald, Robert H. (1993), *Sons of the Empire: The Frontier and the Boy Scout Movement, 1890–1918*, Toronto, Buffalo and London: University of Toronto Press.

McGibbon, Robin (1990), *Gazza!*, London: Penguin Books.

Madge, Charles and Tom Harrisson (eds) (1938), *First Year's Work 1937–38 by Mass-Observation*, London: Lindsay Drummond.

— (1937), *Mass-Observation*, London: Frederick Muller.

Mailey, Arthur (1933), *And Then Came Larwood: An Account of the Test Matches 1932–33*, London: John Lane/The Bodley Head.

Mais, S. P. B. (1964), *Round Britain Coach Tour*, London: A.Redman.

— (1940), *'There'll Always Be an England'*, London: Hutchinson.

— (1930), *It Isn't Far From London*, London: Richards.

— (1922), *Oh! To Be in England: A Book of the Open Air*, London: Grant Richards.

Mason, Tony (1990), 'Stanley Matthews', in Richard Holt (ed.), *Sport and the Working Class in Modern Britain*, Manchester and New York: Manchester University Pres, 159–78.

— (ed.) (1989), *Sport in Britain: A Social History*, Cambridge: Cambridge University Press.

Mass-Observation [1943] (1987), *The Pub and the People: A Worktown Study*, London: Century Hutchinson.

— [1939] (1986), *Britain*, London: Century Hutchinson.

Massingham, H. J. (1950), *The Curious Traveller*, London: Collins.

— (1942), *Remembrance: An Autobiography*, London and Malvern Wells: B. T. Batsford.

— (1935), *Through the Wilderness*, London: Cobden-Sanderson.

Masterman, Len (1988), 'The Battle of Orgreave', in Len Masterman (ed.), *Television Mythologies: Stars, Shows and Signs*, London: Comedia and Routledge, 99–109.

Matheson, Hilda (1933), *Broadcasting*, London: Thornton Butterworth.

Matthews, Stanley (2000), *The Way It Was: My Autobiography*, London: Headline.

Mayer, J. P. (1948), *British Cinemas and Their Audiences: Sociological Studies*, London: D. Dobson.

Medhurst, Andy (1991), 'That Special Thrill: *Brief Encounter*, Homosexuality and Authorship', *Screen* 32.2, 197–208.

Mee, Arthur (1936), *Enchanted Land: Half-a-Million Miles in the King's England*, London: Hodder & Stoughton.

Meisl, Willy (1955), *Soccer Revolution*, London: Phoenix Sports Books.

Merrick, Gil (1954), *I See it All*, London: Museum Press.

Millennium Experience: The Guide (1999), London: The New Millenium Experience Company Ltd.

Miller, Patricia Delphine (1975), 'Marcus Garvey, Garveyism, and Britain', M.Litt. Thesis, University of Edinburgh.

[Mills, Elliott] (1905), *The Decline and Fall of the British Empire*, Oxford: Alden & Co.

Milne, Seamus (2004), *The Enemy Within: The Secret War Against the Miners*, 3rd edn, London: Verso.

Milner, Alfred [1913] (1998), *The Nation and the Empire*, London: Routledge and Thoemmes Press.

Montague, C. E. (1924), *The Right Place: A Book of Pleasures*, London: Chatto & Windus.

— (1922), *Disenchantment*, London: Chatto & Windus.

Morton, Andrew (1997), *Diana: Her True Story – In Her Own Words*, London: Michael O'Mara Books.

Morton, H. V. (1942), *I Saw Two Englands*, London: Methuen.

— (1928), *The Call of England*, London: Methuen.

— (1927), *In Search of England*, London: Methuen.

Mosley, Oswald (1932), *The Greater Britain*: London: British Union of Fascists.

Mosse, George L. (1985), *Nationalism and Sexuality: Respectability and Abnormal Sexuality in Modern Europe*, New York: Howard Fertig.

Moules, Joan (1983), *Our Gracie: The Life of Dame Gracie Fields*, London: Robert Hale.

Mulhern, Francis (1979), *The Moment of 'Scrutiny'*, London: Verso.

Mulvey, Laura (1975), 'Visual Pleasure and Narrative Cinema', *Screen* 16.3, 6–18.

Murray, Fred and Edgar Bateman (1902), *Making Room for Mighty London Town*, London: Francis, Day & Hunter.

Nairn, Tom (2002), *Pariah: Misfortunes of the British Kingdom*, London and New York: Verso.

— (2000), *After Britain: New Labour and the Return of Scotland*, Cambridge: Granta.

— (1997), *Faces of Nationalism: Janus Revisited*, London and New York: Verso.

— (1988), *The Enchanted Glass: Britain and its Monarchy*, London: Radius.

— (1981), *The Break-up of Britain: Crisis and Neo-Nationalism*, revised edn, London: Verso.

Nava, Mica (1999), 'Diana and Race: Romance and the Reconfiguration of the Nation', in Adrian Kear and Deborah Lynn Steinberg (eds), *Mourning Diana: Nation, Culture and the Performance of Grief*, London and New York: Routledge, 108–19.

Neal, Mary (1940), 'The Broken Law', *The Adelphi* 16.4, 147–50.

— (1911a), *The Espérance Morris Book*, 2nd edn, London: J. Curwen.

— (1911b), 'Folk Art', in Reginald R. Buckley, *The Shakespeare Revival and the Stratford-upon-Avon Movement*, London: George Allen, 189–227.

— (1910), *The Espérance Morris Book, Part 1*, London: J. Curwen.

Nehls, Edward (ed.) (1959), *D. H. Lawrence: A Composite Biography, Vol. 3, 1925–30*, Madison, WI: University of Wisconsin Press.

— (1958), *D. H. Lawrence: A Composite Biography, Vol. 2, 1919–25*, Madison, WI: University of Wisconsin Press.

— (1957), *D. H. Lawrence: A Composite Biography, Vol. I, 1885–1919*, Madison, WI: University of Wisconsin Press.

Nicolson, Adam (1999), *Regeneration: The Story of the Dome*, London: HarperCollins.

O'Hear, Anthony (1998), 'Diana, Queen of Hearts: Sentimentality Personified and Canonised', in Digby Anderson and Peter Mullen (eds), *Faking It: The Sentimentalisation of Modern Society*, London: Social Affairs Unit, 183–90.

Orwell, George (1970a), *The Collected Essays, Journalism and Letters, Vol. 2: My Country Right or Left, 1940–1943*, ed. Sonia Orwell and Ian Angus, Harmondsworth: Penguin Books.

— (1970b), *The Collected Essays, Journalism and Letters, Vol. 3: As I Please, 1943–1945*, ed. Sonia Orwell and Ian Angus, Harmondsworth: Penguin Books.

— [1937] (1962), *The Road to Wigan Pier*, Harmondsworth: Penguin Books.

Padmore, George (ed.) [1947] (1963), *Colonial and . . . Coloured Unity: A Programme of Action*, London: Hammersmith Bookshop.

Parker, Andrew, Mary Russo, Doris Sommer and Patricia Yaeger (eds) (1992), *Nationalisms and Sexualities*, New York and London: Routledge.

Paul, Kathleen (1997), *Whitewashing Britain: Race and Citizenship in the Postwar Era*, Ithaca, NY and London: Cornell University Press.

Perry, Roland (1995), *The Don*, Sydney: Pan Macmillan.

Phillips, Andrew (2000), 'The Resurrection of England', in Tony Linsell (ed.), *Our Englishness*, Hockwold-cum-Wilton: Anglo-Saxon Books, 37–48.

Pickles, Wilfred (1949), *Between You and Me*, London: Werner Laurie.

Pilkington, Edward (1988), *Beyond the Mother Country: West Indians and the Notting Hill White Riots*, London: I. B. Tauris.

Pilton, Patrick (1976), *Every Night at the London Palladium*, London: Robson Books.

Pimlott, Ben (1996), *The Queen: Elizabeth II and the Monarchy*, London: HarperCollins.

Pitt, Malcolm (1979), *The World on Our Backs: The Kent Miners and the 1972 Miners' Strike*, London: Lawrence & Wishart.

Powell, J. Enoch (1969), *Freedom and Reality*, ed. John Wood, London: B. T. Batsford.

Powell, Michael (1986), *A Life in Movies: An Autobiography*, London: Heinemann.

Power, Mark (2000), *Superstructure*, London: HarperCollins.

Powers, Alan (2001), 'The Expression of Levity', in Elain Harwood and Alan Powers (eds), *Festival of Britain*, London: Twentieth Century Society, 47–56.

Priestley, J. B. [1934] (1968), *English Journey*, London: Heinemann.

Puskas, Ferenc (1997), *Puskas on Puskas: The Life and Times of a Footballing Legend*, ed. Rogan Taylor, trans. Klara Jamrich, London: Robson Books.

Rajagopalachar, C. and J. C. Kumarappa (eds) (1932), *The Nation's Voice*, Ahmedabad: Navajivan Press.

Randall, Harry and Edgar Bateman (1898), *It's a Wonder I'm Alive to Tell the Tale (Household Remedies)*, London: Francis, Day & Hunter.

Reith, J. C. W. (1924), *Broadcast Over Britain*, London: Hodder & Stoughton.

Reynolds, E. E. (1950), *The Scout Movement*, London: Oxford University Press.

Rhys, Ernest (1931), *Everyman Remembers*, London and Toronto: J. M. Dent & Sons.

Richards, Andrew J. (1996), *Miners on Strike: Class Solidarity and Division in Britain*, Oxford and New York: Berg.

Richards, Jeffrey and Dorothy Sheridan (eds) (1987), *Mass-Observation at the Movies*, London and New York: Routledge & Kegan Paul.

Richards, Jeffrey, Scott Wilson and Linda Woodhead (eds) (1999), *Diana: The Making of a Media Saint*, London and New York: I. B. Tauris.

Robinson, Sugar Ray [1970] (1992), *Sugar Ray: The Sugar Ray Robinson Story*, London: Robson Books.

Rosenthal, Michael (1986), *The Character Factory: Baden-Powell and the Origins of the Boy Scout Movement*, London: Collins.

Routledge, Paul (1999), *Mandy: The Unauthorised Biography of Peter Mandelson*, London: Simon and Schuster.

Rossiter, A. P. (1953), *Our Living Language: An English-Man Looks at his English*, London: Longman, Green & Co.

Russell, Dave (2004), *Looking North: Northern England and the National Imagination*, Manchester: Manchester University Press.

— (1997), *Football and the English: A Social History of Association Football in England, 1863–1995*, Preston: Carnegie Publishing.

Sampson, George (1921), *English for the English: A Chapter on National Education*, Cambridge: Cambridge University Press.

Samuel, Raphael (1994), *Theatres of Memory, Volume 1: Past and Present in Contemporary Culture*, London and New York: Verso.

Samuel, Raphael, Barbara Mitchell and Guy Boamas (eds) (1986), *The Enemy Within: Pit Villages and the Miners' Strike of 1984–5*, London: Routledge & Kegan Paul.

Scargill, Arthur (1975), 'The New Unionism', *New Left Review* 92, 3–33.

Schofield, Derek (2004), 'Sowing the Seeds: Cecil Sharp and Charles Marson in Somerset in 1903', *Folk Music Journal* 8.4, 484–512.

Schwarz, Bill (2003), 'Crossing the Seas', in Bill Schwarz (ed.), *West Indian Intellectuals in Britain*, Manchester and New York: Manchester University Press.

— (2002), 'Unspeakable Histories: Diasporic Lives in Old England', in Peter Osborne and Stella Sandford (eds), *Philosophies of Race and Ethnicity*, London and New York: Continuum, 81–96.

— (2000), 'Actually Existing Postcolonialism', *Radical Philosophy* 104, 16–24.

— (1996), ' "The Only White Man in There": The Re-Racialisation of England, 1956–1968', *Race and Class* 38.1, 65–78.

— (1987), 'Englishness and the Paradox of Modernity', *New Formations* 1, 147–53.

Scott, Maurice and Edgar Bateman (1910), *I'm Using Sunday Language All the Week*, London: Francis, Day & Hunter.

Scott, Maurice, Eustace Baynes and Edgar Bateman (1901), *A Nice Quiet Day; or The Postman's 'Oliday*, London: Francis, Day & Hunter.

Scruton, Roger (2004), *News from Somewhere: On Settling*, London and New York: Continuum.

— (2000), *England: An Elegy*, London: Chatto & Windus.

Seago, Edward (1943), *Peace in War*, London: Collins.

Seldon, Anthony (1997), *Major: A Political Life*, London: Weidenfeld & Nicolson.

Seymour, Anne (1991), 'Walking in Circles', in Richard Long, *Walking in Circles*, London: Thames & Hudson, 7–39.

Sharp, Cecil J. (1907), *English Folk-Song: Some Conclusions*, London: Simpkin & Co./Novello & Co.

Sharp, Cecil J. and Herbert C. MacIlwaine (1912), *The Morris Book, Part I*, 2nd edn, London: Novello.

— (1907), *The Morris Book*, London: Novello.

Shaw, Denis J. B. (1990), *Selling an Urban Image: Blackpool at the Turn of the Century*, Birmingham: University of Birmingham School of Geography Working Paper Series No. 54.

Sherwood, Marika (1999), *Claudia Jones: A Life in Exile*, London: Lawrence & Wishart.

Sinclair, Iain (1999), *Sorry Meniscus: Excursions to the Millennium Dome*, London: Profile Books and London Review of Books.

Skinner, Susan Maxwell and Anwar Hussein (1998), *Diana: An English Rose*, London: Leppi.

Smart, Carol (1996), 'Good Wives and Moral Lives: Marriage and Divorce 1937–51', In Christine Gledhill and Gillian Swanson (eds), *Nationalising Femininity: Culture, Sexuality and British Cinema in the Second World War*, Manchester and New York: Manchester University Press, 91–105.

Southerton, Sydney J. (1934), 'The Bowling Controversy', in *John Wisden's Cricketers' Almanack for 1934*, London: John Wisden, 332–5.

Stacey, Tom (ed.) (1970), *Immigration and Enoch Powell*, London: Tom Stacey Ltd.

Steedman, Carolyn (1986), *Landscape for a Good Woman: A Story of Two Lives*, London: Virago.

Stoddart, Brian (1979), 'Cricket's Imperial Crisis: The 1932–33 MCC Tour of Australia', in Richard Cashman and Michael McKernan (eds), *Sport in*

History: The Making of Modern Sporting History, St Lucia, Queensland: University of Queensland Press.

Sturge Gretton, M. (1914), 'Folk Dancing In and About Burford', *English Folk-Dance Society's Journal* 1.1, 1.

Swanton, E. W. (1985), *Gubby Allen: Man of Cricket*, London: Hutchinson/ Stanley Paul.

Taylor, Carol (1963), 'A Date with Sugar Ray', *Flamingo* January, 10–11.

Taylor, Ian (1991), 'Football in the 1990s: Taking Hillsborough Seriously?', in John Williams and Stephen Wagg (eds), *British Football and Social Change: Getting Into Europe*, Leicester, London and New York: Leicester University Press, 3–24.

Taylor, Rogan and Andrew Ward (1995), *Kicking and Screaming: An Oral History of Football in England*, London: Robson Books.

Theroux, Paul (1983), *The Kingdom By the Sea: A Journey Around the Coast of Great Britain*, London: Hamish Hamilton.

Theweleit, Klaus (1987), *Male Fantasies I: Women, Floods, Bodies, History*, tr. Stephen Conway with Erica Carter and Chris Turner, Cambridge: Polity Press.

Thomas, Edward [1906] (1982), *The Heart of England*, Oxford: Oxford University Press.

— (1913), *The Icknield Way*, London: Constable.

Thompson, E. P. (1991), *Customs in Common*, London: Merlin Press.

— (1978), *The Poverty of Theory and Other Essays*, London: Merlin Press.

Trevelyan, G. M. (1929), *Must England's Beauty Perish?*, London: Faber & Gwyer.

Trowell Festival of Britain Committee (1951), *Trowell: Official Programme*, Nottingham: Trowell Festival of Britain Committee.

Trudgill, Peter (1975), *Accent, Dialect and the School*, London: Edward Arnold.

Trueman, Myfawny, John Balmer and Daragh O'Reilly (2001), *Desperate Dome, Desperate Measures!: Managing Innovation at London's Millennium Dome*, Bradford: Bradford University School of Management.

Tschiffely, A. F. (1936), *Bridle Paths*, London: William Heinemann.

Turner, W. J. (ed.) (1945), *The Englishman's Country*, London: Collins.

Utley, T. E. (1968), *Enoch Powell: The Man and His Thinking*, London: William Kimber.

Waller, Robert J. (1983), *The Dukeries Transformed: The Social and Political Development of a Twentieth Century Coalfield*, Oxford: Clarendon Press.

Walton, John K. (1998), *Blackpool*, Edinburgh and Lancaster: Edinburgh University Press and Carnegie Publishing.

Walton, John K. and Robert Poole (1982), 'The Lancashire Wakes in the Nineteenth Century', in Robert D. Storch (ed.), *Popular Culture and Custom in Nineteenth-Century England*, London, Canberra and New York: Croom Helm and St Martin's Press, 100–24.

Walvin, James (1986), *Football and the Decline of Britain*, Basingstoke: Macmillan.

— (1975), *The People's Game: A Social History of British Football*, London: Allen Lane.

Warner, Sir Pelham (1951), *Long Innings*, London: George G. Harrap.

Warren, Allen (1987), 'Sir Robert Baden-Powell, the Scout Movement and Citizen Training in Great Britain, 1900–1920', *English Historical Review* 101, 376–98.

Webster, Wendy (1998), *Imagining Home: Gender, 'Race' and National Identity, 1945–64*, London and Bristol, PA: UCL Press.

Wiener, Martin J. (1981), *English Culture and the Decline of the Industrial Spirit 1850–1980*, Cambridge: Cambridge University Press.

Wilhide, Elizabeth (1999), *The Millennium Dome*, London: HarperCollins.

Williams, John and Rogan Taylor (1994), 'Boys Keep Swinging: Masculinity and Football Culture in England', in Tim Newburn and Elizabeth A. Stanko (eds), *Just Boys Doing Business: Men, Masculinities and Crime*, London and New York: Routledge, 214–33.

Williams, Linda Ruth (1993), *Sex in the Head: Visions of Femininity and Film in D. H. Lawrence*, Hemel Hempstead: Harvester Wheatsheaf.

Williams, Philip Martin and David L. Williams (2006), *Wired to the Moon: Frank Randle – A Life*, Ashton-under-Lyne: History on Your Doorstep.

— (2001), *Hooray for Jollywood: The Life of John E. Blakeley and the Mancunian Film Corporation*, Ashton-under-Lyne: History on Your Doorstep.

Williams, Raymond (1971), *Orwell*, London: Fontana.

— (1979), *Politics and Letters*, London: NLB.

Williamson, Bill (1988), 'Memories, Vision and Hope: Themes in an Historical Sociology of Britain Since the Second World War', *Journal of Historical Sociology* 1.2, 161–83.

Williamson, Judith (1986), *Consuming Passions: The Dynamics of Popular Culture*, London and New York: Marion Boyers.

Wills, Charlie (nd) *Charlie Wills*, CD Folktrax BD22.

Wilson, Peter (1959), *More Ringside Seats*, London: Stanley Paul.

Winn, Christopher (2005), *I Never Knew That About England*, London: Ebury Press.

Woolf, Virginia [1938] (1943), *Three Guineas*, London: Hogarth Press.

Wright, Basil (1974), *The Long View*, London: Secker & Warburg.

Wright, Patrick (1985), *On Living in an Old Country: The National Past in Contemporary Britain*, London: Verso.

YouGov (2005), 'Britishness', http://www.yougov.com/uk/archives.

Young, Hugo (1991), *One of Us: A Biography of Margaret Thatcher*, final edn, London: Macmillan.

Index

About England, 67
Accent, Dialect and the School, 149
Adeney, Martin, 56–7
After Britain, 18
After Empire, 23
Ali, Muhammad, 116, 120
Allen, George 'Gubby,' 127, 128
Allen, Vic, 56
America *see* United States
Anderson, Benedict, 5, 6, 13, 111
Anderson, M. D., 82
Anderson, Perry, 3, 17–18, 179
Angry Island, The, 2, 83
Appleyard, Bryan, 53
Archetti, Eduardo, 121, 138
Arliss, Leslie, 165
Ashes 1932–3, 122–9
Ashley, Peter, 2
Atlantic City, 99

Baddiel, David, 134
Baden-Powell, Agnes, 35
Baden-Powell, Robert, 6, 20, 28–36, 45
Bagehot, Walter, 172–3
Baker, Baron, 110
Baldwin, Stanley, 19, 77, 113, 179
Balfour, A. J., 104
Barfield, Julia, 65
Barnes, John, 132, 134
Bateman, Edgar, 8, 140, 141, 152, 153–5
Batsford, Harry, 82
Battersea Pleasure Gardens, 49–50
Battle of Orgreave, The, 48, 59–60
Baucom, Ian, 20
BBC, 140, 143, 146–7, 158
    B. B. C. Handbook, 146
Beatles, 100–1
Being Gazza, 138
Belloc, Hilaire, 12, 71, 79, 80
Bennett, Tony, 99
Benyon, Huw, 56
Berry, Ian, 83
Best, George, 134
Beyond a Boundary, 21–2, 106–7, 124
Bhabha, Homi, 20

bicycles, 15
Billy Elliot, 48, 55
Birmingham, 62, 63
Black Jacobins, 91
Blackpool, 86, 97–100, 101–2, 179
    Illuminations, 99
    Tower, 99
Blahnik, Manolo, 176
Blair, Eric *see* Orwell, George
Blair, Tony, 61, 62, 63
Blakeley, John E., 100, 101
Blatchford, Robert, 85, 86
Blunden, Edmund, 67
Blyton, W. J., 67
Body-Line?, 127–8
'bodyline,' 7, 122–4, 127–8, 138
Bolton, 85–6, 87–9, 155–6
boxing, 116, 117, 119; *see also* Ali,
    Muhammad; Robinson, Sugar Ray;
    Turpin, Randolph
Boy Scouts, 6, 20, 28–36, 45, 178–9
    girls in, 34
    imperialism of, 32–3
Boyes, Georgina, 41
Boys' Brigade, 31
Bracken, Brendan, 147
Bradman, Donald, 121, 122, 123, 124,
    125–6, 127, 128, 129, 138
Bragg, Billy, 2, 4, 16
Brandt, Bill, 83
Brassed Off, 48, 55, 59
Break-Up of Britain, The, 18
Brewster, Achsah Barlow, 144
Brief Encounter (film), 8, 159–60, 164–5,
    166–72, 177
Britain, 88
British National Party, 6, 9–10, 11–12, 20
British Nationality Act 1948, 107–8
Britishness, 18–19
Britons, 4
Brown, Gordon, 14, 16
Bryson, Bill, 83
Burchill, Julie, 175
Bushaway, Bob, 162
Buzanszky, Jeno, 130

Calder, Angus, 23
Call of England, The, 69–70
Campbell, Beatrix, 26, 175
Canterbury Tale, A, 7, 77, 78–82
Cartland, Barbara, 172
Case for West Indian Self-Government, The, 91
Cavalcade, 157
Centre for Contemporary Cultural Studies, Birmingham, 23
Chamberlain, Joseph, 113
Charter for Ramblers, A, 69
Chesterton, G. K., 12
Chidell, E. F., 21
cinema *see* film
class, 6, 36
    boxing, 119
    Boy Scouts, 33–4, 36
    Coward, 157
    cricket, 91, 123, 126, 127, 128
    Fields, 92, 93–4
    folk-dance, 36, 41, 44–5
    football, 122, 129, 134, 136–7
    Gandhi, 90
    in *Lady Chatterley's Lover*, 8, 145–6, 163
    in language, 148–9
    Randle, 97
Clifford, Sue, 2
coal mining *see* Miners' Strike
Colley, Linda, 4, 18
Colls, Robert, 4, 16
Colyton, Lord, 108
Comedians, 101
Commonwealth Immigration Act 1968, 113
Commonwealth of Nations, 50–1
Conekin, Becky, 49, 51
Coney Island, 99
Constantine, Learie, 90, 91, 121
Correia, Alice, 60
costers, 153–4, 179
Countryman's England, The, 67
Coward, Noël, 141, 156, 157–8, 159, 167, 170
Crick, Michael, 55
cricket, 1, 7, 90, 106–7, 122–9
Cricket: How to Succeed, 122
Critcher, Chas, 132
Croft, Andy, 75
Crossman, Richard, 172–3
Crystal Palace, 48, 49

Ða Engliscan Gesiðas, 10, 19
Daldry, Stephen, 48
dance *see* folk-dance
Darwen, 86
Davies, Jude, 175
Decline and Fall of the British Empire, 20–1
Deller, Jeremy, 48, 59–60
Design for a Journey, 82
devolution, 1, 12, 62
dialect, 140–1, 143, 145–6, 147, 149, 150
Diana, Princess of Wales *see* Spencer, Lady Diana
Dilke, Sir Charles, 21, 114

Disenchantment, 72
Doane, Mary Anne, 168
Dodds, Philip, 3–4
Does Accent Matter?, 150
'double consciousness,' 22, 106
Double Indemnity, 166
Douglass, Dave, 59
Doyle, Brian, 3
Du Bois, W. E. B., 22, 106
Dyer, Richard, 94

Ealing Studios, 168
Easthope, Anthony, 4
Edinburgh People's Festival, 53
Education Act 1944, 147
Edward VIII, King, abdication, 88, 173–4
Elen, Gus, 154
Ellis, Sam, 137
elocution, 8, 141–2
Emery, Winifred, 144, 145
Emil-Behnke, Kate, 141–2
Empire *see* imperialism
Enchanted Land, 67
England, John, 150–2
England: an Elegy, 13
England in Particular, 2
English, The, 83
English Cavalcade, 67
English Constitution, The, 172
English Culture and the Decline of the Industrial Spirit, 14, 57–8
English Folk-Dance Society, 28, 38, 39, 42, 178–9
English Folk Dance Society's Journal, 42, 44
English Folk-Song, 151
English Folk Songs for Schools, 151
English for the English, 143
English Journey, 66
English Nationalism, An, 10
English Ways, 74–5
Englishman's Country, The, 82
Englishness, 3–4
Englishness and National Culture, 4
Epstein, Brian, 100–1
Espérance Girls Club, 28, 37, 39, 41, 178–9
Espérance Morris Books, 39
Europe, 5, 11, 51
European Football Championships 1996, 1, 134

Faiers, Roy, 10, 11
Falklands War 1982, 54–5
Fallen Angel, 166, 168
fanzines, 133, 134
'fast leg theory' *see* 'bodyline'
Federation of Women's Institutes, 25
Ferrier, Bob, 132
Festival of Britain 1951, 6, 47, 48–53
festivals, 47–65
Fever Pitch, 133, 134, 136, 137
Fields, Gracie, 7, 86, 92–5, 141, 156, 157–8, 181
Figgis, Mike, 60
film, 4, 7, 77–82, 94, 100, 165–8

Fingleton, Jack, 127
flag, George, 1, 2, 3, 19, 178
folk-dance, 6, 28, 36–45
folk-song, 8, 37, 40, 42–3, 141, 150–2
football, 1, 7, 122, 129–39
  racism, 135
  violence, 135
Forever England, 4, 26
Fox, Kate, 2, 4
Francis, Day and Hunter, 141, 153, 155
Frayn, Michael, 49
Frith, Simon, 156
Frost, Frank, 49–50
Fussell, Paul, 72

Gandhi, Mohandâs, 86, 90, 91
Garnett, David, 145
Garvey, Marcus, 7, 103, 104–5, 107, 115,
  120, 179–80
Gascoigne, Paul, 7, 122, 132–3, 134–5,
  137–8
Geertz, Clifford, 5
gender, 6, 8, 23–6, 159–60, 177; *see also*
  masculinity
  Boy Scouts, 34–5, 36
  in *Brief Encounter*, 164–5, 168, 169, 170,
    171
  employment, 98
  folk-dance, 36–7, 41–2, 45
  in *Lady Chatterley's Lover*, 160, 164
Geordies, 4
George, St, 1–2; *see also* flag, George
German, Sir Edward, 52
Gerrard, Michael, 134
Giddens, Anthony, 133, 136
Gill, A. A., 2, 4, 83
Gilroy, Paul, 4, 6, 12, 23, 26, 27, 51, 103–4,
  107, 120, 180
Girl Guides, 34–5, 36
Giulianotti, Richard, 134
Glanville, Brian, 132, 133, 136
Glass, Ruth, 109, 110
Gledhill, Christine, 4
Golding, Florence, 42
Grace, W. G., 121
Great Exhibition 1851, 48
Green, Geoffrey, 130–1
Greenwood, Ron, 129–30
Griffin, Nick, 11–12
Griffiths, Trevor, 101
Grimethorpe colliery, 55
Grosics, Gyula, 130
Guides *see* Girl Guides
Gurney, Ivor, 73

Hall, Stuart, 4, 6, 20, 103–4, 108, 109,
  119–20, 180
Hamilton, Ian, 133
Hammond, Wally, 128
Handbook for Girl Guides, The, 35
Handler, Andrew, 130
Hardy, Bert, 83
Harrison, Tony, 54, 140, 141, 148–50
Harrisson, Tom, 85–6, 87–9, 155–6, 173–4

Hartley, Dorothy, 67
Haynes, Richard, 134
Headington Quarry morris dancers, 37,
  43–4
Heart of England, The, 70
Heffer, Simon, 4, 6, 12, 13, 27, 111
Henderson, Eugene, 117
Henderson, Hamish, 53
Henry, John, 146
Henry, Lez, 19–20
heritage, 57–8, 59–60
Heritage Industry, The, 57–8
Herman, Mark, 48
Heseltine, Michael, 61, 62
Hewison, Robert, 57–8
Hidekúti, Nándar, 130, 131
Higson, Andrew, 4
Hillsborough, 133
Hilton, Jack, 74–5
Hissey, James John, 69
Hitchens, Christopher, 17
Hobsbawm, Eric, 5
Hoggart, Richard, 22–3, 87
holidays, 98–9, 154
Holt, Richard, 4
Home Front, 25
Homecoming, 83
Honey, John, 150
Hopcraft, Arthur, 137
Hopkins, Harry, 50
Hornby, Nick, 133, 134, 136–7
housing, 50
How to See the Country, 82
Howe, Margery, 44–5
Hughes, M. V., 67
Hull, 70
Hungarian football team, 7, 122, 129–31

I Know Where I'm Going, 166
I Never Knew That About England, 2
I Saw Two Englands, 82
Icknield Way, The, 70, 71–2
Identity, 11
Identity of England, 4, 16
immigration, 19, 107, 108–9, 180
imperialism, 5, 27, 50–1, 179–80; *see also*
  postcolonialism
  Boy Scouts, 32–3
  Powell (Enoch), 108, 111–12
In Flagrante, 83
In Quest of the Ashes, 126
In Search of Albion, 2
In Search of England, 66, 67, 68, 69
industry, 68, 70
Irwin, Colin, 2
It Isn't Far From London, 68
It Isn't Far from London, 84
Italian Job, The, 157
It's a Royal Knockout, 173

Jackson, Brian, 147–8
James, C. L. R., 6, 7, 21–2, 86, 90–1, 103,
  105–7, 115, 120, 121, 124, 136, 138,
  179–80

Jardine, Douglas, 122–9, 138, 179
jazz, 155–6
Joad, C. E. M., 69, 75
Johnson, Jack, 116
Jones, Claudia, 120
Jones, Daniel, 142
Jones, Vinnie, 135
journeys, 7, 41, 66–83
Joyce, Patrick, 4, 89

Karpeles, Maud, 40
Kennedy, Peter, 152
Kerr, Rose, 34, 35
khaddar, 90
Killip, Chris, 83
Kim, 32
Kimber, William, 37, 41, 44
King, Anthony, 135
Kingdom by the Sea, The, 83
Kipling, Rudyard, 32
Kirby, John, 52, 53
Krasker, Robert, 168, 170
Kumar, Krishan, 4

Lady Chatterley's Lover, 8, 141, 144,
    145–6, 159–64, 177, 181
Lamming, George, 107, 110
'Lancashire Blues,' 94
Lancaster, Bill, 4
Landes, Ruth, 108
Landscape for a Good Woman, 26
language, 3
Larwood, Harold, 123–4, 127–8, 129,
    138–9
Lawrence, D. H., 8, 140–1, 143–4, 145–6,
    160–4, 181
Le Quesne, Laurence, 124
Lean, David, 8, 164, 167–8
Liebling, A. J., 121
Life and Death of Colonel Blimp, The, 77,
    78
Light, Alison, 4, 26
Lineker, Gary, 134
Linsell, Tony, 10
'Lion and the Unicorn, The,' 15, 16, 159
lion and unicorn, 48
literary studies, 3, 4
Livesey, Roger, 80, 81
Lloyd, Bella, 154
Lloyd, John, 56–7
Lloyd, Marie, 154
Lloyd James, A., 146
London, 27, 62, 68, 84
London Eye, 65
Long, Richard, 83
Looking North, 4
Lovejoy, John, 10

McCall, Cicely, 25
MacColl, Ewan, 96
McCullin, Don, 83
MacDonald, Robert H., 33
MacIlwaine, Herbert C., 38, 42
Madge, Charles, 87–8, 173–4

Madina, Alex, 61, 63
Mailey, Arthur, 124, 125
Mais, S. P. B., 66, 68–9, 82, 84
Major, John, 11, 14, 15, 16
Making of English National Identity, The, 4
Making of the English Working Class, The,
    148
Male Fantasies, 24
Mancunian Films, 100
Mandelson, Peter, 63, 64
Maradona, Diego, 121–2, 138
Marks, David, 65
Marsden, Dennis, 147–8
Marxism, British, 18
masculinity, 24, 25, 134, 159–60
Mason, Tony, 4, 131
Mass-Observation, 7, 85–6, 87–9, 99, 165,
    173–4, 181
Massingham, H. J., 7, 66, 70, 75–7, 82, 84,
    179
Masterman, Len, 59
Matheson, Hilda, 146–7
Matthews, Stanley, 131, 133, 134, 139
Mayer, J. P., 165
Mee, Arthur, 67
Meisl, Willy, 131
Menzies, Robert, 126
Merrick, Gil, 130
Merrie England (Blatchford), 85
Merrie England (German), 52, 53
Millennium Dome, The, 61
Millennium Experience 2000, 5, 6, 47,
    61–5, 182
    failure of, 64
Mills, Elliott, 20–1
Milner, Lord Alfred, 21
mimicry, 8, 144–5, 147–8, 149, 150, 156
Miners' Strike 1984–5, 6, 47–8, 54–60, 61,
    179
monarchy, 8, 14, 172–3, 174, 176, 177
Montague, C. E., 7, 66, 70, 72–4, 82, 179
Morris Book, The, 38, 42, 43
morris dancing, 37–42
    origins, 43–4
Morrison, Herbert, 48, 50, 52, 54, 63
Morton, H. V., 66, 67, 68, 69–70, 82, 85
Mosley, Oswald, 24
Mosse, George L., 24, 159
motoring, 69
Mulhern, Francis, 3
Mulvey, Laura, 167
Munich crisis, 88
music halls, 5, 153, 155, 179

Nairn, Tom, 2–3, 4, 6, 9, 17, 18–19, 84,
    173, 176, 179
national service, 35–6
National Socialism, 24
National Trust, 14, 58, 75
National Union of Mineworkers, 54, 56, 57,
    58–9
nationalisation, 54
Nationalising Femininity, 4
nationalism, 3, 9–14, 16, 18, 178

Nationalisms and Sexualities, 177
Nava, Mica, 175
Neal, Mary, 6, 28, 36–7, 39–45
Nelson, 86, 90, 91
New Left Review, 16, 17, 18, 55
New Millennium Experience Company, 61, 63, 64
Newbolt, Sir Henry, 142
Nor Shall My Sword, 12
North, the, 4, 68, 70, 73, 84–102, 181
North West, the, 7
Notes from a Small Island, 83
Notting Hill Carnival, 120
Notting Hill riots 1958, 7, 103–4, 107, 109, 110–11, 120, 180

O'Hear, Anthony, 174
Old Road, The, 71, 79, 80
On Living in an Old Country, 57–8
Orwell, George, 6, 7, 14–17, 27, 49, 75, 85, 86–7, 95, 96, 159, 179, 181

Page, Jennie, 64
Pan-African Congress, Fifth, 91–2
Parker, Andrew, 177
patriotism, 16
Paul, Kathleen, 107
Paxman, Jeremy, 4
Paxton, Sir Joseph, 48
Peace and War, 82
Pearson, Arthur, 30
performativity, 5
  cricket, 123, 124
  Miners' Strike, 54
photography, 83
Pickles, Wilfred, 147
Pilkington, Edward, 108–9, 110
pillar boxes, red, 15
Pimlott, Ben, 175
Pitt, Malcolm, 56
place, 5, 7
  coalfields, 55–7
  in *Lady Chatterley's Lover*, 160–3, 181
  see also journeys; North, the; individual place names
Playford, John, 41
Plumpton, 66
Portman, Eric, 81
postcolonialism, 6, 7, 19–23, 103, 104, 105, 107, 180
  in the North, 89–92
Pound, Ezra, 143, 144
Powell, Enoch, 7, 13, 18, 104, 107, 108, 111–15, 116, 180
  'rivers of blood' speech, 113–14, 115
Powell, Michael, 7, 66, 77–9, 80, 81, 82, 166, 179
Powers, Alan, 51
Preminger, Otto, 166
Pressburger, Emeric, 7, 66, 77–8, 79, 80, 81, 82, 166, 179
Pride and Prejudice (film), 166
Priestley, J. B., 66, 95, 97–8, 146

Progressive Patriot, The, 2
Pronunciation of English, The, 142
Pub and the People, The, 89
Puskas, Ferenc, 131

race, 6, 7, 23, 103–20, 180
  Boy Scouts, 33–6
  cricket, 90, 106–7
  Festival of Britain, 51
  folk-dance, 36, 41, 42–3
  and imperialism, 20
  Powell (Enoch), 107, 108–9
  Union Jack, 26
  whiteness, 20, 21, 109–10, 120
Race Relations Act 1968, 113
Ramblers' Association, 75, 77
Ramsey, Alf, 131
Randall, Harry, 152
Randle, Frank, 7, 86, 92, 95–7, 100, 101, 179, 181
Reece, Arthur, 153
regionalism, 4, 5, 7, 181–2
Reith, John, 146
revivalism, 5–6, 178
Rhys, Ernest, 143–4
Richards, Andrew, 57
Right Place, The, 72–4
Road to Wigan Pier, The, 75, 85, 86–7, 95, 96
Robinson, Sugar Ray, 111, 116–18, 119, 120, 121, 122
Robson, Bobby, 132
Rochdale, 92, 93, 94
romance, 159–77
Rosenthal, Michael, 30
Rossiter, A. P., 147
Round Britain Coach Tour, 82
Royal Family *see* monarchy
Royal Family, The, 173
rural journeys, 70, 72, 73, 75, 179
Russell, Dave, 4

Said, Edward, 20
Salisbury Review, 13
'Sally,' 156
Sampson, George, 143, 144, 151
Samuel, Raphael, 54, 57, 58
Saturday's Boys, 136
Savage Civilisation, 88
Scargill, Arthur, 54, 55
School of Eloquence, The, 141, 148, 150
School of Scottish Studies, Edinburgh University, 3, 53
Schwarz, Bill, 86, 104, 107, 109, 111
Scouting for Boys, 29, 30–1, 35, 45
Scouts *see* Boy Scouts
Scruton, Roger, 4, 6, 13, 27, 77, 84
Seago, Edward, 82
Sebes, Gusztáv, 130
'Seeds of Love, The,' 151, 152
Seventh Veil, The, 165
sexuality, 8, 159–77
Shakespeare Festival Summer School 1911, 40

Sharp, Cecil
  dance, 6, 28, 36–45, 151
  song, 8, 40, 141, 150–2, 155
Sinclair, Iain, 61
Sing as We Go, 94, 98
Skinner, Frank, 134
Sobers, Garfield, 121
Somewhere in Camp, 96–7, 100
Somewhere on Leave, 100
song *see* costers; folk-song; music halls
South Africa, 121
South Bank Exhibition 1951, 48–9, 50–1,
  52–3, 54, 179
Speakers' Corner, 104
Spencer, Lady Diana, 8, 159–60, 172, 174–7
sport, 4, 7, 121–39; *see also* boxing; cricket;
  football
Sport and the British, 4
Sport in Britain, 4
Stalky and Co., 32
Standard English, 140, 141, 143, 145
Steadfast, 10, 20
Steedman, Carolyn, 26
Street, A. G., 67
Sturge, M. Gretton, 44
suburbanisation, 76
Swanson, Gillian, 4

Taylor, Rogan, 131
Teaching of English in England, The, 142
teeth, 96–7
Thatcher, Margaret, 11, 54–5
theories of Englishness, 5–6, 9–27
There Ain't No Black in the Union Jack, 26
There'll Always Be an England, 82
Theroux, Paul, 83
Theweleit, Klaus, 24
This England, 10–11, 12, 19, 23
Thomas, Edward, 7, 66, 70–2, 74, 79, 82,
  179
Thompson, E. P., 18, 54–5, 148, 161
Three Guineas, 6, 24–5, 159
'Three Lions,' 134, 135
Through the Wilderness, 75–7
travel *see* journeys
Trevelyan, G. M., 75
Trowell, 51–2
Trudgill, Peter, 149, 150
Tschiffely, A. F., 67, 68, 85
Turner, W. J., 82
Turpin, Dick, 116
Turpin, Randolph, 7, 104, 107, 111,
  115–20, 121, 122, 180–1
Tynan, Kenneth, 119

UK Independence Party, 9–10
United States, 5, 51
  African Americans, 103, 106; *see also*
    Robinson, Sugar Ray

Fields and, 94, 95
  music, 155–8
  resorts, 99
Universal Negro Improvement Association,
  103
Unmitigated England, 2

v., 54, 150
Venglos, Jozef, 132
Visions of the People, 4
voices, 8, 140–58

Waddle, Chris, 132, 134
Wakes weeks, 98, 99, 179
Waller, Robert J., 55
Walton, John K., 98, 99
Walvin, James, 129
War, First World, 72, 74
War, Second World, 77, 82, 147, 165,
  177
Warner, Sir Pelham (Plum), 124, 125,
  128
Watching the English, 2
Waterloo Road, 165–6
Waving the Flag, 4
West Indian Federation, 110
When Saturday Comes, 133
When You Come Home, 97
whiteness, 20, 21, 109–10, 120
Wicked Lady, The, 165, 167
Wiener, Martin J., 14, 57–8, 89, 99
Wigan, 69, 70, 85, 86, 95
Wigan Pier Revisited, 26
Wilder, Billy, 166
Wilhide, Elizabeth, 61
Williams, David L., 100
Williams, John, 131
Williams, Linda Ruth, 160
Williams, Philip Martin, 100
Williams, Raymond, 15, 16–17, 22–3, 87,
  95, 96
Williamson, Judith, 173
Wills, Charlie, 152–3
Wilson, Peter, 117–18
Windsor, Barbara, 173
Winn, Christopher, 2
Winterbottom, Walter, 129
Wisden, 125
Women's Institutes, 6, 25–6
Woodfull, Bill, 123, 124
Woolf, Virginia, 6, 24–5, 26, 159
'Worktown' *see* Bolton
World Cup 1990, 122, 134, 135
World On Our Backs, The, 56
Wright, Ian, 19
Wright, Patrick, 57–8

Yeats, W. B., 143, 144
Youth Hostel Association, 75